Business Intelligence in Microsoft® SharePoint® 2010

Norm Warren

Mariano Teixeira Neto

John Campbell

Stacia Misner

Published with the authorization of Microsoft Corporation by:
O'Reilly Media, Inc.
1005 Gravenstein Highway North
Sebastopol, California 95472

Unless otherwise noted, the example companies, organizations, products, domain names, email addresses, logos, people, places, and events depicted herein are fictitious. No association with any real company, organization, product, domain name, email address, logo, person, place, or event is intended or should be inferred.

Microsoft Press titles may be purchased for educational, business, or sales promotional use. Online editions are also available for most titles (*http://my.safaribooksonline.com*). For more information, contact our corporate/ institutional sales department: (800) 998-9938 or *corporate@oreilly.com*.

Printed and bound in the United States of America.

1 2 3 4 5 6 7 8 9   M   6 5 4 3 2 1

Microsoft, Microsoft Press, the Microsoft Press brand, Access, ASP.NET, DirectX, DreamSpark, Deep Zoom, Excel, Expression Blend, Expression Design, Expression Encoder, Expression Studio, Expression Web, FrontPage, .NET, Office, Silverlight, SQL Server, Visual Basic, Visual C++, Visual C#, Visual Studio, Visual Web Developer, Web Platform, WebsiteSpark, and Windows are either registered trademarks or trademarks of Microsoft Corporation in the United States and/or other countries.

This book expresses the author's views and opinions. The information contained in this book is provided without any express, statutory, or implied warranties. Neither the author, O'Reilly Media, Inc., Microsoft Corporation, nor their respective resellers, or distributors will be held liable for any damages caused or alleged to be caused either directly or indirectly by this book.

Acquisitions and Development Editor: Russell Jones
Production Editor: Adam Zaremba
Editorial Production: Octal Publishing, Inc.
Technical Reviewer: Kevin Donovan
Indexing: Potomac Indexing, LLC
Cover: Karen Montgomery
Compositor: Octal Publishing, Inc.
Illustrator: Robert Romano

978-0-735-64340-6

Contents at a Glance

Table of Contents

What do you think of this book? We want to hear from you!

Microsoft is interested in hearing your feedback so we can continually improve our
books and learning resources for you. To participate in a brief online survey, please visit:

microsoft.com/learning/booksurvey

What do you think of this book? We want to hear from you!

Microsoft is interested in hearing your feedback so we can continually improve our
books and learning resources for you. To participate in a brief online survey, please visit:

microsoft.com/learning/booksurvey

What do you think of this book? We want to hear from you!

Microsoft is interested in hearing your feedback so we can continually improve our
books and learning resources for you. To participate in a brief online survey, please visit:

microsoft.com/learning/booksurvey

Introduction

Whether you are a SQL Server business intelligence (BI) developer or a SharePoint Administrator, this book shows you how Microsoft is delivering on its commitment to provide useful, usable BI to its customers. It provides a quick dive into new Microsoft SharePoint 2010 BI features and offerings as well as new SQL Server BI offerings.

The book provides a getting started guide for each of the SharePoint application services dedicated to BI. Additionally, the book introduces features for managing SQL Server 2010 Reporting Services reports and Excel 2010 PowerPivot add-in reports in SharePoint.

The SharePoint Server 2010 application services that provide self-service BI include:

- **Excel Services**   A Microsoft SharePoint Server 2010 service application that you can use to manage, view, interact, and consume Microsoft Excel client workbooks on SharePoint Server.

- **PerformancePoint Services**   A performance management service that you can use to monitor and analyze your business. This service provides flexible, easy-to-use tools for building dashboards, scorecards, reports, and key performance indicators (KPIs).

- **Visio Services**   A service that allows users to share and view Visio diagrams on a SharePoint website. This service also enables you to refresh and update data-connected Microsoft Visio 2010 diagrams from a variety of data sources.

- **PowerPivot**   A SharePoint 2010 application service (included in SQL Server 2008 R2) and an extension to Excel that adds support for large-scale data. It includes an in-memory data store as an option for Analysis Services. Multiple data sources can be merged to include corporate databases, worksheets, reports, and data feeds. You can publish Excel documents to SharePoint Server 2010.

SharePoint administrators, business users, and BI developers, as well as other users and consumers of BI, will want to understand each of these services and how they work together to bring BI to more people through SharePoint.

Which Tool Do I Use?

BI in SharePoint is less about a specific technology or product that meets the needs of a small percentage of users and more about a "buffet" of offerings for the customer who is trying to solve a specific problem. Customers complain that much of the documentation and content that is published is too product-specific. They need to see the big picture. More importantly, customers want to know which specific Microsoft BI tools can best meet their needs.

Perhaps one day the seven tools that each offer a product-dependent method to create KPIs will merge into a single dynamic BI product. But for now, customers need to know when they should choose SQL Server Reporting Services in SharePoint over PerformancePoint Services. Or why they would use the Excel 2010 PowerPivot add-in versus Excel or Excel Services. Each connects to a database and surfaces data from an OLAP cube.

BI Maturity Model

Whatever stage your company has reached in its ability to provide your business users with optimal decision-making data, this book can help you advance that capacity by providing a selection of "crawl, walk, and run" scenarios.

How Do the Tools Work Together to Help Me Solve My Needs for BI?

SharePoint 2010 (enterprise license) now offers several BI tools. We show how they work together in compelling ways.

This book's approach is unique in the following ways:

- The book clearly defines Microsoft BI tools in a matrix. It speaks to the different stages and problems that teams and companies are trying to solve by categorizing the tools according to the specialized BI services they provide and by presenting a maturity model.

- Rather than focusing on the BI features of a single product, the book uses the rich palette of available BI tools from Microsoft to create the big picture that a business enterprise needs to succeed in a competitive global marketplace. It discusses which Microsoft BI tool is best for different scenarios and what costs and products are associated with each.

- The book treats SharePoint-based BI tools both individually and as a whole to show how they work together to provide a complete solution. For example, it explains how you can use the SharePoint 2010 PerformancePoint Services as an aggregator for the other reporting tools such as Excel Services, SQL Server Reporting Services reports, and Microsoft PowerPivot for Excel.

Who Should Read This Book

While anyone interested in using advanced tools to gather and present BI can benefit from this book, it should prove especially valuable to the SharePoint administrators, business users, and BI developers.

SharePoint Administrator

Just as a SQL BI developer peeks into SharePoint 2010 products, we want SharePoint administrators to peek into the tasks involved in developing BI solutions and the inherent difficulty in getting to trusted data. A SharePoint administrator must be aware that you typically can't just "turn on" BI in SharePoint or in SQL Server. Instead, you follow a process. A SharePoint administrator should also be aware of the newest BI features and tools, as well as existing technologies, and have some idea of how to set them up. In this book, we give SharePoint administrators an overview of the latest available BI tools and how they work with SharePoint 2010. This book strives to give SharePoint administrators an understanding of the work and expertise required for an extensive range of possible BI implementations.

Business User

In this book, the term "business user" describes people who are eager to understand the technologies that can help them, their teams, and their organizations measure, analyze, forecast, and report on the most important aspects of the company's business data. A business user may also be a technical decision-maker, deciding which products work best for the individual, team, or organization. By understanding how technology and business needs meet through reporting, measuring, analyzing, and more, we hope that business users will see a return on investment through increased accountability and better alignment with organizational goals.

Using SharePoint 2010 and other stand-alone tools, business users can benefit from learning about the end-to-end process for surfacing and presenting insights to decision-makers. Business users know that trusted insights can change behavior and decisions, which can ultimately help to lead a company in the right direction.

Business users who can benefit from the integrated BI tools offered by Microsoft Office, SharePoint, and SQL Server include:

- Business analysts

- Business decision-makers

- Knowledge workers

- Line workers

Each of the preceding roles has its own unique accountabilities. For each role, we provide simple examples showing how to create BI end results such as the following:

- Reports

- A dashboard in PerformancePoint Services

- KPIs that can be presented using various tools

- PivotTables in Excel

End users may also want to know how to do some tricks in SharePoint, such as how to add a rating system in a SharePoint list, view a blog post, implementing collaborative decision-making in Share-Point 2010, or rating BI assets.

BI Developer

Put simply, the BI developer's task is to establish trusted data sources (tabular data and OLAP cubes) in SQL Server for the various services (Excel, Visio, PerformancePoint) and for PowerPivot and SQL Server Reporting Services. BI developers also help create connections to the trusted data sources and help ensure that the data is the right data.

Organizational BI begins by establishing a single source for trusted data. If users cannot trust the data that's in front of them to make decisions, they won't trust the tools that deliver the data. They will abandon those tools to seek some other way to get the right data, which likely means abandoning their considerable investment in those tools, in both time and money, to invest in new ones.

Data can come from a variety of sources, and in many cases, companies have spent lots of money and time to establish a repeatable ETL (Extract, Transform, and Load) process. This requires a BI developer who knows something about data warehouses (SQL Server), integrating data from various sources using SQL Server Integration Services, and developing T-SQL procedures. If a company decides that creating OLAP cubes is worth the effort, it will also hire (or train) SQL Server Analysis Services experts to do the job. Microsoft has provided the tools to tie all this data together, and this book can help you use them to get the best value from your data management tools.

Using the information in this book, BI developers can help decide which tools to use to surface the data. They can also communicate closely with the SharePoint Administrator in cases where trusted data must be shared.

In this book, the authors provide a discussion of SQL Server Analysis Services OLAP cubes because OLAP cubes are the ideal data sources for organizational BI using PerformancePoint Services, for data sources used by the other services (such as Excel Services, Visio Services, and others), and now for "personal BI" using PowerPivot for Excel and PowerPivot for SharePoint.

Scope of This Book

Before starting to write this book, the authors went back and forth over exactly what to include. For example, we chose not to include information about setting up all the various tools and databases—although we did include a synopsis of best practices for planning, deployment, and configuration. Because this book is aimed primarily at three different audiences—SharePoint administrators, business users, and BI developers—we were forced to sharpen our focus and choose only the most relevant BI products from Microsoft for these audiences.

Those products are:

- SharePoint Excel Services

- SQL Server 2008 R2 PowerPivot

- SharePoint Visio Services

- SharePoint PerformancePoint Services

Organization of This Book

The following sections provide a brief synopsis of what you can expect to learn from each chapter of this book, including the appendixes.

Chapter 1, Business Intelligence in SharePoint

BI is a difficult concept to pin down precisely, because it covers a wide range of products and technologies and thus means slightly different things to different people. This chapter discusses exactly what the authors mean by the term "business intelligence," the Microsoft approach to BI, and how SharePoint fits into the picture.

Chapter 2, Choosing the Right BI Tool

Customers often ask which tools they should use when trying to select among a variety of Microsoft offerings. They're often confused and need information as to why they might want to prefer SQL Server Reporting Services in SharePoint over PerformancePoint Services, or why they might use the Excel 2010 PowerPivot add-in instead of Excel or Excel Services. After all, each product connects to a database and surfaces data from an OLAP cube.

The difficulties of making such decisions are compounded because different teams and companies are at different stages in their ability to surface data to business users for optimal decision-making. Overall, this chapter attempts to answer questions about which tools to use, clarifying the purposes and capabilities of the various products, and helping you choose which ones are most appropriate for your situation.

Chapter 3, Getting to Trusted Data

This chapter discusses how a company can surface reliable data that business users can work with to author reports and make decisions. Historically, BI started in SQL Server, so we take you on a tour that starts with disparate data sources and then we provide step-by-step exercises showing how to create your own mini-data warehouse—and then show you how to create a multidimensional cube.

Chapter 4, Excel Services

Most business intelligence begins in Excel, which can be considered the most pervasive BI tool that exists. But sharing Excel files has always been a huge challenge. Excel Services not only provides the ability to share Excel-based content safely and securely—it also adds powerful management capabilities. Such features as the PivotTable, PivotChart, and Sparklines in Excel improve the look and feel of how data is presented. Among several hands-on examples, you'll see how to create a PivotTable, sparklines, and slicers to provide slice-and-dice capability on the screen for analysis, and how to add your pivot table to a simple dashboard webpage so that you can share it.

Chapter 5, PowerPivot for Excel and SharePoint

A PowerPivot workbook looks like an Excel workbook, and that's how it is supposed to look. The PowerPivot experience is designed to feel as seamless as possible to an Excel user. The difference is under the hood, where PowerPivot enhances Excel. Because PowerPivot uses the VertiPaq engine, it extends Excel so that you can work with millions of rows. Moreover, operations—even with huge volumes of data—are fast! Aggregations that might have taken a day to calculate in SQL Server Analysis Services take only seconds in PowerPivot. In this chapter, you'll see how to mash-up data from different sources, share that data securely via SharePoint, create Data Analysis Expressions (DAX) queries, and more.

Chapter 6, Visio and Visio Services

This chapter shows you how to create data-driven diagrams that provide interactive processes and context.

Chapter 7, PerformancePoint Services

One exciting solution that PerformancePoint Services offers is the ability to show a dashboard that reflects KPIs, such as the available disk space of managed servers. This chapter explains how to create a dashboard with scorecard, KPIs, reports, and connections to data sources.

Chapter 8, Bringing It All Together

In this chapter, you'll capitalize on the concepts and products discussed in all the preceding chapters by walking through the steps to create a dashboard that shows data from various sources, such as PerformancePoint Web Part, Visio Services, Excel Services, and PowerPivot.

Appendix A: Virtual Machine Setup and SharePoint Configuration

In this appendix, you'll find detailed setup instructions, including helpful screen captures, so that you can get up-and-running quickly to work through the book's exercises. We also provide some instruction for configuring SharePoint Server 2010, along with links to relevant sites.

Appendix B: DAX Function Reference

This appendix provides a reference to DAX, introduced in Chapter 5, "PowerPivot for Excel and SharePoint." DAX is an expression language based on Excel formula syntax and is designed to work with multiple tables of data. DAX includes functions that implement relational database concepts.

Appendix C: SharePoint As a Service—"Office 365"

This appendix discusses how Microsoft enables disparate businesses—from the smallest one-person home office to the largest enterprises—to experience the benefits of SharePoint without needing to know how to install, manage, deploy, patch, back up, scale out, or generally maintain the machines or software. The authors anticipate more breakthrough cloud features for BI in the future and encourage readers to get a better understanding of the relationship between the cloud and SharePoint.

Finding Your Best Starting Point in This Book

The different Microsoft tools cover a wide range of technologies associated with BI. Depending on your needs and your existing understanding of Microsoft data tools, you might want to focus on specific areas of the book. Use the following table to determine how best to proceed through the book.

If you are	Follow these steps
New to Microsoft business intelligence	Focus on Chapters 1 and 2.
New to SQL Server 2008 R2, data warehousing, and OLAP concepts	Focus on Chapter 3.
New to SharePoint 2010 services dedicated to BI	Read and perform exercises for Excel, Visio, and PerformancePoint services as well as PowerPivot in Chapters 4, 5, 6, and 7.
New to how the services dedicated to BI work together in dashboards	Read Chapter 8.
New to setting up the virtual machines you will need for this book	Refer to Appendix A.
New to DAX as the PowerPivot extension to the Excel formula language	Refer to Appendix B.
New to Office 365 and cloud-based BI services	Refer to Appendix C.

Many of the chapters in this book include step-by-step exercises so that you can try out the concepts discussed in a hands-on fashion. No matter which sections you choose to focus on, be sure to download and install the sample code on your system.

What's Not in This Book

While this book covers a wide range of products, it doesn't cover everything. We chose to concentrate instead on those technologies that we believe make up the core Microsoft BI tools. Three of the following BI tools are a part of SharePoint Server 2010 and one, Reporting Services, is part of the SQL Server 2008 R2 platform, offering strong reporting and report management features in SharePoint. All these are either up-and-coming or already adopted and in use by the BI community. This brief section explains which technologies we chose not to discuss, but if these technologies also suit your needs, you might consider how you can implement them.

Access Services

Microsoft Access is a relational database management system. Software developers and data architects can use Access to develop application software, and "power users" can use it to build individual and workgroup-level applications.

Access Services is a service application that lets you host Access databases within SharePoint Server 2010. Through Access Services, users can edit, update, and create linked Access 2010 databases, which are then both viewed and manipulated using either a web browser or the Access client. In other words, Access services extends "access" to Access, so that even users who don't have the Access client installed on their desktop can perform operations with the Access application through Access Services.

Access Services can also generate the RDL language used by SQL Server Reporting Services. This is important because it enables you to quickly and easily report on SharePoint data.

There is a self-service element to Access that lets users incorporate rapid application development principles (RAD) to more quickly create data-driven websites without coding in ASP.NET. This is attractive to smaller companies that have a small IT department—sometimes only one or two IT workers. Access and Access Services also become attractive to larger companies when projects are prioritized into already-full IT development schedules, or when users want to provide a very quick proof-of-concept data-driven website.

SQL Server 2008 R2 Reporting Services in SharePoint

SQL Server 2008 R2 Reporting Services with SharePoint integration has several new features, including support for multiple SharePoint Zones, support for the SharePoint Universal Logging service, a new data extension, and a query designer for SharePoint Lists as a data source. The SharePoint List data extension supports getting data from the following SharePoint technologies: SharePoint lists for SharePoint Foundation 2010, SharePoint Server 2010, Windows SharePoint Services 3.0, and Office SharePoint Server 2007.

SQL Server Reporting Services Report Builder 3.0 is a report-authoring tool that enables you to create ad-hoc reports quickly. The tool helps report creation, collaboration, and consistency by enabling business users to create and share report components that can be accessed via a shared component library.

We didn't quite omit this topic entirely; we did include a somewhat longer summary of what SQL Server Reporting Services is in Chapter 3, "Getting to Trusted Data."

Business Connectivity Services

Microsoft Business Connectivity Services (BCS), formerly named the Business Data Catalog, provides read/write access to external data from line-of-business (LOB) systems (such as Microsoft Dynamics, Oracle, or Siebel), web services, databases, and other external systems from within Microsoft SharePoint 2010. SharePoint 2010 has product features that can use external data directly, both online and offline. BCS enables tools such as Microsoft Visual Studio 2010 and Microsoft SharePoint Designer 2010 to help make connections to the external data.

How Is BCS Different from BDC in SharePoint 2007?

BCS lets users read and write external data into Microsoft SharePoint and into Microsoft Office applications. In contrast, BDC was designed to give users a read-only window into external systems. Using BCS, solution designers can now describe the structure of the external system as well as determine how that data should behave within SharePoint and Office.

Duet Enterprise

You may have asked, "How is Duet Enterprise different from BCS if it connects to ERP data?" Duet Enterprise is an application built on the SharePoint 2010 platform, and it uses BCS in conjunction with SAP data. Duet Enterprise was developed jointly by two companies: SAP and Microsoft. SAP is a German software company known primarily for its SAP Enterprise Resource Planning and SAP Business Objects products. Duet Enterprise enables all employees to consume and extend SAP applications and data through Microsoft SharePoint 2010 and Microsoft Office 2010. Duet Enterprise combines the collaboration and productivity supported by Microsoft SharePoint and Microsoft Office with the business data and processing functionality of SAP applications.

For SAP users, Duet reduces the learning curve and provides wider access to enterprise information and policies—resulting in greater user adoption. As a result, organizations can increase corporate policy compliance, improve decision-making, and save time and money. We mention the product here because there are a lot of SAP customers and a lot of SAP data; making that data available to many users was previously difficult or impossible.

Duet's plan is to continue developing interoperability between SAP and SharePoint in areas such as system management, single sign-on, and more. By blending the worlds of process and collaboration, end-to-end solutions will form as tools and feature extensions become available. To learn more, see *http://www.sap.com/solutions/duet/index.epx* or *http://www.duet.com/index.aspx*.

Web Analytics

Web Analytics helps you collect, report, and analyze usage data so that you can measure the effectiveness of your SharePoint Server 2010 deployment. The following is an overview of the new Web Analytics features:

- Traffic reports that provide the following metrics:

    - Number of Page Views: Track site usage and popularity.

    - Top visitors: Discover who is visiting your site.

    - Top Referrers: Determine how visitors arrive at your site.

    - Daily Unique Visitors, Top Destinations, Top Browsers, and so on.

- Search reports that provide insights into what users search for, including the following:

    - Number of Queries: Learn how many times users took advantage of search.

    - Top Queries: Identify the most-used search terms.

    - Failed Queries: Hone in on queries that fail for users.

    - Best Bet Usage, Search keywords, and so on.

- Inventory reports that display metrics about the inventory of your sites, such as the following:

    - Storage usage: See the total disk drive space consumed by each user.

    - Number of sites: Track how many sites exist.

    - Top Site Product Versions, Top Site Languages, and so on.

Conventions Used in This Book

This book presents information using the following conventions, which are designed to make the information readable and easy to follow:

- In most chapters, you'll see general concepts and explanations of the technology in that chapter.

- Some chapters contain hands-on exercises. Each exercise consists of a series of tasks, presented as numbered steps (1, 2, and so on) listing each action you must take to complete the exercise.

- Boxed elements, with labels such as "Note," provide additional information or alternative methods for completing a step successfully.

- Text that you type (apart from code blocks) appears in bold.

- A plus sign (+) between two key names means that you must press those keys at the same time. For example, "Press Alt+Tab" means that you hold down the Alt key while you press the Tab key.

- A vertical bar between two or more menu items (for example, File | Close) means that you should select the first menu or menu item, and then the next, and so on.

System Requirements

This book addresses several different types of audiences, not all of whom might want to install software and follow along. If you do want to perform the exercises, you should first read Appendix A, "Virtual Machine Setup and SharePoint Configuration."

Code Samples

Several chapters in this book include exercises that let you interactively try out concepts or techniques discussed in the main text. Some of these require setup and configuration or scripts to set up the example scenarios. Before working with the exercises, read Appendix A, and follow the download and configuration instructions carefully. The accompanying sample scripts are available for download from the book's page on the website for Microsoft's publishing partner, O'Reilly Media, at *http://oreilly.com/catalog/9780735643406/*.

Click the Examples link on that page. When a list of files appears, locate and download the BiInSharePoint_Examples.zip file.

> **Note** In addition to the code samples, you should have SQL Server 2008 R2 installed as part of the virtual machine installation. The instructions below use SQL Server Management Studio 2008 R2 to set up the sample database used with the practice examples. If available, install the latest service packs for each product.

Installing the Code Samples

To install the code samples on your computer so that you can use them with the exercises in this book, unzip the BiInSharePoint_Examples.zip file that you downloaded from the book's website.

Using the Code Samples

The folder created by unzipping the BiInSharePoint_examples.zip program contains several files:

- **Sample Database**   Optional SQL scripts to build the sample database, NorthwindOrdersDW, and scripts to add dimension and fact tables if you don't want to create the tables manually.

- **SQL Scripts**   Scripts for creating the underlying data for the NorthwindOrdersDW, which is the sample Northwind database that emulates a simplified transactional database.

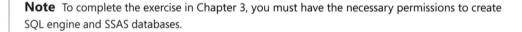

> **Note** To complete the exercise in Chapter 3, you must have the necessary permissions to create SQL engine and SSAS databases.

Acknowledgments

Norm Warren would like to first thank his wife, KarAnn, and children for their patience while writing the book. He would also like to thank the people that have helped contribute in one way or another to this book.

Kevin Donovan, Technical Reviewer of the whole book and Program Manager at Microsoft.

Trevor Dywer, Director at Avanade, Bruno Ferreira, BI Developer for Accenture, all who have offered chapter review and support.

Joe Hutchison, BI architect, who provided invaluable guidance for several areas of the book.

All the others who have helped provide support or information that made this book a reality.

John would like to thank Mark Kashman for his review of the SharePoint Online content as well as the other authors for their reviews and hard work. Most importantly, John would also like to thank his beautiful wife, AnnMarie, for her unending patience, love, and support.

Mariano would like to thank Kay Unkroth, program manager, and Lee Graber, developer, (both from Analysis Services team at Microsoft) for reviewing his chapter. And, most importantly, to thank his family—Bárbara, Sofia, and Miguel—for their support and love.

Errata and Book Support

We've made every effort to ensure the accuracy of this book and its companion content. If you do find an error, please report it on our Microsoft Press site at *oreilly.com*:

1. Go to *http://microsoftpress.oreilly.com*.

2. In the Search box, enter the book's ISBN or title.

3. Select your book from the search results.

4. On your book's catalog page, under the cover image, click **View/Submit Errata** in the list of links.

You'll find additional information and services for your book on its catalog page. If you need additional support, please send email to Microsoft Press Book Support at *mspinput@microsoft.com*.

Please note that product support for Microsoft software is not offered through the addresses above.

We Want to Hear from You

At Microsoft Press, your satisfaction is our top priority, and your feedback is our most valuable asset. Please tell us what you think of this book at:

http://www.microsoft.com/learning/booksurvey

The survey is short, and we read every one of your comments and ideas. Thanks in advance for your input!

Stay in Touch

Let's keep the conversation going! We're on Twitter: *http://twitter.com/MicrosoftPress*.

Chapter 1
Business Intelligence in SharePoint

After completing this chapter, you will be able to

■ Understand the definition of business intelligence.

■ Understand why business intelligence is important.

■ Preview the business intelligence stack (Office + SQL Server + SharePoint Server).

■ See examples of business intelligence in SharePoint at work.

■ Create a collaborative decision-making environment in SharePoint 2010.

Introduction

This book is a collaborative effort to show how Microsoft and Microsoft SharePoint business intelligence (BI) offerings can help businesses and technical personnel solve common business problems.

BI in SharePoint is less about a specific technology or product tailored to the needs of a small percentage of users, and more about a "buffet" of offerings that can aid customers who are trying to solve a specific problem. One common customer complaint is that much of the published documentation and content is too product-specific. That makes it difficult to get the big picture—and providing that big picture is one rationale for this book.

Even more importantly, customers need to know which Microsoft offerings they should choose from the buffet. Perhaps one day the seven tools that offer a method for creating key performance indicators (KPIs) will merge into a single product, but for now, customers are confused and need guidance as to when they should use SQL Server Reporting Services in SharePoint 2010 rather than PerformancePoint Services, or why they would use PowerPivot for Excel 2010 instead of Excel or Excel Services. Chapter 2, "Choosing the Right BI Tool," gives this guidance, looking at the tools from a few angles, including a BI maturity model.

This chapter introduces the definition for BI and explains why it is important to you, your team, and your organization. It also discusses the platforms and tools used to deliver pervasive BI for a wide variety of users. At the end of the chapter, we provide a peek at what you can do with BI in SharePoint.

Leading Up to Business Intelligence

So, exactly what does "business intelligence" mean? The authors could provide a simple, tool-centric definition, but we have decided to give you the context that can help you make the most sense of what BI is, why it's important, and what forces are driving its popularity.

Observations from Steven R. Covey's book, *The Seven Habits of Highly Effective People*, show that an airplane that travels from Boston to Los Angeles is off-course for 90 percent of the journey, but the airplane successfully reaches its destination because the pilot makes continuous course corrections based on instruments that monitor the flight and provide feedback.

Much like an airplane, if a company is not steered, it will inevitably be off course more than 90 percent of the time. Most companies have a goal or destination and, to gain necessary business insights, use instruments or measurement tools to help monitor and analyze past, current, and projected future performance. Those insights give managers the information they need to make changes, or "course corrections." Insights come in the form of reports, scorecards, KPIs, dashboards, and other information vehicles, driven by a concept called "trusted data."

These scorecards, dashboards, KPIs, reports, and other tools can help a company see the relationships between their business and its highest priorities and strategies. Decision-makers want the visual experience that dashboards offer so that they can feel as if they're driving their company to its destination.

Fortunately, airplanes are predictably more successful at reaching their destinations than companies are in successfully reaching their goals. Is this success due to the science and precision of the measurement tools used in the aviation industry?

Over the years, weather conditions, patterns, and other variables that affect flight and direction—originally considered unmeasurable—have become increasingly measurable. New instruments were developed and produced to give pilots precise location coordinates. Now the same is occurring for businesses. Douglas W. Hubbard, in his book *How to Measure Anything; Finding the Value of "Intangibles" in Business*, lists a few real-life examples of variables that companies previously chose not to measure because they were presumed to be unmeasurable, including:

- The flexibility to create new products
- Management effectiveness
- Productivity of research
- Risk of bankruptcy
- Quality

Accounting professionals and academics, including Robert S. Kaplan, Baker Foundation Professor at Harvard Business School, have developed methodologies for measuring many elements in business that were previously thought of as unmeasurable in the performance of companies. Kaplan and David Norton proposed the concept of a Balanced Scorecard (BSC) as a means of measuring the performance of a business strategy. The BSC encapsulates four main areas that capture performance metrics:

- **Financial**   Measures of profitability and market value to satisfy owners and shareholders
- **Internal business processes**   Measures of efficiency and effectiveness for producing a product or service
- **Customer satisfaction**   Measures of perceived quality, low cost, and other related factors to show how well a company satisfies its customers
- **Innovation and learning**   Measures of a company's ability to develop and utilize human resources to meet strategic goals in the present and future

The preceding four areas can be simply referred to as Finance, Operations, Sales, and Human Resources or—to simplify even further—FOSH metrics.

Additional perspectives can include community and social impact, government relations, and others. These measures of success are sometimes called critical success factors. The BSC and other methodologies, such as Six Sigma,[1] help companies follow the pattern shown in the following illustration.

---

[1] Originators of Six Sigma: *http://web.archive.org/web/20051106025733/http://www.motorola.com/content/0,,3079,00.html*.

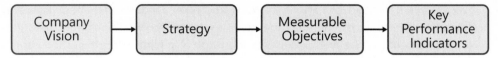

A company vision statement or mission statement is important for getting a company to focus on what makes it successful. Someone said, "You must stand up for something, or you will fall for everything." The vision statement helps a company filter which voices it will listen to, because the vision defines its purpose and reason for existence. Typically, upper management communicates the vision or mission statement to the company.

A strategy is a set of policies, procedures, and approaches to business that is intended to produce long-term success. The strategy reflects the mission of the company.

The mission is also used to develop measurable objectives. When established, objectives help determine KPIs, which are quantifiable measurements that reflect critical success factors.

KPIs allow for monitoring of metrics that are aligned with principal objectives. Then managers or employees can analyze issues that surface from data that indicate conditions that need more attention (once called "exception reports"). Action can then be taken to "correct the course" so that the company reaches its destination.

For illustration purposes, the following example shows how an organization designs a KPI, turning data into actionable information:

> **Mission:** For Mtn. Bike Company to design, build, and market bikes to meet the needs of the mountain bike community
>
> **Strategy:** To improve Mtn. Bike customer's satisfaction
>
> **Objective:** To increase repeat Mtn. Bike customer store sales by 20 percent
>
> **KPI:** The number of quarterly repeat sales for Mtn. Bike customers

To achieve the objectives, the decision-makers in the company ask the following questions about the business:

- What *has* happened? (monitoring)
- What *is* happening? (monitoring)
- *Why* is it happening? (analyze)
- What *will* happen? (forecast based on analyzing)
- What do we *want* to have happen? (new hunches spurring new actions based on what you know)

Part of the problem when trying to arrive at the answers to these questions is that much of the data needed is in a raw format stored in line-of-business (LOB) systems and other disparate business areas. Chapter 3, "Getting to Trusted Data," explains how companies accomplish providing access to this data in a usable form.

Beware of Losing Sight of What Matters Most

Companies that develop a vision or mission statement (define who they are and what success is), make goals, and monitor those goals can then reevaluate and flourish. This approach is used by corporations, teams, departments, and not least, individuals (us). Unfortunately, what happens often is that organizations lose focus of the vision and are deterred or distracted.

This is illustrated in the experience of a tragic airplane accident[2] that occurred over 36 years ago. In the middle of the night, a Lockheed 1011 jumbo jet fatally crashed into the Florida Everglades. All vital parts and systems of the airplane were working perfectly, and the plane was only 20 miles away from its landing site.

During the approach, a green light failed to illuminate, and the pilots discontinued the approach. The aircraft was set to a circling holding pattern over the pitch-black Everglades while the crew focused on investigating the failed light. The pilots became so preoccupied with the light that they failed to notice that the plane was gradually descending toward the dark swamp. By the time someone noticed what was happening, it was too late to avoid the disaster.

The malfunctioning light bulb didn't cause the accident; it happened because the crew placed its focus on something that seemed to matter at the moment while losing sight of what mattered most.

The tendency to focus on the insignificant at the expense of the profound happens not only to pilots but to companies, departments, teams, and individuals. Sometimes the things that distract are not necessarily bad, and often they seem right.

As you will see, BI helps bring to life the mantra, "what is measured gets managed." We believe it is worth the time and effort to make sure you are measuring the right things. When you know what to measure, you can stay on course and not be distracted by the insignificant.

---

[2] The Crash of Flight 401 (source: *http://www.suite101.com/content/the-crash-of-flight-401-a97138*).

What Is BI?

Simply put, BI comprises the tools that help companies execute performance management. And performance management can be defined as a series of organizational processes and applications designed to optimize the execution of business strategy.

In this book, we extend this definition of BI to include tools that that help individuals, teams, and organizations simplify information discovery and analysis, making it possible for decision-makers at all levels of an organization to more easily access, understand, analyze, collaborate, and act on information—anytime and anywhere.

In this way, to improve organizational effectiveness, Microsoft BI tools enable you to create and manage information through an integrated system that includes core business productivity features, such as collaboration tools, search capabilities, and content management.

This book provides high-level information about the available tools so that you can determine which tools can best help you reach your destination as an individual, team, or organization.

The Need for Business Intelligence Today

This following story[3] illustrates the importance of winnowing the data that's truly important from massive amounts of raw data and explains how to incorporate that important data into a BI solution:

> *Two men formed a partnership. They built a small shed beside a busy road. They rented a truck and drove it to a farmer's field, where they purchased a truckload of melons for a dollar per melon. They drove the loaded truck to their shed by the road, where they sold their melons for a dollar per melon. They drove back to the farmer's field and bought another truckload of melons for a dollar per melon. Transporting them to the roadside, they again sold them for a dollar per melon.*
>
> *As they drove back toward the farmer's field to get another load, one partner said to the other, "We're not making much money on this business, are we?"*
>
> *"No, we're not," his partner replied. "Do you think we need a bigger truck?"*

You'll probably agree that we don't need a bigger truckload of information. Like the partners in the story, our bigger need is a clearer focus on how to value and use the information we already have. Today's workplace tends to inundate people with information instead of using the right amount of data to focus on the right problems.

---

[3] Do you think we need a bigger truck? (Source: *http://www.hort.wisc.edu/cran/pubs_archive/newsletters/2002/news_2002_09_05.pdf*).

The amount of data businesses accumulate will continue to grow—and Microsoft and other companies will continue to develop better methods for moving, storing, retrieving, and displaying that data in meaningful ways. Companies must continue to increase their capacity to discover useful data, which will likely come from various systems and will require planning and collaboration to utilize effectively. Best practices must be developed for getting that relevant information into different forms or visualizations that can help provide insights and change behavior.

In the words of Bill Baker, former general manager of BI applications for the Microsoft Office Business Platform, "There is no substitute for getting the design right, getting the data right, training your users and in general providing them the least amount of data and the most amount of guidance."

T. S. Eliot, in his poem "Choruses from The Rock," described the situation as an "endless cycle" in which "wisdom" is "lost in knowledge" and "knowledge" is "lost in information."

Focusing on good BI addresses that exact problem. It simplifies information discovery and retrieval, making it possible for decision-makers at all levels of an organization to more easily access, understand, analyze, share, and act on information by helping them reach insights. Insights provide the impetus to improve the behavior of individuals, teams, and organizations. "Insights" is the word Microsoft uses to encapsulate what SharePoint 2010 provides to customers in the way of BI.

Microsoft's Vision for BI

It is Microsoft's goal to provide BI tools that give employees access to the data required for making informed decisions and that have the flexibility to work in familiar ways, using tools such as Excel and Visio.

The "analytical paradox" described by Joey Fitts (*http://vimeo.com/11756037*), author of the book *Drive Business Performance: Enabling a Culture of Intelligent Execution*, states, "Those who make the most decisions have the least information. Those who make the fewest decisions in the middle of the organization have the most information." Employees on the front line have the ability to take action on insights derived from analytical capabilities but rarely have the information required to reach those insights on their own. They must ask the IT department—and then get in line when requests for information from systems are backlogged. The following illustration summarizes the vision Microsoft has to deliver BI to more people to solve the analytical paradox (source: *http://www.slideshare.net/nicsmith/business-intelligence-deck-final*).

Modern computing power is making BI more and more available to the individuals in an organization so that they can make faster, more informed decisions. Microsoft has worked hard to deliver on the vision and strategy by building the tools that are highlighted in this chapter and in this book.

The preceding illustration shows the flow of right information being delivered at the right time and in the right format. Finding the right amount of information to deliver is critical so as not to overwhelm business users and, at the same time, to help them stay focused. The flow of information in the illustration touches three decision levels: Strategic, Tactical, and Operational:

Strategic: At the executive level, decisions are made that center around what a company is going to do at large, comprising choices such as product lines, manufacturing methods, marketing techniques, and channels.

Tactical: Decisions made at this level support the strategic decisions made at the executive level. At this level, analysts examine whether forecasts meet the financial targets set forth in the 1-to-5-year plan. If they do not, the elements of the forecasts must be changed. For example, a financial forecast is created in part for the purpose of measuring and monitoring against a firm's own general targets as compared to investor expectations. Investor expectations are based on a number of variables, which include industry average, the economy, and so on.

At this level, pro forma statements are used to accomplish the following objectives:

- Estimate the effect of proposed operating changes, enabling managers to conduct "what if" analysis.

- Anticipate the firm's future financing needs.

- Forecast free cash flows under different operating plans, forecast capital requirements, and then choose the plan that maximizes shareholder value.

Operational: Operational decisions comprise those made daily by all employees to support tactical decisions. Their impact is immediate, short term, short range, and usually low cost. The consequences of a bad operational decision are usually minimal, although a series of bad or sloppy operational decisions can cause harm. But when taken together, operational decisions can have an impact on the vision of the company.

Is all of this just another attempt toward a "BI for everyone" utopia? We don't believe it is. We think it is important for you to be aware of the work that may be necessary to prepare data so that insights can be made available to more people in positions to do something about problems. We believe it's worth your time to review the BI maturity model discussed in Chapter 2, "Choosing the Right BI Tool," that gives you an idea of where your department or company is in terms of making trusted data available and of having a culture geared toward executing on intelligence. The BI maturity model leads to a well-supported, concerted effort to get data from systems in a state that can be trusted to help support agile decisions.

Many companies use Excel and access to SQL Server for gathering BI and yet still have an infinite number of "versions of the truth." Also, companies often have some people who are louder than others or have more clout, so those are the folks who end up getting what they need from the IT department to create reports. Others know how to create more visual reports and, as a result, are more successful in getting their data in front of the decision-makers, even when their data is not validated.

We wouldn't have written this book if we didn't genuinely believe that you can make a difference in this space to help make the promises of BI become reality.

What SharePoint Does for BI

SharePoint Server 2010 can be used with SQL Server reporting and BI tools to surface BI data in meaningful ways. SQL Server provides the primary data infrastructure and BI platform for giving report authors and business users trusted, scalable, and secure data.

Many good reasons support the partnering of SQL Server and SharePoint product groups to integrate products such as PowerPivot and SQL Server Reporting Services, enabling you to share and organize BI assets in SharePoint lists and document libraries.

The following is a list of benefits that SharePoint Server products provide:

- Users can capitalize on SharePoint Server scalability, collaboration, backup and recovery, and disaster recovery capabilities to manage BI assets created in PowerPivot, Excel, Visio, Report Builder, and PerformancePoint Dashboard designer.

- Use of trusted locations protocols limits access to PerformancePoint Services content types, Excel Services, and Visio Services files.

- When security and data source connections are established, publishing to a SharePoint Server website is a quick way to share BI assets that ultimately help employees make better decisions, faster.

- In SharePoint Server, with Excel Services, Visio Services, and PerformancePoint Services functioning as service applications, Visio Web Drawing files, Excel workbooks, and PerformancePoint dashboards and dashboard items are stored and secured within SharePoint lists and libraries, providing a single security and repository framework.

The BI Stack: SQL Server + SharePoint + Office

The following architectural diagram, described in detail on the Microsoft TechNet site in "Architecture for Business Intelligence in SharePoint Server 2010," at *http://technet.microsoft.com/en-us/library/ff475895.aspx*, provides another, more technical, visual aid for how each of the pieces work together.

Presentation Tier

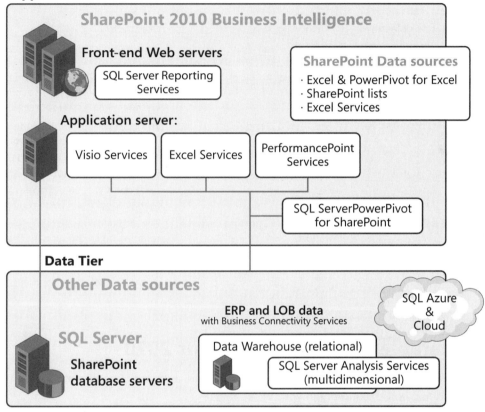

Report authoring is discussed in the next section. Report viewing can occur in just about any browser, in Microsoft Office, on Windows 7 phones, and in SharePoint Search.

Authoring in Microsoft BI Tools

When it comes to SharePoint and BI, the essential objective is to have the ability to create insights in the authoring tools that are spread among Office, SharePoint, and SQL Server (see the following table) and then to share the results in charts, reports, dashboards, and KPIs. These insights can be shared with the organization, the team or community, or with the individual via a browser.

Product or platform	Authoring tool	Comments
Microsoft Office 2010 desktop applications	Excel 2010 and Visio 2010 (Professional or Premium) and PowerPivot for Excel 2010	Before publishing a worksheet to SharePoint Server by using Excel Services or Visio Services, you must have already authored and—if applicable—connected to a data source.
SharePoint Server 2010	Dashboard Designer and Web Parts that offer KPIs	You start Dashboard Designer from a SharePoint Server 2010 website. BI Web Parts are available to use individually to create simplified KPIs. Each client tool also provides Web Parts to extend your ability to render reports.
SQL Server 2008 R2	SQL Server Reporting Services Report PowerPivot for SharePoint	Report Builder was originally designed to help you create reports. PowerPivot for SharePoint is a SharePoint shared service that integrates PowerPivot into your SharePoint environment.

Some Examples of BI in SharePoint 2010

The following sections look at ways you can take advantage of SharePoint 2010 features for developing and strengthening your BI capabilities.

PerformancePoint and the BI Stack

The following example of BI shows how a solution using PerformancePoint Services in SharePoint 2010, integrated with SQL Server 2008 R2, provides KPIs that drive decisions in an IT department. The IT Operations scorecard shows how simple it is to see where database space, as a percentage, is not meeting its target. After the following illustration is a brief explanation that maps what is going on underneath the hood.

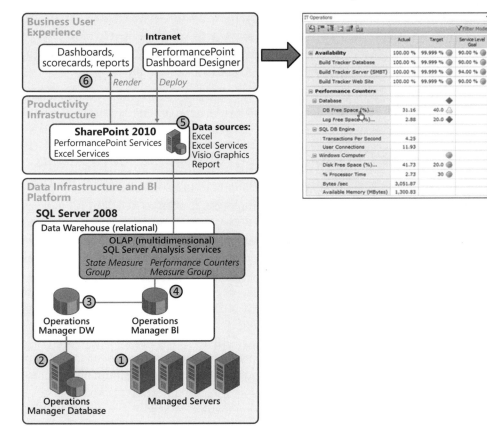

1. System Center Operations Manager collects monitor state and performance counter data from managed servers.

2. The Operations Manager database collects data from the managed servers. Data is pre-aggregated and stored in tables designed to support production reporting requirements.

3. A small subset of data in the Operations Manager data warehouse (OperationsManagerDW) is transformed and loaded into the BI framework database (Operations Manager BI). This database contains the star schemas for the Analysis Services OLAP cubes.

4. Analysis Services OLAP cubes are built and processed from data stored in the Operations Manager BI database.

5. Data from the OLAP cubes is used to populate PerformancePoint Server scorecards, dashboards, and analytic reports. These components are originally created using the Office PerformancePoint Services 2010 Dashboard Designer.

6. Scorecards, dashboards, and analytic reports are made available to the user community through SharePoint Server. After the scorecards, dashboards, and analytic reports are initially created and deployed, they should not need to be deployed again. These components are refreshed as new data becomes available in the OLAP cubes.

The IT Operations scorecard on the right side of the illustration reveals (flagged by the red diamonds) that free-space targets for the database are not being met.

Collaborative Decision Making: BI in Social Computing

Companies can combine social networking and BI to foster collaborative decision-making. In a way, this is a form of BI that empowers employees to vote on decisions for the organization. It promotes collaborative decision-making (CDM) as described in Wikipedia, "a recursive process where two or more people or organizations work together in an intersection of common goals—for example, an intellectual endeavor that is creative in nature—by sharing knowledge, learning and building consensus."

Because of the "SharePoint effect"—a phrase used in the book *SharePoint Deployment and Governance Using COBIT 4.1: A Practical Approach*—sites, lists, and documents are being created and stored in ever-increasing quantities. Organizations can quickly be overwhelmed by lists and libraries. The problem requires some techniques to help filter all the information. For this reason, companies might consider using some of the social computing features available in SharePoint 2010, such as the Rating Setting or tagging documents, so that focus is on the most useful BI assets. Other social networking features in SharePoint can also prove useful. Consider how the following can be used for collaborative decision making:

- **Social networking** The ability to connect with others in the organization
- **Social content** Communication venues such as blogs and wikis for sharing content
- **Social feedback** The ability to tag documents and other content

Following is an example of the Rating Setting for lists; to the right of the large arrow, you can see a list that has a rating system, generated by BI users. This example demonstrates "leadership that can be social" and puts decisions in the hands of those who review dashboards, scorecards, and reports, perhaps daily. This type of feature improves the level of trust in BI assets.

To add a rating feature to a list

1. In the library where you have your BI assets listed, click the Library tab.

2. In the Settings group, click Library Settings.

3. Under General Settings, click Rating Settings.

General Settings

Title, description and navigation
Versioning settings
Advanced settings
Validation settings
Column default value settings
Rating settings
Audience targeting settings
Metadata navigation settings
Per-location view settings
Form settings

4. In the Rating Setting dialog box, select Yes and then click OK.

5. Navigate back to the Library to see that the rating setting is viewable.

Note No ratings are viewable until users begin to rate the files in the Library.

Summary

In this chapter, we discuss the purpose and need for BI in language that is directed at the business user. We show that companies are much like aircraft in that they have a destination or goal and must constantly react to feedback provided by instruments that measure and monitor. Those instruments are the BI tools we implement so that we have a method for visualizing metrics that tell us what has happened, what is happening, why it is happening, and what will happen to our business.

We explain Microsoft's vision for BI. We also explain what SharePoint does for BI and provide a couple of examples to show the benefits of using SharePoint 2010 in any BI implementation.

As you can see, there is a lot to cover in this book. We are excited to show what you can do with BI in SharePoint 2010.

Chapter 2
Choosing the Right BI Tool

After completing this chapter, you will be able to

- Differentiate between business communities that consume BI.
- Understand the typical progression of BI.
- Determine the best BI tools for your needs.

Introduction

As described in Chapter 1, "Business Intelligence in SharePoint," business intelligence (BI) is a general term used to describe the development of insights from one or more tools that allow information workers and decision-makers in a company to understand what has happened in the past and to compare past events to what is happening now. With these insights, they can set appropriate goals for the company, monitor ongoing progress towards those goals, and take corrective action whenever necessary. This chapter focuses on the reporting and analysis tools that make these insights possible. In turn, these tools rely on a supporting infrastructure of trusted data, described in Chapter 3, "Getting to Trusted Data."

If you're a business user, your primary interaction with a BI solution is with the presentation layer. However, the Microsoft stack includes a variety of tools with overlapping capabilities that can seem confusing at first glance. This chapter can help you understand how these tools support different scenarios, how your choice of which tool to use can change over time, and how to select the right tool for the task at hand.

If, on the other hand, you're a BI developer or SharePoint administrator, this chapter can help you develop and support a successful BI implementation. You need to understand the different ways that users can interact with data, now and in the future, and the implications of tool selection for the overall architecture.

This chapter starts by examining the analysis needs of business user communities and how the Microsoft reporting and analysis tools serve these communities. It then reviews the typical progression of competency with BI within a company and how that progression affects the mix of tools for business users. Finally, it provides a guide to selecting the right tool for the community and analytical requirements applicable to you.

Business User Communities

When it comes to BI, business users are likely to have different information needs, depending on their technical skills, the types of decisions they make, and how they need to save and share their insights. In several different ways, business users with common characteristics can be grouped into separate user communities. By understanding the needs of these business user communities from a variety of perspectives, you can select the tools that best support those needs.

Casual Users vs. Power Users

One common way to differentiate business users is to separate them into two communities—casual users and power users. Casual users might be department managers, executives, or even external stakeholders such as customers or suppliers. Casual users tend to be infrequent users of BI, perhaps once per week or less, whereas power users are often daily users of BI.

Because casual users spend less time with BI, their skill level with BI tools is much lower than that of power users. Therefore, the interfaces to such tools must be simple so that they can find the information they need on their own. For these users, a web-based reporting application works well. The tools that help a casual user interact with data and develop insights tend to be very simple and focused on specific sets of data.

But making tools simple for casual users often makes them too simple for power users, who typically require access to a wide variety of data and need more on-demand analytical capabilities. Power users spend enough time working regularly with BI tools that they develop advanced technical skills. These users, typically business analysts and analytical modelers, need tools that give them the ability to explore the data without restraint.

Another way to distinguish casual users and power users is by assessing their familiarity with the data. It's quite possible that a person can be quite knowledgeable about the data in his or her own department and thus qualify as a power user, requiring a more analytical BI tool for daily work. It's also possible that this same person has access to data in another department but is less familiar with that data. For that situation, this user needs a basic reporting tool that simplifies information access.

In their book *Business Intelligence: Making Better Decisions Faster*, Elizabeth Vitt, Michael Luckevich, and Stacia Misner break down the casual users down into two groups—information users and information consumers, as shown in the following illustration, in which the pyramid shows the relative size of all three groups of business user communities.

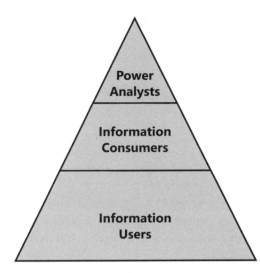

The largest community consists of information users, who rely on standard reports that BI developers publish to a central location. These reports may be accessible either online or in print, depending on the distribution mechanism that the report administrators implement. For this business user community, SQL Server Reporting Services is a good solution, either running as an independent application or integrated with SharePoint Server 2010. It provides a scalable online environment for viewing reports that administrators can secure, and it can deliver reports in a variety of formats on a scheduled basis via email or to a network file share.

Information consumers are the second community of casual users. They tend to explore the data more than the information users, but they lack the expertise necessary to query a database directly. They can get the information they need by working with interactive reports that include parameters for filtering and sorting or that include options to change the visibility of selected report elements. Interactive reports can also include the ability to drill down to more detail, either by displaying the details in the same report or by opening a separate report for the details. Again, Reporting Services is the best choice for meeting the needs of this community. With a proper understanding of information consumers' needs, a report author can incorporate a variety of interactive features into reports.

At the top of the pyramid, power analysts are the smallest community. Power analysts might use existing reports as a starting point for analysis, but they also need the ability to define and execute their own queries. In some cases, they might even build reports for the other communities. For example, a power user can use Report Builder 3.0 to create a report based on their own queries and then publish the entire report (or even individual elements of the report, called report parts) for the other user communities to access. Information consumers can build up a customized report from these report parts without knowing anything about how to construct a query or how to design the report part.

As flexible as Reporting Services is, it's still a reporting tool and has limited support for the type of ad hoc analysis that power analysts frequently perform. A more commonly used tool for analysis is Microsoft Excel 2010. A power analyst can group and filter data in a pivot table and create additional calculations to supplement analysis of the data. If analysis requires integrating data from multiple data sources, the power analyst can use PowerPivot for Excel.

Organizational Hierarchy

The position of a business user within the organizational hierarchy and the decision-making associated with that position often play a role in the type of information and the BI tool that the user requires. The higher the business user is in the hierarchy, the more likely that the user is an information consumer as described in the preceding section. Furthermore, the higher in the hierarchy a user is, the more likely it is that the information that user relies on is already cleansed and highly processed, is already compatible with data from different sources, and has been restructured for reporting and analysis.

Because this information has long-term value and is vital to strategic planning, a solid BI infrastructure exists to automate the necessary cleansing and processing. Usually this information is provided to upper management in a summarized, structured format with limited analytical capabilities. Reporting Services can be useful as a delivery mechanism for this type of information online, in print, or via email. Other online viewing options include dashboards and scorecards in SharePoint Server 2010 or PerformancePoint Services.

As business users move closer to the operations of the business, their information needs diverge, depending on the type of work a user performs. People at this level of the organizational hierarchy can be information users, information consumers, or power analysts.

The information requirements of these users differ from those of upper management because these users often combine official corporate data from a BI system with other data either created manually or obtained from external sources. This combination of data might occur only occasionally or might be an ongoing exercise. Either way, this type of quick and dirty data mash-up typically has only short-term value, so it's not a candidate for a formal BI implementation. On the other hand, it's a perfect scenario for PowerPivot for Excel, which very easily accommodates this type of ad hoc data integration.

BI Communities

Microsoft has another way of grouping users, which focuses instead on how users work with BI and how much collaboration they require. These BI communities, and the BI tools designed for each community, are shown in the following illustration. As you can see in this diagram, some overlap of tools exists between communities.

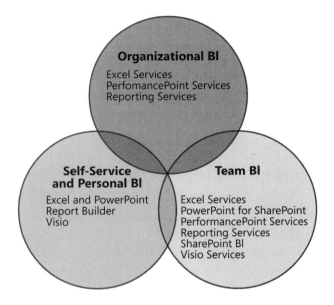

Organizational BI

Some popular ways to deliver BI to all employees in a company are to provide access to metrics that show progress towards organizational goals or to compare a current state to historical trends. Ideally, users of organizational BI can break down this information to see how their individual departments contribute to current conditions. Because the intended audience of information is the entire company, you can anticipate that the audience consists largely of information users and information consumers. Therefore, an organizational BI solution needs to support only online viewing, with limited interaction.

Typically, this information comes from approved data sources that have been staged, transformed, and restructured into a data warehouse. Ideally, this data has also been incorporated into an Analysis Services cube to provide both faster reporting to all business users and more flexible analysis for the power analysts.

Whether the data is stored in a relational database or a cube, the three primary tools for consuming this data at the organizational level are Excel Services, PerformancePoint Services, and Reporting Services. Excel Services and PerformancePoint Services require a SharePoint Server 2010 installation, with scalability achieved by setting up a SharePoint farm to distribute the workload. Reporting Services can be integrated into a SharePoint farm or can run independently. All these services require IT support to install and configure the environment.

In organizational BI solutions, business users tend to be consumers of published content rather than contributors. Content contributors are usually BI developers, IT professionals, and, in some cases, power analysts. The prevailing concept in organizational BI is to centralize content by using defined standards for layout, naming conventions, and color schemes. This BI can be consumed as is or can be used as base components by power users, who aggregate these with other content suitable for a targeted audience.

Each of the tools discussed in this section solves specific problems for organizational BI, starting with the most commonly implemented tool. The following descriptions of each tool aren't intended to be comprehensive; they focus on the features that address specific challenges that organizations face when implementing BI.

Reporting Services   Many organizations start with standard reports by implementing Reporting Services. If it's set up to run in SharePoint integrated mode, Reporting Services relies on the same security model and centralized storage that SharePoint uses, which makes it easier to administer. Report administrators can control how reports execute to balance performance against timeliness of data, either by setting up a report to run on-demand to view current data or to use caching to execute it in advance and minimize the wait time for viewing.

Having reports available in a SharePoint document library also makes it easier for business users to find information for online viewing. Users have only one place to go for all corporate information, whether that information is in the form of Reporting Services reports, Excel workbooks, or other content. The interface is simple for users to access because reports are stored like any other content on the SharePoint server, making it a good option for information delivery to a wide audience of casual users. (Even if you run Reporting Services in native mode—without SharePoint Server 2010—the interface remains easy to use.) As an alternative, reports can be sent directly to users via email as often as necessary.

Reporting Services is also popular for its ability to produce pixel-perfect reports. The report author, typically an IT professional, has a high degree of control over the appearance and behavior of report elements to produce just the right layout, whether users view the report online or export it to another format. Also, with some advance thought about the types of questions that a user might ask when viewing a report, the report author can build in parameters for filtering and can add interactive features that lead the user to additional answers.

Crossing over into the team and personal BI communities, Reporting Services also supports a variety of export formats, allowing any user to save the report in a print-ready format such as a Portable Document Format (PDF) file or to incorporate information into a Word document. Moreover, the user can reuse the information in a report simply by using a Web Part to include it in a dashboard. Users with more advanced skills can export report data for further analysis into Excel or can set up a report as a data feed for ongoing analysis with PowerPivot for Excel. In addition, BI developers can incorporate reports into PerformancePoint Services dashboards. And reusability doesn't stop there. In companies with mature BI implementations, application developers can embed Reporting Services content in custom analytical applications through application programming interfaces (APIs).

Excel Services   Although Reporting Services can produce some reports with complex calculations, it is limited in what it can do. It isn't meant to be a replacement for Excel. On the other hand, Excel isn't meant to be a corporate reporting solution. Although it provides a lot of formatting options and can handle complex calculations, Excel does not support the same control over formatting that's available in Reporting Services and it has limits on the amount of data that can be stored in a workbook. (If you're creating workbooks with PowerPivot for Excel, the limits are much higher.) However, sharing Excel workbooks through Excel Services can be a reasonable reporting alternative for organizations that aren't using Reporting Services.

Excel Services runs as a SharePoint Server 2010 service application. The advantage of using Excel Services is that organizations can take advantage of the SharePoint infrastructure to deliver information contained in workbooks to a wide audience, which is a much better approach than sending them to users through the email system. Users don't need to have Excel or any other type of application or plug-in installed on their computer; they just need to use a supported browser—Internet Explorer or Mozilla Firefox on a computer running a Windows operating system, or Safari on a non-Windows system. And because the workbooks are stored in SharePoint, the users need only to learn how to use one interface to access any corporate content.

Excel Services also provides a more secure and scalable approach than email distribution. Administrators and content owners can control whether users can only view a document online or whether they can download it. It's also possible to restrict viewing to certain sheets or selected items in the workbook when it's important to hide intellectual property or the detailed data behind a particular cell value. Furthermore, the Excel Services calculation engine handles all the complex calculations for multiple concurrent users, thus sparing hardware resources on the user's computer.

When an Excel workbook sources data from an Analysis Services cube, Excel Services supports drilling, filtering, and sorting data in a pivot table. Although the user cannot replace dimensions on the pivot table's rows, columns, or filter axes, the interactivity is still better than Reporting Services can support. For organizational BI, in which dissemination of information is a higher priority than supporting analysis, this limitation of Excel Services should not be an obstacle.

The workbook author can configure the report to accept parameters from the user for another type of interactivity. When the user views the workbook in Excel services, the user can type in the parameter values, which can in turn be input values for a calculation. This feature allows the user to dynamically change workbook content using a simple interface.

Another benefit of Excel Services is the reusability of information contained in workbooks for the team and personal BI communities. Users can reference cell values in an Excel workbook published to SharePoint to create status indicators, which are a very simple type of key performance indicator (KPI) having only three possible levels. Also, by using Excel Web Access Web Parts, more advanced users can use workbooks, in whole or in part, in dashboards. Parameters in the workbook can be connected to Filter Web Parts, allowing users to change content for multiple Web Parts on the same dashboard page with a single filter. In addition, an Excel workbook can provide source data for a Chart Web Part.

BI developers can take advantage of Excel workbooks in several ways. Data in a workbook can be a data source for various content types in PerformancePoint Services, while a workbook itself can display in a PerformancePoint Services dashboard. For customized web-based analytical applications, application developers can use the Excel Services REST API or the ECMAScript object model to display and interact with workbooks as described in Chapter 4, "Excel Services."

PerformancePoint Services   Companies with a clearly defined performance management strategy use PerformancePoint Services to communicate progress towards established goals. The basic dashboard capabilities in SharePoint Server 2010 might be the first step that some companies take as they develop corporate performance analytics, but PerformancePoint Services is preferred for its advanced dashboard functionality. It also includes components such as scorecards, analytical reports, strategy maps, and filters that BI developers and power analysts can use with either PerformancePoint or SharePoint dashboards.

The best data source for PerformancePoint Services components is an Analysis Services cube, which delivers the best performance for viewing and interacting with content. With respect to the analytical grid, analytical charts, and decomposition tree, a cube is the only type of data source these reports can use. The analytical reports are the best way to support drilling and pivoting in a web browser environment. BI developers can structure dashboards to simplify the use of analytical reports for casual users who might feel overwhelmed by the functionality these reports provide, but the decomposition tree cannot be built in advance. Power analysts who fully understand the data source and the tool's capabilities will appreciate the support for ad hoc analysis in these report types.

Apart from the analytical components in PerformancePoint Services, dashboards and scorecards are simple enough for the casual user to explore. A benefit of using PerformancePoint content types to build dashboards and scorecards is the ability for the BI developer to integrate multiple data sources so that business users can see related content in one location. For example, rather than opening an Excel workbook to see the established organizational goals and then opening a Reporting Services report to see the current status from an operations data source, the user can instead see the goals and the status side by side in one report, no matter where the source data is actually stored.

Although plenty of advantages are gained by using PerformancePoint Services, some disadvantages must be pointed out: First, the formatting options are limited as compared to Reporting Services or Excel. Second, developers can use PerformancePoint Services dashboards to combine a lot of content built for other purposes and can reuse many PerformancePoint content types in SharePoint dashboards, but that's it. The only other way to reuse content built for PerformancePoint Services is to build custom applications by using the PerformancePoint Services API.

Team BI

An easy way to get started with BI is to focus on a single community within an organization, which might be preferable because it's faster to deliver initially than an organization-wide initiative. The target community might be an entire department or perhaps a small team within a department. Or it could be a project team in which multiple departments are represented, or it could even be a group of people external to the organization, such as customers.

The key differentiators between team BI and organization BI are the scope of the information provided to the target audience and a greater participation in the content development process by the team community. Consequently, the ideal BI infrastructure provides an opportunity for the team to use the information collaboratively as they work toward a common goal.

Like organizational BI, data for a team BI solution often comes from approved, cleansed, and processed sources and is quite possibly stored in an Analysis Services cube. However, the scope of the data tends to be more limited. For example, a data mart built from a single data source might be the primary data of interest for team BI.

Team BI solutions can use the same tools that are prevalent in organizational BI. In addition, team BI might also include SharePoint BI, Visio Services, and PowerPivot for SharePoint as additional options for creating and sharing content. Casual users can easily view content produced with any of these tools within SharePoint as part of a dashboard or as individual documents stored in a document library. Power analysts and BI developers typically share responsibility for creating and managing content for team BI.

Let's start by reviewing the three new tools added to the mix, and then we can revisit the other tools to learn how their usage changes when implemented for team BI communities.

SharePoint BI   SharePoint Server 2010 includes several features that make it ideal for team BI, especially for teams without much existing infrastructure already in place. In fact, once IT has given a team access to a SharePoint site, power analysts on the team can manage content for consumption by the team BI community with relatively little effort. The ease of implementation translates to simple capabilities, but for teams that are new to BI, these simple capabilities might be all that casual users need.

Another benefit of SharePoint BI is the ability to combine content in a single location from team members who are using different tools. That way, no one is forced into learning a new tool for content creation or investing in the hardware, software, and processes necessary to support even a small data mart before the migration to a new tool or process is absolutely necessary.

To get started quickly, a SharePoint site collection owner can create a specialized site type called Business Intelligence Center. It includes a set of libraries and supports content types specific to BI, such as Excel workbooks and dashboards. It can also store reports if Reporting

Services is configured to run in SharePoint integrated mode. In addition, the Business Intelligence Center includes a special document library for data connections that power analysts and BI developers can use to create new workbooks, reports, Visio diagrams, and PerformancePoint content.

SharePoint BI also includes a special type of SharePoint list for storing status indicators which, as explained earlier in this chapter, are a simple type of KPI. Status indicators are simple enough for business users to use for reporting progress on activities just by updating fixed values manually or by finding a KPI stored in an Analysis Services cube. More adventurous users can also build a status indicator from an Excel workbook or a SharePoint list. It's important to note that these status indicators are really intended as a baby step into the world of performance management. Users can view them only in status indicator lists and dashboards. They can't be reused in any other tool that has a KPI capability.

We've already mentioned SharePoint dashboards as a way to present workbooks, reports, and PerformancePoint components. Dashboards can include all kinds of other content, such as status indicators, Visio Services diagrams, Chart Web Parts, and Filter Web Parts. They're supposed to be simple enough to enable anyone to build a dashboard page, but in reality, power analysts and BI developers are the creators of dashboards.

Chart Web Parts provide a way for more advanced users to display data visually if using a workbook or using Reporting Services isn't an option. It supports only a few data sources, but it can be a quick way to add a chart to a dashboard. The chart can display data from another Web Part on the same dashboard page or from a SharePoint list, a Business Data Catalog, or an Excel workbook. It's not reusable by any other tool.

Filter Web Parts on the dashboard make it easy to customize content on a dashboard page for each user. The same filter value can update multiple Web Parts on the same page. Working with dashboard pages is not difficult when merely adding a group of Web Parts. However, it can be a bit more challenging to configure correctly when attempting to link these Web Parts together for use with a filter, especially if the Web Parts come from different data sources. For this reason, constructing anything but the simplest of dashboards is usually a task assigned to a BI developer.

Visio Services   Visio Services provides a whole new to way visualize data. It supports live connections to data sources for use in web-based Visio diagrams that display information ranging from a color-coded status about projects to the current state of processes, to the availability of servers, and so on. Conceptually, the purpose of a Visio diagram is similar to that of a dashboard because it helps business users see trends and outliers at a glance.

Visio diagrams are accessible in a document library or can be added to a SharePoint dashboard by using a Visio Web Access Web Part, so they are just as easy for users to consume as any other content available in SharePoint. Like Excel Services with workbooks, Visio Services does not require users to have Visio installed on their computers before they can view a diagram published to SharePoint.

The development of Visio diagrams is in the realm of a specialist who understands how to build Visio diagrams and how to connect the data to the diagram properly by using the desktop application Visio 2010. Supported data sources for Visio Services include SQL Server, SharePoint lists, Excel Services, Access, and any source accessible with an OLE DB or ODBC provider. No other tool provides functionality like Visio Services, so the diagrams are not reusable for team BI outside of SharePoint unless the team develops a custom application.

PowerPivot for SharePoint PowerPivot for SharePoint is a service application that relies on Excel Services to execute queries and render PowerPivot for Excel workbooks on demand and includes management capabilities unique to PowerPivot workbooks. It requires a separate installation and configuration process on a SharePoint farm. Its purpose is to provide a link between self-service BI and team BI.

Business users, usually power analysts, can publish their PowerPivot for Excel workbooks to SharePoint, either in a standard document library or in a specialized document library that displays thumbnail images of workbooks to enable users to find the workbook they want without first opening it. Just as with Excel workbooks, administrators and workbook owners can control access and restrict users to online viewing only, thereby protecting the data contained in the workbook.

Beyond enabling the sharing of information with other team members and supporting concurrent access in a scalable environment, PowerPivot for SharePoint has several other benefits for business users. PowerPivot workbooks do not maintain live connections to the data sources, so a periodic refresh is necessary to keep the information as current as possible. PowerPivot for SharePoint can manage the data refresh process on a schedule and send out notifications if a problem occurs. In addition, PowerPivot for SharePoint can become a data source for another PowerPivot workbook, a Reporting Services report, and any other tool that can use Analysis Services as a data source.

PowerPivot for SharePoint has features for IT professionals as well. Often, any information that gets managed by users rather than IT can go undetected. A user might create a report to answer a one-time question, and then, under certain circumstances, the report suddenly can become a mission-critical application that IT knows nothing about. PowerPivot for Excel gives users the freedom to compile information as they see fit, while publishing the results to SharePoint allows IT to use management features in PowerPivot for SharePoint to maintain some oversight over the users' activities. IT can see what data sources are being used, which workbooks are popular, and how many server resources are necessary to render a report for the team community. When appropriate, IT can recommend a proper BI solution to take the place of a PowerPivot workbook.

Excel Services   Excel Services can be just as important to a team BI community as it is to an organizational community, if not more so. To support this community and encourage power users to develop content, IT can supply a set of data source connection files in a data connections library.

Reporting Services   As with Excel Services, a good strategy for IT (or power analysts) to adopt in support of team BI is to create and publish reusable content that users can access for team content development. In the case of Reporting Services, three types of content support this strategy: shared data sources, shared datasets, and report parts.

Shared datasets contain the query strings necessary to retrieve data from a data source and hide the technical details from the user who can take the dataset and build up a report completely from scratch, using the Report Builder 3.0 authoring tool. This tool is much simpler to use than the report designer used by BI developers, providing enough flexibility and freedom for power analysts to construct a report according to their needs but also providing wizards to guide less-technical users through the process of building simple report layouts.

The use of report parts is another option available to further simplify the report development process for users who might otherwise fall into the category of information user. Report parts, as mentioned earlier in this chapter, are individual elements in a report, such as a map, a chart, or a table, which can be published independently of the original report in which they were created. Report Builder 3.0 includes a Report Part Gallery that users can browse to locate items they would like to include in a report and arrange in any way they like. Everything necessary for the report part to work gets added to the report along with the report part, so the user doesn't need to know how to set up data sources, datasets, or parameters in order to build a report successfully by using report parts. If the user has enough technical skill to create a Word document, that user probably is capable of building a report entirely from report parts.

PerformancePoint Services   A team BI community can use PerformancePoint Services for department-focused dashboards and scorecards. As with report parts, an IT professional or a designated power user can construct individual components, such as data sources, KPIs, filters, scorecards, and reports that users can use in a SharePoint dashboard, which would be easier to construct for the more advanced information user or power analyst than a PerformancePoint dashboard.

Self-Service and Personal BI

The whole point of building BI infrastructures that contain a data warehouse, data mart, or Analysis Services cube is to allow users to get information when they need it, on a self-service basis. But in many companies, users still rely on standard reports that have limited interactivity. The reports might have parameters that allow users to filter the reports, or they might allow the users to drill down into more detail. Regardless, these reports are typically built to answer one question but not necessarily the next question that the user might have. So when these new questions arise, users wind up going back to IT to get those reports.

As an alternative, users start looking outside the approved sources because they need to get information to make decisions. They may get information from wherever they can find it internally; they may get it from external business partners; and maybe they'll find some data on industry trends that they can download from an Internet site. In short, they wind up manually compiling a lot of data. The bottom line is that the data they need for decision-making on a day-to-day basis is not getting integrated into the corporate system, and that's the problem that self-service BI is intended to solve.

Due to the overlap with organizational and team BI communities, we've already touched on the tools commonly used by this community: Excel, PowerPivot for Excel, Report Builder, and Visio. Casual users are more likely to use Excel and Report Builder, while power users may use any of these tools as applicable to the task at hand. A user can use any of these tools to create a document for personal reference or can share the document with a team BI community by publishing it to a SharePoint document library.

How would a user decide which tool to use? Let's review the characteristics of the documents produced by each tool.

Excel   Excel is a tool commonly preferred by users of all skill levels for ad hoc reporting and analysis. Users can retrieve data from data sources and combine it with manual data. A user can import data and then manipulate the data by creating charts, sorting, filtering, and applying a wide range of calculations from simple to complex. Casual users might use Excel for simple summing and averaging of data, whereas power users might create complex forecasting models. Power users can also create PivotTables from raw data or from Analysis Services data sources for analysis using aggregate functions to summarize data grouped on rows and columns and using filters and slicers to focus on a subset of data. Although the creation of a PivotTable is generally a task for the power user, a casual user can easily explore a PivotTable that has already been created.

Excel is ubiquitous in many organizations, so most users already have a passing familiarity with this tool. Even if they don't create the workbooks themselves, they can access workbooks from SharePoint and, as long as they have the right permissions, download workbooks for personal use. Then they can apply calculations, filter the data, and make other changes to the data without affecting the original workbook.

PowerPivot for Excel   As flexible as Excel can be, it can also be a challenge to combine data from multiple data sources for analysis and to keep the data refreshed. That's where PowerPivot for Excel comes in. It can also use reports as one of its data sources. As another plus, PowerPivot can handle much more data than Excel. Like standard Excel, it's good for interactive exploration of data.

Users don't need to understand relationships between tables created by drawing together data from disparate sources, and PowerPivot can recommend relationships based on its analysis of the contents of data from each source. Calculations can be added by using Data Analysis Expressions (DAX), as described in Chapter 5, "PowerPivot for Excel and SharePoint." This language is Excel-like, which makes it easier for users to create calculations if they're already comfortable with Excel functions. PowerPivot for Excel does make self-service BI easier, but primarily for power users. Casual users benefit most from PowerPivot for Excel when power users publish workbooks to SharePoint.

Report Builder   Report Builder is a desirable tool for users who want to produce a specific type of report layout and also want to store reports in a centralized location, whether for personal use or for sharing with others. Even if a user creates a report for personal consumption, the user can subscribe to the report to receive a report with fresh data on a regular schedule.

Visio   Visio is the only tool that provides data-driven diagrams. Of all the self-service BI tools, Visio is least likely to be used for personal consumption. For example, if a user is monitoring the status of a process, it's easier to build a simple report by using one of the other tools. It's more likely that a power user or BI developer will use Visio to create diagrams to publish to SharePoint for sharing with a team BI community.

The Progression of BI

The Microsoft vision for BI can be summarized simply as the delivery of the right information at the right time in the right format to users at all levels of a company. It's a noble goal, and the Microsoft tools can indeed help companies attain this goal, but not from day one. Instead, the democratization of BI across the organization occurs incrementally. The length of time required depends on many factors, such as the corporate culture overall, management's attitude towards BI, and a support system for users, among others.

An understanding of the typical progression that many companies experience as they expand their use of BI can help in many ways. It can affirm that your company is moving in the right direction, and it can also show you the possibilities that remain for further progression. It can also help you determine which tools are best suited for your current stage and help you prepare for the next.

BI Maturity Model

Wayne Eckerson developed the Business Intelligence Maturity Model for The Data Warehousing Institute™ (TDWI) as a means for organizations to benchmark their deployments against other companies. At a high level, the model identifies six stages that mark the progression of BI from a cost center to a strategic asset. As shown in the following illustration, by plotting the typical user adoption rate along the six stages of the model, Eckerson's research revealed a bell curve in most organizations in stages 2 and 3. It's important to understand that companies don't necessarily follow a linear progression from stages 0 to 5. Stages often overlap, and the length of time that a company remains in a particular stage can vary.

> **Note** You can download a poster illustrating the Business Intelligence Maturity Model from *http://tdwi.org/pages/posters/business-intelligence-maturity-model.aspx*. You can also use TDWI's online assessment tool to benchmark your company's BI maturity by completing the survey at *http://tdwi.org/pages/assessments/benchmark-your-bi-maturity-with-tdwis-new-assessment-tool.aspx*.

TDWI's BI Maturity Model—User Adoption Curve

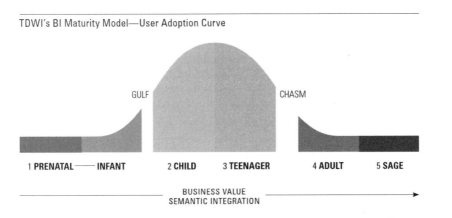

Notable aspects of the model are the Gulf and the Chasm, which highlight the reality that BI implementations are not likely to proceed smoothly from one stage to another. As Eckerson discussed these findings with BI implementers, he discovered that the inclusion of these two obstacles in the model validated their experience that setbacks in BI implementations and flagging enthusiasm for pursuing pervasive BI are a normal part of the process. Perseverance pays off for teams that can stay focused on the steps necessary to expand the capabilities of their BI infrastructure.

Even within the same company, it's very likely that each department will mature at different rates. That's okay. The good news is that wherever people are, they have tools to support them, they can transition to higher levels of maturity over time, and the tools can adapt accordingly. Each successive step in the maturation process translates into greater business value.

In this section, we provide an overview of the characteristics of each stage of the BI Maturity Model and describe the tools that are useful in each stage.

Stage 0: Prenatal

In the prenatal stage, a company has yet to create a data warehouse to support information requirements. Instead, all reports are sourced from operational systems, with no consolidation of information across systems without special processes in place. That is, there are no formal Extract, Transform, and Load (ETL) processes. Financial applications often have the richest set of reports available in the company and are the primary source for management reports. At this point, the available reports are static and focus on historical events to help users understand what has happened. Any changes desired by users require customization by IT, but it's not uncommon for such requests to take weeks or months to fulfill.

To transition from the rigid reporting system typical of this stage to a formal BI solution, many companies start by reproducing their existing reports in Reporting Services. Although the problems associated with responding to requests for customization don't go away, with some forethought, parameterization of reports can enable users to make changes to the report content, which in some cases might forestall the need for one-off report development.

Stage 1: Infant

When users can't get what they need from the operational reports, they often develop their own solutions, which leads to a proliferation of reports based on spreadsheets or Microsoft Access databases that users have cobbled together. Such user-developed data collections are also described as spreadmarts, shadow systems, or skunkworks projects.

Executives often enlist analysts to compile briefing books based on these informal data collections. The focus begins to shift from trying to understand what has happened in the past to attempting to understand how past results might influence what happens in the future.

What starts as a compilation of official data for a specific need can grow into a mission-critical solution that people come to rely on, yet it's unmanaged, unsecured, and unauditable. It can take a lot of manual labor to gather and manipulate the data, leaving little time to analyze the data collected before a decision from the user is required. The concern of each user in this stage is to produce information that supports personal decision-making. Little regard is given to reconciling results with other users producing comparable information, and no official system of record exists to resolve results that disagree.

In this stage, Excel and Access are popular tools. For organizations that have yet to implement a formal BI environment, PowerPivot for Excel can simplify the effort of gathering and integrating data. But it doesn't solve the more serious problem resulting from a lack of IT oversight.

The Gulf

The Gulf is the first obstacle that must be overcome before moving into real BI. Prior to this obstacle, executives likely view any efforts to promote BI as just another variation of operational reporting. To progress, they need to understand how BI is necessary to improved business processes and decision-making at all levels of the organization. According to an Aberdeen Group study, one of the benefits of a collaborative BI environment is a 30 percent improvement in business processes as compared to other companies without such an environment. Executive support is critical to experiencing similar improvements.

Users need to understand how the next step in the BI progression can shift their workload from mundane data-gathering tasks to analysis tasks that are much more valuable in the long run to employers. If users remain unconvinced, a company can get stuck in the Gulf. Even after crossing the Gulf, companies find that spreadmarts are difficult to completely eradicate and often persist through into the Teenager stage.

To successfully cross the Gulf, BI developers should take an iterative and incremental approach, focusing on small projects that are easier to implement rather than trying to build a solution to be all things to all people. Ideally, the first effort should focus on a single source system that contains well-understood data sources. Frequent prototype reviews with users can help the team stay focused on the requirements of this first official BI project. BI developers must remain diligent to counteract scope-creep as user requests continue to outpace IT's ability to deliver new information.

Fortunately, the Microsoft platform can help here. It's very easy to prototype and develop solutions from those prototypes in an iterative fashion, working closely with the user community to get it right. One option is to build prototypes with Analysis Services to build a model and then use Excel to validate it with users. Another option is to let users model their data the way they want to see it using PowerPivot for Excel. In the latter case, IT can take the design and reproduce it in Analysis Services.

Stage 2: Child

At last, the company begins to demonstrate progress with BI, with the first project typically focused on a single subject area. Most companies in this stage have no previous experience with managing BI projects, so the early projects focus on building a data mart without attempting to align metrics with corporate objectives.

The novelty of BI in this stage can generate excitement among users, who are motivated to abandon their labor-intensive past for the new and improved way of finding answers to their questions. Power users who understand the business well can learn the new tools quickly so that they can drill into trends over time, to determine why things happened the way they did.

If an organization has yet to start with Reporting Services, this stage is a common place to introduce it to users. The first set of reports is usually based on department-level standard reports developed in earlier stages with parameterization and drilldown capabilities built in to enable casual users to successfully explore the data. Behind the scenes, the BI team builds a data mart and possibly an Analysis Services cube as data sources for these reports.

To support the ad hoc analysis requirements of power users, the BI team gives users access to cubes using Excel. In addition, these users continue to use PowerPivot for Excel to get answers to questions that can't be answered by the data mart.

Stage 3: Teenager

Having successfully implemented BI at a department level during the Child stage, many companies next take steps in an attempt to prevent each department from setting up its own data mart. In the Teenager stage, the company establishes a formal data warehouse not only to consolidate resources but also to bring consistency to BI processes and company metrics. By adding experienced BI practitioners to the team or by engaging consultants, the company begins to formalize BI across departments and to adopt best practices.

During this stage, the BI solution grows to accommodate more casual users, but this growth also results in an increased demand for standard parameterized reports that can be filtered and dashboards that can be tailored to specific audiences. Also during this stage, the use of BI expands to include KPIs to help management monitor progress towards goals.

Reporting Services continues to be a dominant technology in this stage, with greater emphasis on developing reports that can be used in multiple ways by the addition of parameters, including filters that tailor information to the user. Team BI communities also begin to emerge, with power users publishing shared datasets and report parts that enable casual users to build their own versions of reports. To promote collaboration, the BI solution expands to include the use of SharePoint for dashboards and possibly PerformancePoint Services for scorecards.

The Chasm

Unfortunately, the Chasm is a more challenging obstacle to cross than the Gulf. If the problem of spreadmarts and independent data marts across the company have not been addressed by this point, the next step in the maturation process might be exceedingly difficult to obtain. Any change in the company's business strategy can also pose problems for the BI team, but ironically, that's when the organization needs BI most of all.

To successfully move to the next stage, developing a flexible architecture for the company's BI solutions is mandatory. As difficult as it might be, the company must commit a key group of users to the development of a common glossary for terms and calculations used in reports, workbooks, and other BI-related documents. Support from the top down is necessary. One characteristic of the Chasm is the inevitable struggle between team BI and organizational BI communities. In the end, corporate IT standards must prevail so that the departmental BI systems can properly align at the corporate level.

During this stage, self-service BI is perceived to be the goal by many users, but over-reliance on this approach to information management can lead to chaos, with unmanaged reports proliferating throughout the company. Reports developed by one person might be useful to another, but if that other user can't find what they need, time is wasted to develop a duplicate report.

To counteract this type of problem, the BI team needs to focus on building datasets, interactive reports, report parts, and dashboards that address the range of broad questions that users ask regularly. In particular, this is the very type of problem that the self-service BI features in Reporting Services and PowerPivot for SharePoint are intended to solve. These tools can be introduced during the Teenager stage, but they can't solve the unification problem, which is typically not a technical challenge but an organizational behavior challenge.

Stage 4: Adult

When a company can successfully define standards, a common set of terms, and consistent rules, it's ready to develop an enterprise data warehouse and move to the Adult stage, which yields several significant advancements in BI capabilities. The enterprise data warehouse transitions the use of BI from the support of departmental objectives to the support of organizational objectives. Performance management expands beyond the use of dashboards for monitoring processes to include scorecards that enable individuals to see how their respective decisions impact corporate performance.

The addition of real-time data feeds, as well as forecasting and modeling tools, enables users not only to analyze the past to better understand what happened but also to apply that knowledge to the current situation and to anticipate the future. This maturation of BI capabilities enables proactive management of the company based on predictive analytics as an alternative to the reactive management approach in earlier stages in which only historical analysis was possible.

Furthermore, the flexibility previously missing in the BI solution architecture finally arrives. Abstraction layers insulate users from changes to the underlying system as alignment of sources continues to occur. Users can now repurpose data and reports to suit their needs rather than wait for BI developers to respond to a new report request.

The Microsoft platform continues to support the BI requirements of a company in the Adult stage. The BI team can roll out PerformancePoint Services, if it hasn't already been implemented in an earlier stage, in support of the new performance management activities. In addition, Analysis Services supports the development of forecasting models, the results of which can be accessed in any of the self-service BI tools.

In terms of tool usage, most of the time casual users still want prepackaged content to monitor events or conditions relevant to their daily tasks. This can be accomplished through dashboards presenting a combination of scorecards, reports, and Excel workbooks. Each of these tools can present a view of the current state, support filtering to allow the user to focus on particular items of interest, and provide the ability to drill down to more detail. The enterprise search capability in SharePoint provides these users with another way to find relevant content. If users still need to create something themselves, they can use Report Builder to create data mash-ups from reusable components in Reporting Services, SharePoint lists, and PowerPivot workbooks published to SharePoint.

Stage 5: Sage

In the final stage, companies establish a BI center of excellence to promote and sustain best practices for the current platform, to support user adoption, and to drive innovation. Rather than maintain the centralized management of BI that emerged in the Adult stage, the company allows departments to assume control once again over BI processes with the mandate that these departmental-level projects adhere to the standards and best practices defined at the corporate level.

BI becomes a strategic asset in this stage as well and transitions to a service-oriented architecture. Developers can then use web services to embed BI into line-of-business applications. The provision of BI to external stakeholders can also become a revenue stream for the company. When this happens, the company continues to make large investments in BI to ensure high levels of service to the external stakeholders.

The entire Microsoft BI stack is in use by the time a company reaches this stage. In addition, the Microsoft platform is fully extensible. Developers can use APIs for any tool in the stack to enable customization at every point of the information management process and can embed that customization into applications. Even without customization and with no additional configuration necessary, Reporting Services can provide data feeds as a service to enable a company to surface data from cubes, mining models, or relational data warehouses.

Road Map to Analytical Competition

Another way to view the progression of BI is provided by a road map developed by Thomas H. Davenport and Jeanne G. Harris in their book *Competing on Analytics: The New Science of Winning*. The purpose of this road map is to provide a realistic view of the stages a company often experiences in its quest to derive value from analytics and to outline a strategy for successfully transitioning to higher stages. As shown in the following illustration, the analytics road map proposed by Davenport and Harris consists of five stages that follow a progression similar to the one in the maturity model described in the previous section, but one that's more compressed and leads to a more specific outcome. Whereas the maturity model views the end state for BI as a pervasive technology and potential revenue stream, the road map assumes that the goal for BI is to produce a distinct competitive advantage.

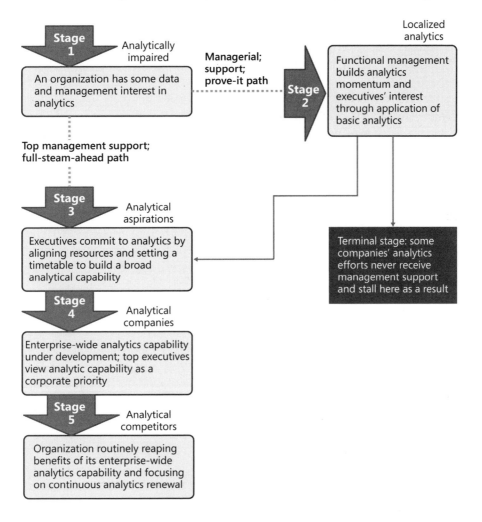

Stage 1: Analytically Impaired

In the first stage, operational data is not ready for analysis. Reporting directly from operational data is fraught with problems and suffers from data quality issues. To progress to the next stage, management needs to be convinced that better decision-making results from access to better data. Meanwhile, some technically savvy business users begin compiling data for personal analysis. Excel is often the tool of choice at this stage.

Stage 2: Localized Analytics

The work begun by the independent analysts begins to show promise in this stage as they develop new insights that have value for the company. One of two things happens at this point: Either executive management agrees that it's time to start formally investing in BI, and the company moves to the next stage, or management remains unconvinced and needs more evidence of successful outcomes from analysis before making the commitment.

As a result, the focus of this stage is to gradually build out a BI infrastructure at a local level with minimal investment, such as a department-level single-subject data mart. Despite the lack of support from executive management, the BI team can use this stage to develop experience before tackling the more comprehensive projects in the next stage. In addition, the department making the investment in BI benefits from the business process improvements resulting from the better analytical capabilities. According to the analytics road map, a company could be in this stage from one to three years.

The BI components in the Microsoft stack are a good starting point for a department-level data mart that could also include a complementary cube to support analysis. Reporting Services can deliver standard reports to department users and provide data feeds for power users to use in PowerPivot for Excel for deeper analysis.

Stage 3: Analytical Aspirations

When a company is ready to commit to analytics at the corporate level, the focus shifts from the tactical BI solutions found at the department level to a company-wide performance management solution. The challenge at this stage is the integration of various tools and processes implemented across departments and to reach agreement regarding the metrics against which to measure progress. In general, the road map indicates the length of time for this stage can be a few months or up to two years.

In this stage, the Microsoft stack scales from a departmental deployment to an enterprise deployment. The Reporting Services platform remains in place for broad distribution of standard reports. SharePoint and PerformancePoint Services now become tools for monitoring and reporting performance management results. Power users can also now share PowerPivot for Excel workbooks by publishing them to SharePoint and thereby promote collaborative analysis.

Stage 4: Analytical Companies

To move into this stage, the company must establish analytics as a priority and the corporate culture must support an ongoing process of experimentation. Management encourages analysts to develop and test hypotheses and to discover new areas worth exploring. The purpose of analytics in this stage is to discover how to use information assets to differentiate the company from its competitors in the marketplace. During this stage, the tools for analysis become more advanced and developers are tasked with embedding analytics into business processes.

Here the BI team can exploit the full range of capabilities in the Microsoft BI stack, including the data mining features in Analysis Services. In addition, developers can integrate BI into the line-of-business applications.

Stage 5: Analytical Competitors

At this stage, analytics aren't just helping management run the company better, as evidenced by strong financial performance, but the insights derived from analytics also create a competitive advantage in the marketplace. The use of BI is now widespread across the company and executive management is fully committed to continued investment in BI technologies.

Additional tools are not a major factor in this stage. Instead, the implementation of the Microsoft tools in earlier stages can help foster an environment that enables business users at all levels of the organization to find the right information at the right time.

Tool Selection

Throughout this chapter, we've identified various characteristics of the user tools, including their appropriateness for different types of users and the suggested level of BI maturity at which each tool can be adopted. We've also pointed out some of the advantages and disadvantages of each tool to help you understand the implications of selecting a tool before you get started on a project. Now we'll summarize this information and provide some additional pointers so that you have a quick reference for all the tools in one convenient location.

The table that follows provides a summary of the tools, with a breakdown of the primary user of each tool by business user community and by BI community. Additionally, the table identifies whether the business user (who can be either a casual user or a power analyst), the power analyst, or the BI developer is responsible for creating content with the tool. Last, the table identifies where the content for the tool can be reused.

Tool	BI community	Content author	Reusability
Excel	Self-service and Personal BI	Business User	■ Excel Services ■ SharePoint BI ■ PerformancePoint Services
PowerPivot for Excel	Self-service and Personal BI	Business User	PowerPivot for SharePoint
Excel Services	■ Team BI ■ Organizational BI	Business User	■ SharePoint BI ■ PerformancePoint Services ■ Customized applications
PowerPivot for SharePoint	Team BI	Business User	■ Excel ■ Report Builder ■ SharePoint BI ■ PerformancePoint Services ■ Customized applications ■ Any tool that connects to Analysis Services
Report Builder (Reporting Services)	■ Self-service and Personal BI ■ Team BI	Business User	■ PowerPivot for Excel ■ SharePoint BI ■ PerformancePoint Services ■ Customized applications
Report Designer (Reporting Services)	■ Team BI ■ Organizational BI	BI Developer	■ PowerPivot for Excel ■ SharePoint BI ■ PerformancePoint Services ■ Customized applications
SharePoint BI	Team BI	■ BI Developer ■ Power User	Content not reusable in other tools
PerformancePoint Services	■ Team BI ■ Organizational BI	■ BI Developer ■ Power User	■ SharePoint BI ■ Customized applications
Visio	Self-service and Personal BI	BI Developer	Visio Services
Visio Services	Team BI	BI Developer	■ SharePoint BI ■ Customized applications

> **Note** In the Content Author column in the preceding table, the BI Developer is omitted in some rows but can often be the primary content author with the respective tool. We've elected to identify the BI Developer in this table only when the BI Developer is most likely to have the primary role for creating the content.

Excel

Excel is a very popular tool, and many, if not most, analysts are already using it. Excel is familiar even to casual users and for this reason gets used for everything from simple To Do lists to complex financial analysis.

Use this tool to:

- Retrieve data from a source without having query language skills.
- Analyze data (that is, group, filter, drill down) containing fewer than one million records.
- Create pivot tables and charts with limited formatting options.
- Apply complex calculations to data.
- Publish workbooks to Excel Services to share insights.
- Store data for use in SharePoint:
    - ❏ Status indicator
    - ❏ Chart Web Part
    - ❏ Visio Web Drawing
    - ❏ PerformancePoint Services KPI or filter
    - ❏ Component in a SharePoint or PerformancePoint Services dashboard

PowerPivot for Excel

PowerPivot for Excel provides power users with a tool that uses familiar Excel features while supporting more advanced analysis.

Use this tool to:

- Analyze small or large amounts of data (millions of records).
- Integrate multiple data sources when no data mart exists or when analysis needs to incorporate data not found in the data warehouse.
- Create pivot tables and charts with limited formatting options.
- Apply complex calculations to data.

- Reproduce the analytical capabilities that Analysis Services supports without waiting for IT to build a cube.

- Publish workbooks to PowerPivot for SharePoint to share insights.

- Store data for use in SharePoint:

    - Status indicator

    - Chart Web Part

    - Visio Web Drawing

    - PerformancePoint Services KPI or filter

    - Component in a SharePoint or PerformancePoint Services dashboard

Chapter 5, "PowerPivot for Excel and SharePoint," provides more information about using this tool.

Excel Services

Excel Services is a SharePoint service application that enables users to share Excel workbooks in a secure, centralized location. The interface is simple for casual users to find and access information.

Use this tool to:

- Enable users to share large workbooks outside of email, even to users who don't have Excel installed.

- Display data in a dashboard-like layout using a familiar interface.

- Provide casual users with collaborative workbook editing and limited analysis capabilities in a browser environment.

- Protect intellectual property in Excel workbooks.

- Embed complex calculation capabilities in custom applications.

You can learn more about this tool in Chapter 4, "Excel Services."

PowerPivot for SharePoint

PowerPivot for SharePoint is another SharePoint service application that uses Excel Services to display PowerPivot for Excel workbooks and provides management oversight of activity related to these workbooks. Because PowerPivot for SharePoint relies on Excel Services, the familiar, simplified interface helps casual users interact easily with the workbooks and to use the workbooks as a data source using self-service BI tools such as Report Builder or Excel.

Use this tool to:

- Enable users to work collaboratively on analytical data compiled in a PowerPivot for Excel workbook.
- Automate the process of refreshing the data sources in a workbook.
- Provide users with a data source for self-service BI tools.
- Discover data sources used in workbooks and monitor workbook usage.

Refer to Chapter 5 to learn how to work with PowerPivot for SharePoint.

Reporting Services

Reporting Services is the best option for delivering standard report content to a wide audience either online or via email. When integrated with SharePoint, it relies on the same storage and security mechanisms but retains all the features available in native mode.

Casual users can easily access reports and, in some cases, might build their own reports. Power users can participate in the content development process.

Casual users can use Report Builder 3.0 to:

- Build reports from published report parts using drag-and-drop.
- Build reports from shared datasets (with no need to know the query details) and design a simple table, matrix, or chart by using a wizard.
- Apply basic formatting to a report.

Power users can use Report Builder 3.0 to perform the same tasks as casual users and to:

- Connect to data sources and create queries to retrieve data for a report.
- Create and publish shared datasets and report parts for use by casual users.
- Build reports using any of the same features supported in the Report Designer available in Business Intelligence Development Studio:
  - Pixel-perfect layout of table, matrix, list, or chart objects
  - Design for online viewing or print format
  - Geospatial mapping
  - Interactive features—sort, filter, drill down, drill through, document maps, tooltips
- Provide a data source of PowerPivot for Excel.

- Create an entire dashboard layout, displaying data from multiple sources on a single page when the following characteristics are desired:
  - ❏ Fine control over the appearance
  - ❏ Interactive features already available in Reporting Services
  - ❏ Distribution of dashboard in print or other formats
  - ❏ Support for subscriptions
- Create content with a specific layout or interactive features for use in a SharePoint or PerformancePoint Services dashboard or in a custom application.

BI developers can use Report Designer to perform the same tasks as power users. However, although Report Designer allows the BI developer to publish report parts, it does not provide access to published report parts to use when designing a new report. Report Designer also allows the Report Developer to work with multiple reports in the same session, whereas Report Builder allows users to work with only one report at a time.

Report consumers can access reports in SharePoint to:

- View and interact with a report online.
- Export a report to a variety of formats, including data feeds.
- Subscribe to a report for scheduled delivery by email or to a network file share.

SharePoint BI

SharePoint BI accommodates a variety of sources, which allows power users or BI developers to consolidate information in a single location even when a formal BI implementation is not yet in place and to change out content when the company eventually develops a data warehouse or Analysis Services cube.

Use this tool to:

- Set up status indicators to track performance using a simple interface and optionally to add to a dashboard.
- Develop Chart Web Parts to add data visualization to a dashboard if other tools are not preferred.
- Build a simple dashboard to display, and optionally filter, information from multiple sources on a single page (such as workbooks, reports, Visio Web Drawings, PerformancePoint Services content, and other content types).

Chapter 8, "Bringing It All Together," provides more information about working with SharePoint's BI features.

PerformancePoint Services

PerformancePoint Services is yet another SharePoint service application that supports the development of content types used in performance-management solutions that users access in SharePoint. BI developers typically produce the complete solutions using the Dashboard Designer tool, although power users might also use this stool to contribute content.

Use this tool to:

- Create data sources for use when developing KPIs, scorecards, reports, and filters.

- Develop both simple and advanced KPIs.

- Create scorecards to display KPIs in asymmetrical or hierarchical structures for use in either a SharePoint or a PerformancePoint dashboard.

- Build an analytic grid report or analytic chart report to support browser-based interactive pivoting, drilling, and filtering of data in an Analysis Services cube.

- Provide access to the decomposition tree visualization by creating a scorecard, analytic grid report, or analytic chart report.

- Build a strategy map as a supplement to a scorecard to illustrate relationships between objectives, goals, and KPIs.

- Design filters to use in a SharePoint or PerformancePoint Services dashboard.

- Develop a dashboard containing one or more pages by using PerformancePoint content types (scorecard, strategy map, analytic reports, and filters).

For more details, see Chapter 7, "PerformancePoint Services."

Visio Services

Visio Services is the final SharePoint service application that we cover in this book. It enables users to securely share Visio diagrams for viewing in a browser. Because designing data-driven Visio diagrams requires a solid understanding of Visio and the data sources, BI developers most likely will be responsible for content development rather than users.

Use Visio 2010 to:

- Produce web diagrams, optionally linked to a data source, to illustrate a business process, condition, or other scenario.

- Build a PivotDiagram as a data-visualization tool for hierarchical data.

Use Visio Services to:

- Enable users to share Visio diagrams with users who don't have Visio installed.

- Embed diagrams in custom applications.

See Chapter 6, "Visio and Visio Services," to learn more about these tools.

Summary

The goal of this chapter is to describe how the various BI tools can work separately or together in different scenarios, for different user communities, and at different stages of maturity with BI capabilities. Don't be overly concerned if you or business users in your company want to start using a certain tool before the maturity model or road map says you're ready for that stage. The whole point of BI is to empower users to access information in any way possible. Just make sure that users aren't trying to use a tool that requires greater technical skills than they possess. If they're willing to learn, support them in their efforts, but don't turn them loose without support, because they might simply give up on all BI out of frustration. For the same reason, don't implement a tool if the necessary infrastructure isn't yet in place or if it doesn't provide the specific functionality that you need. At this point, you should have a better understanding of how the tools available in the Microsoft BI stack work together to support your goals for delivering information to users at all levels of your company, and you should feel better prepared to select a tool. The next chapter explains what you need to do to establish the back-end infrastructure to better support many of these tools.

Chapter 3
Getting to Trusted Data

After completing this chapter, you will be able to

- Understand the term "trusted data."

- Understand SQL Server 2008 R2 and its role in business intelligence (BI).

- Understand the life cycle of a BI implementation.

- Create a data warehouse.

- Move data from a source to the data warehouse.

- Create a SQL Server Analysis Services cube.

Introduction to Trusted Data

The major focus of this book is on how to use SharePoint Server 2010, integrated with SQL Server 2008 R2, to present data to business users. This would be pointless without data you can trust to present to your business user applications. Trusted data comes from business processes occurring in departments such as marketing, finance, e-commerce, and more, and is then transformed for use in decision-making. The transformation lets trusted data be delivered in formats and time frames that are appropriate to specific consumers of reports, spreadsheets, visualizations, and other data rendering tools.

Data that's incomplete, out-of-date, or poorly documented can destroy users' trust. Users who don't have confidence in the data might refuse to use the reports and analyses created from this data. Instead, they might build their own data stores. The solution is a combination of following best practices for data collection, data profiling, and data integration, plus the application of guidelines from related disciplines, such as data quality, master data management, metadata management, and so on. The BI maturity model mentioned in Chapter 2, "Choosing the Right BI Tool," shows that making trusted data available across an organization doesn't occur as a single event; it's a process that occurs in stages.

Another way to look at trusted data is as data "approved for viewing." The viewers are business users who range from front-line employees to executive management and external stakeholders. You can imagine the importance of having trusted data when everything rides on decisions being made at the corporate level.

The broad definition of BI described at the beginning of this book includes both the data warehouse and the tools used to view the data from the warehouse. This chapter explains what a data warehouse is, what online analytical processing (OLAP) is and how it relates to data warehousing, and finally, how Microsoft implements these technologies to deliver the right information and the right amount of information in the right form, fast.

Additionally, for most of the authoring tools, a cube is the ideal data source, because:

- It's not just that it's structured data—it's structured in a way that mirrors how the users already view their business, so it's intuitive.

- Cube data is faster to query, so questions can be asked and answered very quickly.

- The data in a cube is interactive and more easily presented by using a variety of tools for reporting and analysis. While standard reports are frequently referenced, structured reports and analysis are interactive and can be generated for ad hoc exploration of data in search of answers.

- When in place, a cube can help prevent long lines (waiting periods) for the IT department because it enables more self-service authoring.

The authoring tools support drag-and-drop elements for building reports, charts, graphs, and scorecards. The following illustration shows an example using Excel's PivotTable Field List dialog box, which makes data available in a drag-and-drop format for building reports. The data is organized intuitively.

A lot of thought and work goes into warehousing data in such a way that it can be retrieved easily. This chapter provides a broad overview of the steps toward creating trusted data; you can find other resources that provide deeper coverage. Data warehousing and OLAP have developed over decades, and many people have written books about these subjects.

Some of the more popular books come from Ralph Kimball and the Kimball Group, such as "The Data Warehouse Toolkit: The Complete Guide to Dimensional Modeling" and the "Data Warehouse ETL Toolkit: Practical Techniques for Extracting, Cleaning, Conforming, and Delivering Data," both available at *http://www.ralphkimball.com/html/books.html*. A good resource for white papers about BI, managing BI projects, and more is the data warehouse institute (TDWI) (*http://tdwi.org/*). And you can see why they're a primary area of professional focus when you consider how so many companies struggle to harness mountains of data and then try to make that data useful.

This chapter also dives into what SQL Server 2008 R2 offers as the foundation for trusted data and why it is so important to SharePoint Server 2010 services that are dedicated to BI. PowerPivot for Excel and PowerPivot for SharePoint were developed by the SQL Server product team in large part because the client and back-end databases have a symbiotic relationship.

Additionally, this chapter provides examples of the end-to-end BI implementation life cycle.

Finally, at the end of this chapter, you can learn how to create your own cube by using SQL Server Analysis Services.

Before discussing the tools, it's worth taking a look at the concepts that can help you get closer to having trusted data.

SQL Server 2008 R2 + SharePoint 2010 + Office 2010

SQL Server has traditionally been a one-stop shop for customers seeking to implement BI solutions. Many companies still use SQL Server to move data from disparate sources in an extract, transform, and load (ETL) process, develop solutions to surface multidimensional data, and use products such as SQL Server Reporting Services to build reports from relational and multidimensional databases.

The following illustration, sectioned from a downloadable poster on TechNet at *http://www.microsoft.com/downloads/details.aspx?familyid=FC97D587-FFA4-4B43-B77D-958F3F8A87B9&displaylang=en*, shows how SQL Server 2008 R2, SharePoint 2010, and Office 2010 work together to deliver data that helps business users.

> **Note** Microsoft BI authoring tools are available in all three layers shown in the illustration. Some tools come from SQL Server, such as Report Builder; some, like PerformancePoint, are in SharePoint; and others are in Office, including Excel and Visio. See Chapter 2, "Choosing the Right BI Tool."

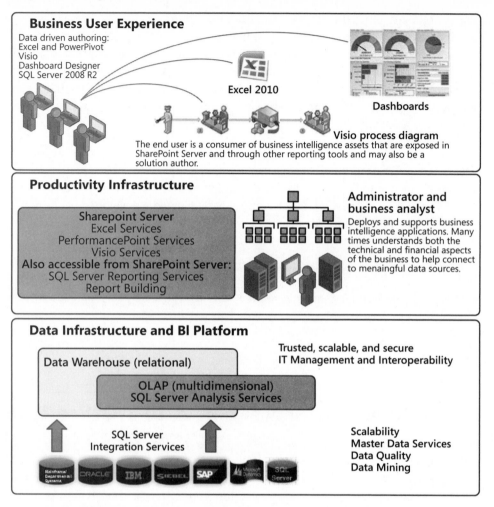

You can use SharePoint Server in conjunction with SQL Server Reporting Services and BI tools to show BI data in meaningful and productive ways. SQL Server provides the primary data infrastructure and BI platform that gives report authors and business users trusted, scalable, and secure data.

The following sections describe the technologies and features in SQL Server that support BI functionality and features.

Important These tools are discussed at greater length in the section "Life Cycle of BI Implementation" later in this chapter, to help you see where and how the tools fit in the context of the phases of an end-to-end scenario.

BI in SQL Server2008 R2

The important products in the Microsoft BI technology stack include Microsoft SQL Server Integration Services, Microsoft SQL Server Analysis Services, Microsoft SQL Server Reporting Services, and Microsoft Business Intelligence Development Studio. These products make up the core of the BI features in SQL Server and are important to understand if you want to understand Microsoft's BI offerings.

Core BI Components

This section describes each of the four core components that make up the SQL Server BI features.

SQL Server Database Engine

The SQL Server database engine is the core service for storing, processing, and securing data; it serves as the engine for both the staging and the data warehouse databases. BI data is derived from databases managed by the SQL Server database engine.

SQL Server Integration Services (SSIS)

Microsoft SQL Server Integration Services (SSIS) gives you data integration and data transformation solutions to help you get to trusted data faster. You can create repeatable data integration using the ETL process. This process can be automated, moving data from sources such as XML data files, flat files, or relational data sources to one or more destinations. Data from disparate sources must often be cleansed.

Features that make SSIS compelling for ETL solution building include:

- A user interface that helps users move data and perform ETL.
- Wizards for importing and exporting data and that help create a package that contains the business logic to handle data extraction, manipulation, and transformation. Workflow elements help process data.
- Runtime debugging so that BI developers can step into code and watch the processes in a package. Reusable event handlers also help developers to create rich, repeatable ETL processes.

On another note, because this book is about SharePoint, it makes sense to mention that SharePoint is also a source and destination system from which to extract and load data. It is becoming increasingly more important to know how to move data from and to SharePoint as companies adopt SharePoint to store business data. Some data will be tied directly to another software product that has partnered with SharePoint for sharing.

We give an example of SSIS in action in the section "Step 3: Create and Populate the Data Warehouse."

For more information, see "SQL Server Integration Services," at *http://go.microsoft.com/ fwlink/?LinkId=199546*.

SQL Server Analysis Services (SSAS)

Microsoft SQL Server Analysis Services (SSAS) is designed to support ad-hoc reporting needs, and multidimensional data is the key to this. Using SSAS, formerly known as OLAP Services, you can design, create, navigate, and manage multidimensional structures that contain detail and aggregated data from multiple data sources. Learn more about multidimensional data in the section "Step 4: Create an SSAS from Warehouse Data."

SSAS uses wizards to simplify the cube development process. Dimensional data or cube data is a common data source for the types of analysis you can perform using Microsoft Office, SQL Server Reporting Services, PowerPivot, and BI-related service applications in SharePoint.

Multidimensional data helps users analyze data. For more information, see "SQL Server Analysis Services—Multidimensional Data," at *http://go.microsoft.com/fwlink/?LinkId=199541*.

Data Mining

SQL Server Analysis Services data mining tools provide a set of industry-standard data mining algorithms and other tools that help you discover trends and patterns in your data. Data mining complements what you do in SSAS by helping you discover surprises in data and often provides a glimpse of "what will happen." This is sometimes referred to as predictive analysis. Also, SSAS helps you validate "what you think happened," to support a belief that is based on historic data.

By looking at the following data mining case studies, available at (*http://www.microsoft.com/ casestudies/*), you can learn more about specific business problems that were solved using SSAS data mining. Here are some examples:

- **Illinois Department of Transportation**   "The Illinois Department of Transportation Saves Lives with Microsoft Business Intelligence Solution" (*http://www.microsoft.com/ casestudies/Case_Study_Detail.aspx?CaseStudyID=4000001842*)

- **The Banca Marche Group**   "New Information System Increases Efficiency and Helps Double Profits at Italian Bank" (*http://www.microsoft.com/casestudies/Case_Study_ Detail.aspx?CaseStudyID=201077*)

- **Zillow.com**   "Database Products Help Real Estate Service Evaluate Millions of Homes Daily, Cut Costs" (*http://www.microsoft.com/casestudies/Case_Study_Detail. aspx?CaseStudyID=1000003853*)

The following Excel add-ins can help you perform predictive analysis:

- Table Analysis Tools for Excel provide easy-to-use features that take advantage of Analysis Services Data Mining to perform powerful analytics on spreadsheet data. For more information, see "SQL Server Analysis Services—Data Mining," at *http:// go.microsoft.com/fwlink/?LinkId=199543*.

- Data Mining Client for Excel enables you to work through the full data mining model-development life cycle within Microsoft Office Excel 2007 and Excel 2010, using either worksheet data or external data available through Analysis Services.

SQL Server Reporting Services

Microsoft SQL Server Reporting Services (SSRS) and SharePoint 2010 are integrated include a full range of tools with which you can create, deploy, and manage reports for your organization. SSRS also has features you can use to extend and customize your reporting functionality.

The following illustration shows the Welcome page of the SSRS Report Wizard, which you can use to create an RDL file that can be stored in SharePoint integrated mode.

SSRS includes Report Builder 3.0, an authoring tool that you can launch directly from SharePoint Products 2010. You can publish report server content types to a SharePoint library and then view and manage those documents from a SharePoint site.

Why use SharePoint for managing SSRS reports? Stacia Misner in "SSRS 2008 R2 and SharePoint 2010"[1] says, "You'll have only one security model to manage and, even better, business users will have only one environment in which to create, find, and share information, whether that information is in the form of reports, lists, documents, or other content types. Furthermore, you can manage reports using the same content management, workflow, and versioning features that you use for other SharePoint content."

In a nutshell, SharePoint provides SSRS with similar or the same BI asset management benefits as other BI assets such as Excel Spreadsheets, Visio diagrams, PerformancePoint Dashboards, and more.

For more information about SSRS, see "SQL Server Reporting Services," at *http://go.microsoft.com/fwlink/?LinkId=199545*.

Business Intelligence Development Studio

Microsoft Business Intelligence Development Studio (BIDS) provides several intuitive wizards for building integration, reporting, and analytic solutions within a unified environment. BIDS supports the complete development life cycle for developing, testing, and deploying solutions. The BIDS development environment uses a Visual Studio shell and includes project templates that make it easy to design solutions for ETL processes, cubes, and reports. The following illustration shows the projects from templates that you can create in BIDS.

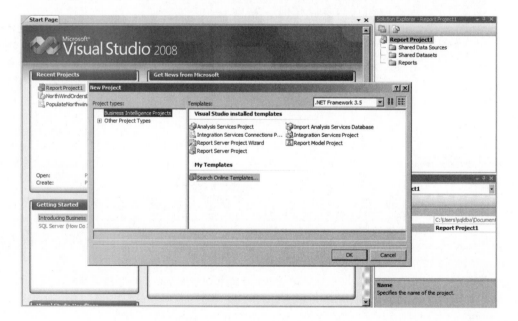

---

[1] Source: *http://www.sqlmag.com/article/sql-server-2008-r2/Reporting-Services-2008-R2-and-SharePoint-Server-2010-The-Next-Generation-of-Integration.aspx*.

Other SQL Server 2008 R2 BI Features

The following sections briefly describe other SQL Server 2008 R2 features that can help you develop more comprehensive BI solutions.

PowerPivot for Excel and PowerPivot for SharePoint

PowerPivot is an add-in for Excel that enables users to create self-service BI solutions. It also facilitates sharing and collaboration on those solutions by using the SharePoint Server 2010 environment. The major components of PowerPivot are as follows:

- PowerPivot for Excel 2010 is a data analysis add-in that delivers computational power directly to Microsoft Excel 2010. PowerPivot for Excel enables users to analyze large quantities of data and integrates with SharePoint Server to help IT departments monitor and manage collaboration. The add-in extends Excel so that it can work with data exceeding one million rows, including external data. PowerPivot includes the Vertipaq engine, which provides rapid calculations over large data sets. For more information, see Chapter 5, "PowerPivot for Excel and SharePoint."

- PowerPivot for SharePoint 2010 extends SharePoint Server and Excel Services to add server-side processing, collaboration, and document management support for the PowerPivot workbooks that publish to SharePoint sites. For more information, see "PowerPivot for SharePoint," at *http://go.microsoft.com/fwlink/?LinkId=199547.*

> **Important** While SSAS is an OLAP engine available for IT professionals to build sophisticated, high-performance solutions to deploy across the organization, PowerPivot for Excel is intended for information workers who build BI solutions for their own use rather than for use across the entire organization.
>
> Users can publish their PowerPivot files to SharePoint Server or SharePoint Foundation for use by a team. To learn more about the differences, see the PowerPivot Team Blog post "Comparing Analysis Services and PowerPivot," at *http://go.microsoft.com/fwlink/?LinkId=192047.*

Master Data Services

You can use SQL Server Master Data Services (MDS) to centrally manage important data assets company-wide and across diverse systems to provide more trusted data to your BI applications. MDS helps you create a master data hub that includes a thin-client data management application. This application is used by a data steward who ensures compliance with rules established as part of a company's data governance initiative. This application can significantly reduce the need to perform ETL because data is being managed with foresight. BI developers can spend less time extracting data from disparate sources and more useful time collecting accurate data from MDS, the "single source of the truth." The benefits also include improving report consistency and a more trusted source. Aligning data across systems can become a reality.

MDS can also apply workflow to assigned owners, apply extensible business rules to safeguard data quality, and support the management of hierarchies and attributes. For more information, see "Master Data Services," at *http://go.microsoft.com/fwlink/?LinkId=199548*.

StreamInsight and Complex Event Processing

Microsoft StreamInsight is a new feature in SQL Server 2008 R2 that helps you monitor data from multiple sources and that can detect patterns, trends, and exceptions almost instantly. StreamInsight also lets you analyze data without first storing it. The ability to monitor, analyze, and act on high-volume data in motion provides opportunities to make informed business decisions more rapidly. For more information, see "Microsoft StreamInsight," at *http://go.microsoft.com/fwlink/?LinkId=199549*.

Life Cycle of a BI Implementation

The best way to explain BI concepts is within the context of a BI implementation life cycle. The diagrams in this section give you a 50,000-foot view of the life cycle of a BI implementation, from determining KPIs to actually surfacing data and monitoring those KPIs in a dashboard. The example in this section is not indicative of the reality that companies face; it's intended only as an illustration of the end-to-end process. However, for the purpose of learning about the major components of an implementation, which include subcomponents for each phase, this example is useful. After the end-to-end example, you can work through a quick hands-on lab to practice creating a cube from a very small data warehouse.

Step 1: Decide What to Analyze, Measure, or Forecast

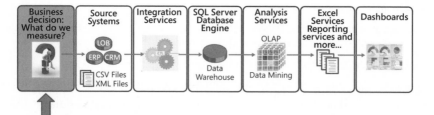

Suppose your company decides it wants to answer questions by using data it has collected from transactional systems. Or perhaps your company wants to improve its forecasting process by collecting the right information, by having more reporting flexibility, or by giving more people access to information. The required steps for these BI initiatives can go wrong in several places. You need to get to what your customer wants, and you want to be effective so that you build the solution the organization needs.

Determining what to do with the data might be the most important—and often the most difficult—step. It's important because you do not want to spend resources collecting data that is not useful. Savvy developers and solution designers must work with users to determine their data requirements in an efficient, iterative manner.

The easier a designer makes it for users to quickly understand the results of a BI solution, the closer a designer can come to delivering a useful solution. For this reason, one of the tools, the SQL Server Business Intelligence Developer Studio (BIDS) browser, enables developers to see the results of data collection and queries, and it is nearly identical to the viewer in Excel. Both tools provide great support for prototyping and scope checking.

Step 2: Inventory the Data You Have

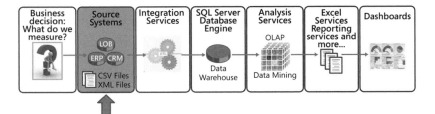

After you know what you want to measure, you must determine where the data will come from and plan how to collect it. The preceding illustration shows data from Line-of-Business (LOB) systems, Enterprise Resource Planning (ERP) systems, Customer Relationship Management (CRM) systems, and flat files, such as CSV and XML files. Other sources, such as Excel files and data from online transaction processing (OLTP) systems, are also common and are valuable as raw data sources that can be cleaned and prepared for BI solutions.

An OLTP system can be defined as a relational store that is designed and optimized for computer-based transactions. Transaction processing is information processing, one transaction at a time. For example, when an item is purchased at a store, the store records that purchase as a single transaction in a computer system that uses an OLTP database. An OLTP system records business transactions as they happen and supports day-to-day operations in an organization. Transactional data is the raw data that the business can use as the basis for fact data and, later, to calculate measures (in cubes), as discussed in the next section.

As you can see, it's common to draw from multiple data sources to deliver a useful BI solution. It's also common to gather data from multiple OLTP systems. Because of the variety of sources, the data very likely contains a variety of different formats for dates, product and category names, and other data. Inconsistent data types used for the same data, different time periods, and other problems require you to consolidate and cleanse the data.

Before cleansing data, your primary goal is to determine where the data is to extract, clean, and conform. Because the ETL process can be the most resource heavy, it's also vital that you understand exactly what the users require before you begin. Best practices for understanding user requirements often include a prototyping and iterative back-and-forth discussion among analysts, report users, and developers. It is particularly important to validate that you're collecting the right amount of information at the right time, in the right format, and with the most helpful visualizations.

Far too often, a company starting a BI initiative wants to integrate the enterprise's data right now, so they're reluctant to take the time to design an extensible and universal solution—but not doing so increases the likelihood of unusable solutions that lead to future rework. It is well worth your time to review the methodologies and literature around BI project management solutions in other books and articles.

You deliver the cleaned source data into a dimensional data store that implements querying and analysis capabilities for the purpose of decision-making. There are excellent books and articles on best practices for ETL data. Ralph Kimball is a pioneer for data warehousing and has published much of the original content for ETL and other data warehousing best practices. You can find his books and articles at *http://www.ralphkimball.com*. Other sources include The Data Warehouse Institute (TDWI), at (*http://tdwi.org*), which is an educational institution for BI and data warehousing. In addition, the "Information Management" site, at *http://www.information-management.com/*, provides news, commentary, and feature content serving the information technology and business community.

Step 3: Create and Populate the Data Warehouse

As the following illustration shows, Step 3 occurs in two phases. First you must design and create a data warehouse in SQL Server. (A number of books have been written on best practices for creating a data warehouse.)

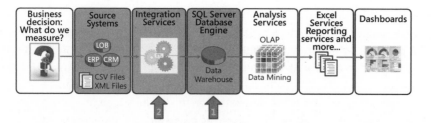

What is not shown in the preceding diagram is a staging database. A staging database is an intermediate storage location used for organizing, cleansing, and transforming data to prepare it for a data warehouse. A staging database helps minimize the impact on the source systems during the ETL process. Basically, you want to get in and out of the data warehouse quickly. If you put everything into a staging database, and then if a transformation step fails, you can restart with the data in staging instead of having to go back and touch (impact) the source systems again. The staging database sits between the various sources and the data warehouse.

After creating a data mart or data warehouse, you can use stored procedures or SSIS to create a repeatable ETL process for getting various sources of data into your data warehouse databases. SSIS is a rich tool that performs useful operations, such as making the data conform to specifications so that you can use it in applications, to create cubes, or to connect directly to it from reports.

Let's look at some of the components of a data warehouse.

What Is a Data Warehouse?

A data warehouse is a database that functions as a repository for storing an organization's data for reporting and analysis. The core data in the data warehouse typically consists of numeric values that you can aggregate in a number of ways. The data is usually stored in a structure called a "star schema" rather than in a more normalized structure found in typical transactional databases. Querying data can be very resource-intensive, so the data warehouse structure provides much better querying times. Ad hoc queries return summed values, similar to queries you would perform in a transactional database to create a report.

Data Warehouse vs. Data Mart

A data warehouse usually contains data from multiple sources and covers multiple subject areas. In contrast, a data mart is subject-specific and contains a subset of data applicable to a specific department or segment of an organization. A data warehouse can contain one or more data marts.

Facts and Dimensions

When you work with data warehouses, you quickly learn that the entire discussion centers on facts and dimensions. Data warehousing is about storing the data that people can use to solve business problems—and you determine what data to store by asking questions like "What number needs to be viewed, and in what manner does the number need to be analyzed?"

The what part is typically a number such as the number of products produced, the defect rate, the manufacturing cost, and so forth. These numbers are called fact data. The values stored in a data warehouse (or data mart) consist primarily of fact data.

After identifying the what, you must determine how users should see the fact data. How the user will analyze the fact data becomes the dimension. The most common dimension is time, which gives context to the facts that are stored. For example, users might want to see trends in manufacturing costs over time, or they might want to see sales volume over time.

A data warehouse has a different structure than a transactional database. The primary reason for the structure change is to improve the speed of querying the data. The following illustration shows a scaled-down version of a star schema. It also illustrates how fact data and dimensions are made available—from which you would choose report elements to create a report. A report is a subset of the data in the relational database, but as you can see, multiple scenarios are available, and the report you want to create is dictated by the data within the facts and dimensions. The schema in the illustration shows only one fact and only a handful of dimensions, but in real-world situations, a schema may hold more facts and many, many more dimensions.

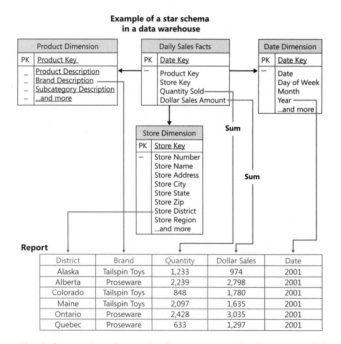

Example of a star schema
in a data warehouse

District	Brand	Quantity	Dollar Sales	Date
Alaska	Tailspin Toys	1,233	974	2001
Alberta	Proseware	2,239	2,798	2001
Colorado	Tailspin Toys	848	1,780	2001
Maine	Tailspin Toys	2,097	1,635	2001
Ontario	Proseware	2,428	3,035	2001
Quebec	Proseware	633	1,297	2001

The information shown in the report at the bottom of the preceding illustration could be a prototype for a customer to communicate requirements to a business user. The report communicates one variation of two facts, Quantity and Dollar Sales. The Date column shows how the two facts are aggregated, in addition to the context provided by the dimensions.

Moving Data by Using SSIS

SSIS is a tool that SQL BI developers use to move data from various sources to the data warehouse. The next section, "From Data Warehouse to Report, Using SSIS," provides an example of how to make a copy of some data and then move it from the original data warehouse to a subset data warehouse.

Other BI developers might prefer to clean and load data to the data warehouse by using T-SQL and stored procedures, but SSIS provides a useful alternative to T-SQL and stored procedures because it can support repeatable ETL processes.

This phase can be the most expensive part of your BI solution because it's typically the most time-consuming part of the project. You can expect a lot of surprises in the data—such as missing or invalid values—and cleaning it is typically a very iterative process during which misunderstandings get ironed out and data quality issues are resolved. The cost of ETL for any BI solution is also affected by other variables, too many to list them all here, but that include issues such as the following:

- How well the project is sponsored, starting from the very top (CIO, CEO, and so on).

- The size of the project and business unit. The solution could reach the organization, department, team, and a group of individuals, each of which vary in size.

- The culture and dynamics of the organization, department, and team and how well they are able to communicate requirements and how well the prototypes are presented. Typically ETL is an iterative process—and even after that, misunderstandings often lead to changes. A good change-management system helps control the scope of the project and, ultimately, the time and money spent.

The preceding is not an all-inclusive list of variables or considerations. You can find several good books that discuss project methodologies, such as agile BI data warehousing, as well as books explaining how to use SSIS for more than just creating a repeatable ETL solution.

From Data Warehouse to Report, Using SSIS

A great example example of SSIS being used with the Contoso data warehouse is given by Valentino Vranken in his blog post "Calculating LastXMonths Aggregations Using T-SQL and SSIS." You can download this sample SSIS package from *http://blog.hoegaerden.be/category/ sqlserver/t-sql/*. Vranken's post shows how you use the Merge Join data transformation in SSIS and Common Table Expressions in T-SQL to calculate aggregations over a specified period of time. The sample also provides a good example of when you don't necessarily need to spend the time to create a cube.

The scenario begins with a database, the Contoso data warehouse, which contains some sales figures. Management asks for sales-related data to be made available somewhere for easy analysis. Ideally, you'd build a cube, but because budgets are currently tight, a less work-intensive temporary solution is appropriate, consisting of an additional table that will be created and populated with the data that management requires. The new table must contain details (number of items and amount of the sale) about products sold, grouped by the date of the sale, the postal code of the location where the sale occurred, and the product category.

Furthermore, each record must contain the sum of all sales of the last month for the postal code and the product category of each particular record. Two additional aggregations should calculate the sales for the last three months and for the last six months, respectively.

The following illustration shows the SSIS Data Flow tab.

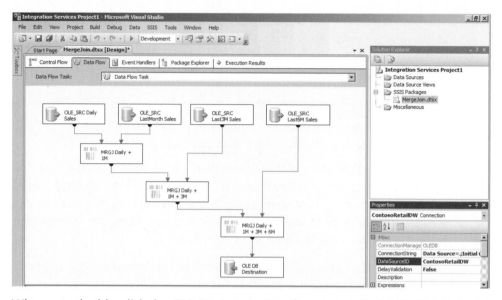

When you double-click the OLE DB Source data flow task called OLE_SRC Daily Sales, you see the source code in the SQL command text of the Ole DB Source Editor dialog box. Each flow task performs an activity that you control. When you run the package, you can see the progress of each flow task. All of this occurs in development, because packages typically run as scheduled unattended processes.

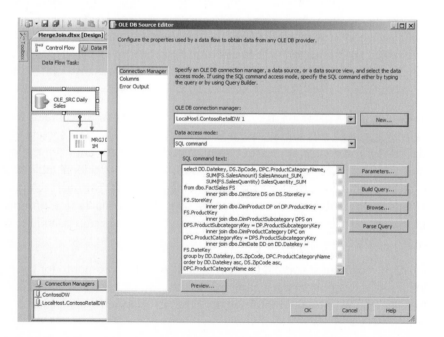

The preceding example provides only a glimpse of what you can do with SSIS to extract, transform, and load data.

Step 4: Create an SSAS Cube from Warehouse Data

This section explains the concepts involved in creating a cube, followed up with a hands-on practice exercise to create your own cube. The following illustration shows where cube creation fits into the overall BI life cycle.

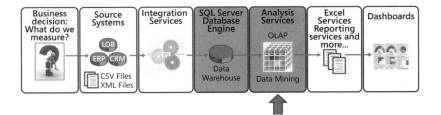

What Is OLAP?

OLAP stands for On Line Analytical Processing, a series of protocols used mainly for business reporting. Using OLAP, businesses can analyze data in a number of different ways, including budgeting, planning, simulation, data warehouse reporting, and trend analysis. A main component of OLAP is its ability to make multidimensional calculations, which means it supports a wide and lightning-fast array of possibilities. In addition, the bigger the business, the bigger its business reporting needs. Multidimensional calculations enable a large business to complete calculations in seconds that would otherwise take minutes to obtain.

OLAP is a technology that stores detail and aggregate data in a multidimensional structure that supports fast queries and on-the-fly calculations. A general way to understand what OLAP does is to see it as part of a specialized tool that helps makes warehouse data easily available.

Why Use SSAS?

In the section "Core BI Components," we provide a brief description of what SSAS is. Here we reiterate why it is important. SSAS provides server technologies that help speed up query and reporting processing. Aggregations can be preprocessed to make querying very, very fast. Analysis Services implements OLAP technology to simplify the process of designing, creating, maintaining, and querying aggregate tables while avoiding data explosion issues.

SSAS allows BI developers to:

- Create KPIs that can later be used in authoring tools such as PerformancePoint Dashboard Designer.

- Create perspectives, which are subsets of data from a cube. Sometimes developers compare perspectives to database views. Perspectives allow BI developers to reduce the amount of data made available so that departments, such as an accounting department, have the data they need.

- Apply cell-level security that affects what data can be used in Office applications such as Excel, SSRS, and PerformancePoint Services.

- Use Multidimensional Expressions (MDX) to query cubes.

The following illustration shows the NorthWindOrdersDW project using SSAS. We hope the illustration gives you a sense of how rich the tool is for designing cubes.

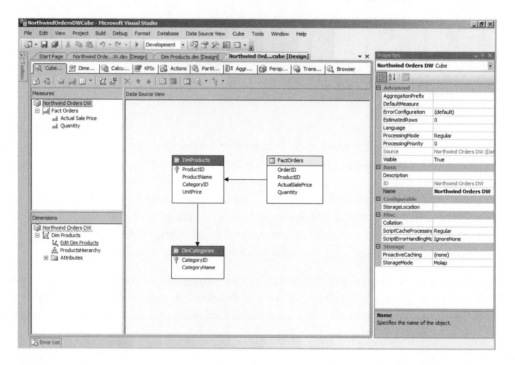

What Is a Cube?

An OLAP cube is a logical structure that defines the metadata of its underlying data warehouse data. The cube provides multidimensional data derived from relational tables or a data warehouse, and it's optimized for rapid querying. In other words, the term cube describes existing measure groups and dimension tables. The "Understanding the OLAP Environment, Basic Terminology" video, at *http://www.microsoft.com/business/performancepoint/productinfo/proclarity/training/WEB50P-1/OLAP_Terminology/OLAP_Terminology.html*, can help you understand OLAP terminology.

Querying a cube is significantly faster than querying the source data directly, but remember that to get these performance gains you must store significantly more data.

Business logic can be encapsulated in the cube so that there is only one way to perform a calculation, to prevent a myriad of versions from user-calculated values.

What Is MDX?

In short, OLAP cubes contain lots of metadata; metadata, in its simplest definition, is data about data. MDX is a metadata-based query language that helps you query OLAP cubes.

You can build MDX calculations, such as sales of a previous week, with great efficiency. This task would otherwise be very difficult to do in a relational language and could include hundreds of lines code to accomplish. In MDX, you would need only one line of code!

Alternatives for Creating Cubes

As shown in the following illustration, the Unified Dimension Model (UDM) defines business entities, business logic, calculations, and metrics and provides a bridge between BI developers and data sources. BI developers can run queries directly against the UDM by using BI tools. To use the UDM, you must have an OLE DB or SQL Server connection.

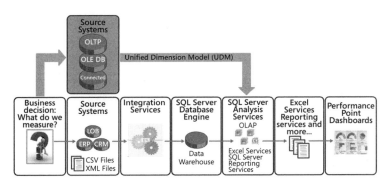

In reality, you can create cubes on OLTP (or relational and normalized data) or almost any other data source, in any format to which you can connect, through SSAS data source providers. This flexibility is both good and bad. If you're new to creating OLAP cubes, you'll want to build projects using the wizards and tools in BIDS. These wizards save you time and are designed to work with traditional star schema source data as depicted in the following diagram.

Step 5: Surfacing OLAP Data to Front-End Tools

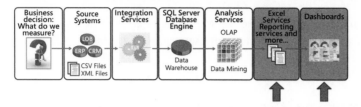

With prepared data ready, you can work on how you want to present the data. (Note that the sequence of events leading up to this point, as presented in this chapter, do not always happen in this exact sequence.) The authoring tools let you connect to data that does not come from a data warehouse or cube but rather directly from SharePoint lists, Excel files, CSV files, OLTP databases, and other sources. In particular, PerformancePoint Services can include data produced in the other BI authoring tools, which enables you to create a dashboard and a mash-up of work performed by other analysts, developers, and business users.

In the following section, to more fully understand the data preparation process, you can walk through an exercise to create your own cube.

> **Note** The remaining chapters of this book discuss each authoring tool as well as how to present the results in SharePoint 2010, providing examples of how to surface data that was prepared for decision-making.

Create a Cube from Data in SalesContosoDM

The lab exercise in this section ties together the information provided earlier in this chapter. You can use this exercise to learn more about the conceptual, physical, and logical models being used—from creating the data warehouse to creating a cube for reporting.

The purpose of this lab is to show how data warehousing and multidimensional concepts are easier to understand when you perform the tasks with a very simplified dataset. Of course, the complexities multiply when you have much larger data sources and real-world data; typically, you would use multiple data sources from disparate systems, or you might find that the data sources for what you want to measure don't even exist in electronic format. There are other complications as well.

The goals for this hands-on lab are as follows:

- Determine the reports that the data warehouse is supposed to support.
- Identify data sources.
- Extract data from their transactional sources.

- Build and populate a dimensional database.

- Build and populate Analysis Services cubes.

- Build reports and analytical views by:

    ❑ Using Excel, PerformancePoint, SSRS, PowerPivot, or Visio.

    ❑ Creating a custom analytical application and writing MDX queries against cubes.

- Maintain the data warehouse by adding or changing supported features and reports.

Northwind Database

This exercise uses the Northwind database, available at the Northwind Community Edition, located at *http://northwindcommunity.codeplex.com/SourceControl/list/changesets*. You might ask, why use Northwind? The answer: because it is easy to use, takes two seconds to install, and is small and simple enough to use for getting-started demos. The Northwind database contains good sample data, so it's an excellent place to show you how to create a data warehouse.

Data Warehouse Scenario

Suppose you work for the Northwind Traders Company. This hypothetical company sells products around the world and records data into the sample database created when you installed the Northwind database. Business owners want views that let them break down the order details by product, product category, quantity, and price. Having such a tool can help stakeholders get quick views of which products are selling.

More typically, a BI solution specialist would extract that information from business users through an iterative process. Business users might not know what they really want until after some interviews and after evaluating several prototypes. For the purposes of this exercise, assume that management has predetermined exactly what they want to see in a report.

This example is simplistic and therefore considerably easier to build than a typical warehouse. Baya Dewald, in his article "Case Study of Building a Data Warehouse with Analysis Services (Part One)," at *http://www.informit.com/articles/article.aspx?p=443594*, describes some of the challenging aspects of creating a data warehouse as follows:

> *"Because data is already in a SQL Server database that has a fairly simple structure, the first few steps of a typical warehouse project are already done for us. In reality, you don't always get this lucky: The DW architect usually has to identify multiple data sources that will be used to populate the warehouse. The organization's data could be stored in various relational database management systems (Oracle, SQL Server, DB2, and MS Access being the most common), spreadsheets, email systems, and even in paper format. Once you identify all data sources, you need to create*

data extraction routines to transfer data from its source to a SQL Server database. Furthermore, depending on sources you're working with, you might not be able to manipulate the data until it is in SQL Server format.

The Northwind database has intuitive object names; for example, the orders table tracks customer orders, employees table for records data about employees, and order details table tracking details of each order. Again, in the real world this might not be the case—you might have to figure out what cryptic object names mean and exactly which data elements you're after. The DW architect often needs to create a list of data mappings and clean the data as it is loaded into the warehouse. For example, customer names might not always be stored in the same format in various data sources. The Oracle database might record a product name as "Sleeveless Tee for Men," whereas in Access you could have the same product referred to as "Men's T-Shirt (sleeveless)." Similarly, the field used to record product names could be called "product" in one source, "product_name," in another and "pdct" in the other.

Once you have determined which data you need, you can create and populate a staging database and then the dimensional data model. Depending on the project, you may or might not have to have a staging database. If you have multiple data sources and you need to correlate data from these sources prior to populating a dimensional data structure, then having a staging database is convenient. Furthermore, staging database will be a handy tool for testing. You can compare a number of records in the original data source with the number of records in the staging tables to ensure that your ETL routines work correctly. Northwind database already has all data I need in easily accessible format; therefore, I won't create a staging database."

Getting Started with the Data Source

The Northwind database is what is generally termed an "OLTP data store." Remember that OLTP databases are structured so that they are capable of storing data quickly—but not optimally structured to retrieve data quickly. Therefore, you want to create a data warehouse from the Northwind OLTP database that you can use to query data for the report.

To download and install the Northwind data source

1. Go to the Northwind Community Edition, located at *http://northwindcommunity. codeplex.com/SourceControl/list/changesets*, on the CodePlex site hosted by Microsoft. CodePlex is a web storage site maintained as a service to the developer community.

2. Click the Download link.

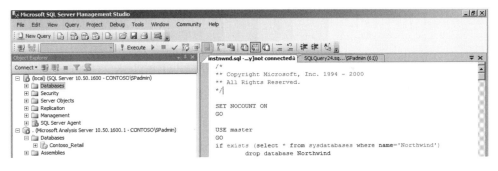

3. Save the downloaded file to a computer that has SQL Server 2008 R2 installed.

4. In the folder where you saved the file, double-click the instnwnd.sql file, which opens the script for creating Northwind database in SQL Server Management Studio. You must have permissions to run the script that creates the database.

5. Click Execute.

> **Note** Make sure you are connected to SQL Server's database engine.

6. In the Object Explorer window, shown in the following illustration, navigate the database to view the tables and columns to ensure everything worked.

> **Note** You might need to right-click the Databases item and select Refresh from the context menu before you can view the Northwind database.

Design and Create the Data Warehouse

People have been creating data warehouses for more than twenty years now, so you can find numerous books and best practices that describe how to improve the return-on-investment (ROI) for your data warehouse. The article "Best Practices for Data Warehousing with SQL Server 2008," at *http://msdn.microsoft.com/en-us/library/cc719165.aspx*, is a good place to start.

For this exercise, there really isn't much complexity to the design. In fact, it is worth noting that this example doesn't include a dimension for time, which is the most common dimension. The design for this exercise comes from the following illustration, which is a simplified snowflake schema. A snowflake schema relates to the dimension structure itself—the dimension is in multiple tables. There is still an overall star schema in that you have a fact and dimension structure, which is the core construct. The snowflake is considered a structure that extends dimensions, such as the product dimension.

NorthwindOrdersDW

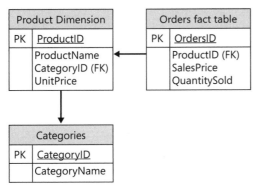

In this section, you will accomplish the following tasks:

- Design the data warehouse (already done)

- Create the fact and dimension tables for the data warehouse

- Populate the fact and dimension tables

- Set relationships between the tables

To create the fact and dimension tables

1. Expand the Databases folder, and then expand the NorthwindOrdersDW database folder. Right-click the Tables folder, and select New Table from the context menu. A Table Designer tab appears, as shown in the illustrations under Steps 2 and 4 of this exercise.

   Note You can also write a script to create databases and populate tables.

2. In your new table, populate the Column Name and Data Type columns with the information displayed in the following table.

SP2010-BI.Nor...bo.DimProducts		
Column Name	Data Type	Allow Nulls
ProductID	int	☑
ProductName	nvarchar(40)	☑
CategoryID	int	☑
UnitPrice	money	☑
		☐

3. Save your new table with the name DimProducts.

> **Note** To demonstrate the flexibility of SQL Server Analysis Services to create relationships defined in the snowflake design shown in the preceding section, you do not set those relationships in the NorthwindOrdersDW database. In other words, this is not a good database design. Typically, you'd define relationships in the data warehouse, which makes creating the cube much easier.

4. Repeat Steps 1–3, populating the Column Name and Data Type values as shown in the following tables. For our purposes, you can select all check boxes in the Allow Nulls column.

SP2010-BI.Nort...dbo.FactOrders

Column Name	Data Type	Allow Nulls
OrderID	int	☑
ProductID	int	☑
ActualSalePrice	money	☑
Quantity	int	☑
		☐

SP2010-BI.Nor....DimCategories

Column Name	Data Type	Allow Nulls
CategoryID	int	☑
CategoryName	nvarchar(15)	☑
		☐

5. Save these two tables as FactOrders and DimCategories.

You have just created your fact and dimension tables! After right-clicking the NorthwindOrdersDW database and selecting Refresh, you can expand the columns. You should see the three new tables, as shown in the following illustration.

Your three-table data warehouse is now in place and ready to populate with data from the Northwind database.

You can choose from several methods for populating data, some more complex than others. In the following exercise, because the source data is already clean, you don't have to deal with the complexity of cleansing the data before populating the data warehouse. This data comes from a single source (SQL Server Northwind database), the tables and columns are intuitively named, the data is clean, and you don't need to put data into a staging database first.

You can use two very simple methods to populate data in this example:

- **SQL Server Import And Export Wizard**   Takes data from Northwind and inserts it into the NorthwindOrdersDW DimProducts and HierarchyCategories tables.

- **An *INSERT* SQL statement**   Takes data from Northwind, aggregates it, and inserts it into the NorthwindOrdersDW FactOrders table.

To populate NorthwindOrdersDW dimensions tables

1. Open BIDS and create a new project, as shown in the following illustration.

2. Select the Integration Services Project type, and type **PopulateNorthwindOrdersDWDimensions** for the project name.

3. From the PopulateNorthwindOrdersDWDimensions menu, select Project | SSIS Import And Export Wizard, as shown in the following illustration.

This starts a wizard where you can select your source and destination databases, tables, and columns.

4. On the wizard's starting page, click Next.

5. On the Choose A Data Source page, select Microsoft OLE DB for SQL Provider Server Data source, type **(local)** in the Server Name field (assuming your database is on your machine; otherwise, select the appropriate server), and select Northwind for the Database. Click Next.

6. On the Choose A Destination page, select Microsoft OLE DB Provider For SQL Server, type **(local)** in the Server Name field (assuming your database is on your machine, otherwise, select the appropriate server), and select NorthwindOrdersDW for the Database. Click Next.

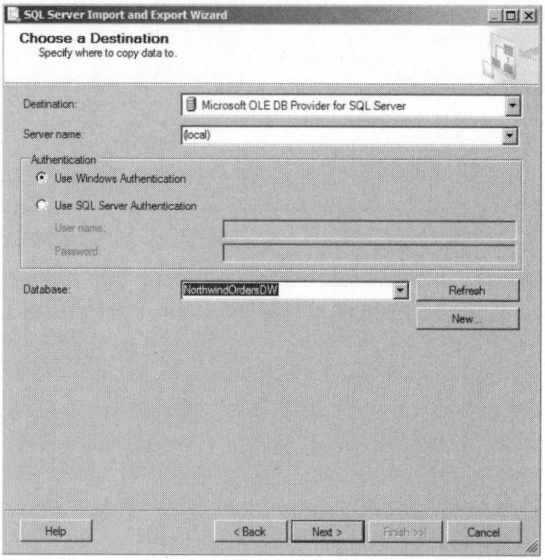

7. Make sure the option Copy Data From One Or More Tables Or Views is selected. Click Next.

8. All the tables in the Northwind database are available for selection, as shown in the following illustration. Select Categories, and in the drop-down list in the Destination column next to Categories, select [dbo].[HierarchyCategories] as the destination table. Click Next.

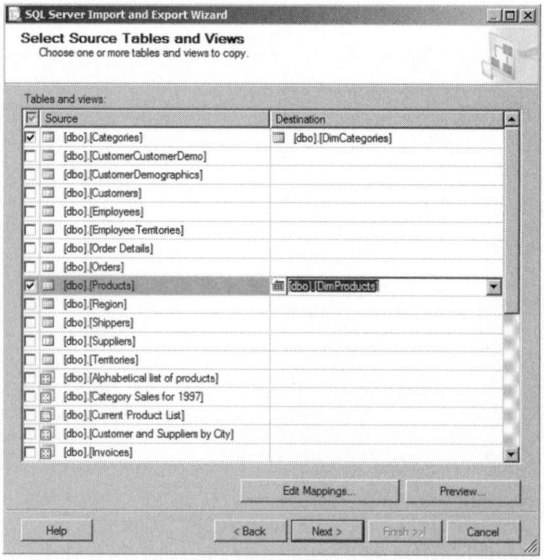

9. Select Products, and in the drop-down list in the Destination column next to Products, select [dbo].[DimProducts] as the destination table.

10. Click Edit Mappings.

Notice that you can edit mappings between source and destination tables. The wizard automatically maps to the columns in the destination table that have the same names as those in the source table. Additionally, the wizard detects that the destination table is only a subset of the source table. It therefore sets <Ignore> on the unused columns, as shown in the following illustration so that those columns are not copied.

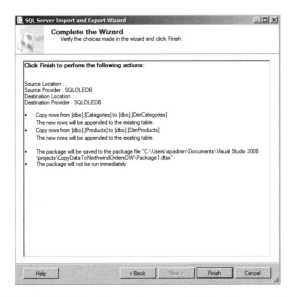

11. Click Next to see a summary of the SSIS project.

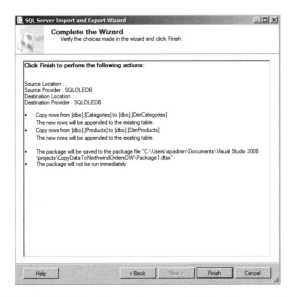

12. Click Finish for the project to validate the operations.

13. Click Close. The wizard closes, and you are taken back to the BIDS project. Right-click the package you just created with the SSIS Import And Export Wizard, and select Execute Package, as shown in the following illustration.

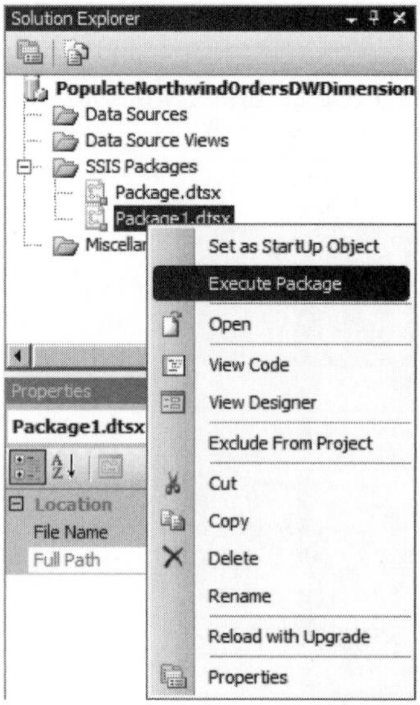

When you execute the package, you can view the progress of the tables moving by clicking the Progress tab.

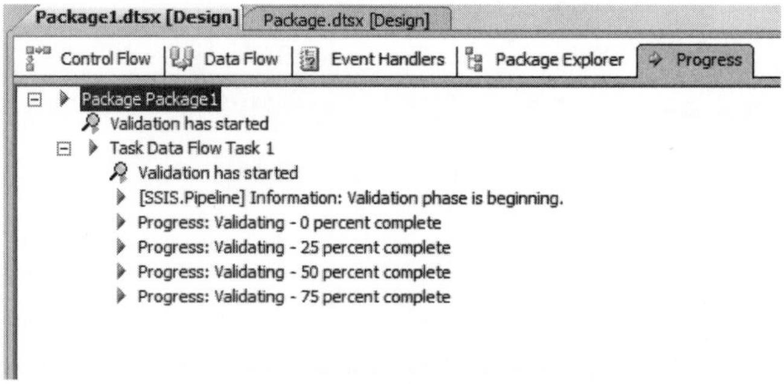

14. When the package completes, query your dimension tables in SQL Server Management Studio to ensure that they were populated with data. To do this, right-click the table and select Script Table As | Select To | New Query Editor Window. Then select Execute.

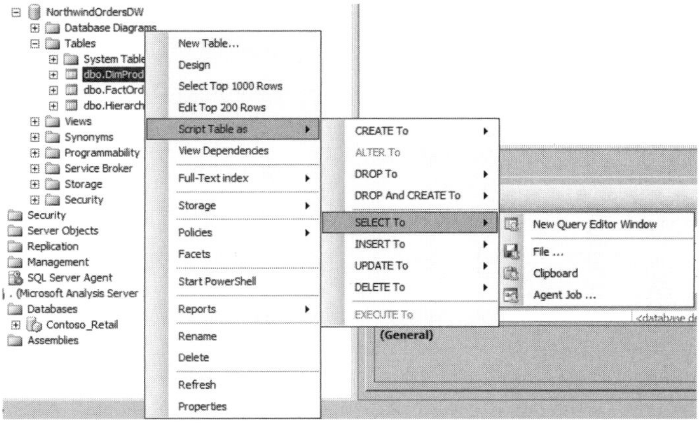

After executing the query, you should see the data in the results table, as shown in the following illustration.

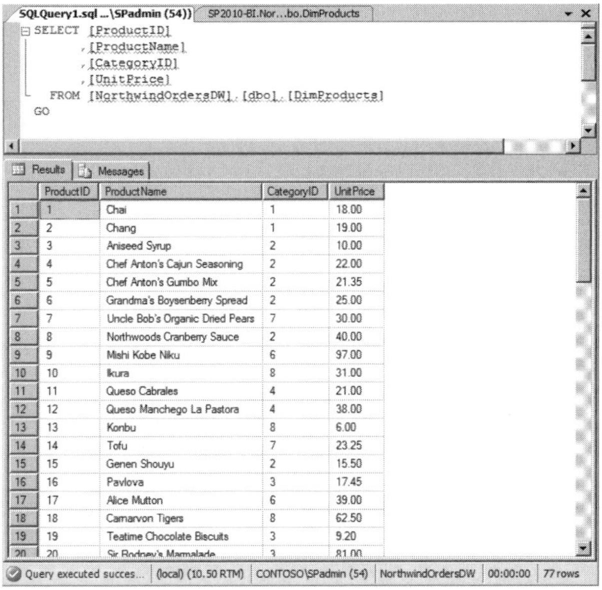

You've populated the two dimension tables. Next you'll populate the FactOrders table.

To populate the NorthwindOrdersDW FactOrders table

1. Type the following INSERT statement in a new Management Studio query window:

```
INSERT FactOrders (
OrderID
, ProductID
, ActualSalePrice
, Quantity
)
SELECT [OrderID]
, ProductID = max(ProductID)
, ActualPrice = Sum(UnitPrice)
, Count = sum(Quantity)
FROM [Northwind].[dbo].[Order Details]
GROUP BY
[OrderID]
HAVING MAX(ProductID) <1000
ORDER BY [OrderID]
GO
```

Make sure you are in the NorthwindOrdersDW database, and select Execute.

830 rows should be affected, as indicated in the Messages pane and as shown in the following illustration.

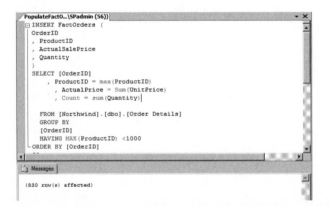

2. To ensure that the FactOrders table was populated, run the query shown in the following illustration.

You should notice that the INSERT statement used a GROUP BY clause that aggregates data. In this example scenario, you need to see only product sales and quantity by order, and you don't care about multiples of the same product on the same order. That level of detail is not necessary, thus the aggregation.

Create an Analysis Services Cube, Based on NorthwindOrdersDW Data

This is the exciting part. If your source data is in good format, the cube wizard for Analysis Services makes the process of creating a cube relatively simple.

> **Note** Before moving on, it's worth explaining why we are creating a cube and not simply building a report from the data warehouse we built. It's true that for this simple example, we could have built reports by querying either the transactional database or the data warehouse directly. Some companies do report off their transactional databases; depending on the situation, that might strain resources. But when transactions and queries across a more complex database structure compete for resources, IT departments might limit analytical queries to times when the transactional databases are not in heavy use.
>
> Even with a data warehouse in place, complex queries to relational tables for reports might take all night or even all weekend to complete. For this reason, a company usually looks first at creating data warehouses or data marts and/or OLAP cubes. Another reason to build cubes is to limit information aggregation to one or more cubes.

Creating a Cube Summarized

Following is a summary of the process using Analysis Services wizards to build a cube based on the data warehouse you created in the previous exercise:

1. Create a data source, pointing to the physical data warehouse.

2. Create a Data Source View, which is a copy of the data in the data warehouse.

3. Create the product dimension and associate it with Categories as a hierarchy.

4. Create the cube.

5. Build the project.

6. Deploy the cube so that the cube database shows in Analysis Services.

7. Process the cube to populate it with data.

Randal Root, a technical consultant and author of BI Solutions with SQL Server 2011 (Apress), created a video that shows you how to create a cube built on the data warehouse you just created. You can view the video at *https://docs.google.com/leaf?id=0B5U6tT4eiM6aNzQyNTg 1YmUtMDRiMi00YTE1LTkxNzUtZTAwMzM1YjlkYTQ1&hl=en&authkey=CIOnzo8N*.

> ⚠ **Important** Notice a difference between the cube I built for this example and the video: I created relationships in the Data Source View rather than in the NorthwindOrdersDW data warehouse. You'll build those relationships in the next exercise.

When you're done creating a cube, you can use the browser to navigate through your data or use it to negotiate requirements with business users as if it were a prototype report.

To create relationships between FactOrders, DimProducts, and DimCategories

1. After running the wizard to create the data source and Data Source View, right-click the Relationships folder to see the FactOrders table, as shown in the following illustration.

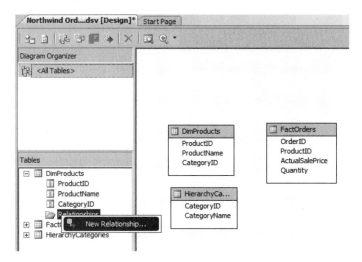

2. In the Specify Relationship dialog box, make sure FactOrders appears in the Source (Foreign Key) Table field and that DimProducts appears in the Destination (Primary Key) Table field. Select ProductID under both Source Columns and Destination Columns, and then click OK to see a line between the FactOrders table and DimProducts table, as shown in the following illustration.

3. Right-click the Relationships folder under DimProducts.

4. In the Specify Relationship dialog box, make sure DimProducts appears in the Source (Foreign Key) Table field and that DimCategories appears in the Destination (Primary Key) Table field. Select CategoryID for under both Source Columns and Destination Columns. Click Ok.

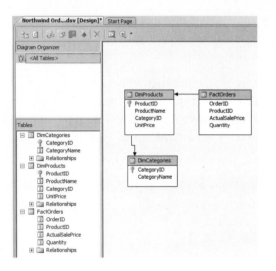

You should now see the relationships shown in the following illustration. Typically, these relationships are defined in the data warehouse, but we wanted to show how you can enhance the Data Source View. Data source views are conceptually similar to relational views because they represent a view of the data from data sources in a project.

Summary

This chapter provides an overview of the major steps involved in getting to trusted data by using SQL Server 2008 R2. Keep in mind that ensuring data quality throughout an organization or even in a department is a process rather than a single event or initiative, and it must typically have backing from the very top of the organization. Creating a repeatable ETL process and getting data from disparate sources to a staging database and then to the data warehouse is a time-consuming process. At this point, you should understand that:

- There is likely to be continuous maintenance on a data warehouse, because it's an entity that grows as the need for more reports develops within an organization.

- The data warehouse grows both in size and complexity as more reports are required.

Using Analysis Services in BIDS by designing, building, deploying, and processing a cube from the data that is established as trusted, ideally from a well-structured data warehouse, is the next step to presenting business users with a cube in useful and meaningful way. As you can see, many steps are involved in getting to trusted data that BI developers and analysts can use in the authoring tools.

Office 2010 is one of those authoring tools, familiar to many, many users, which you can count on for surfacing data prepared for business users to consume and from which they can confidently make decisions, analyze, and predict patterns and behavior in business. SharePoint 2010 is the platform that organizes and shares the results of having authored dashboards, reports, charts, graphs, heat maps, and other products of the Microsoft BI stack. Among other things, SharePoint 2010 provides the following:

- Scalability, collaboration, backup and recovery, and disaster recovery capabilities to manage your BI assets created in PowerPivot, Excel, Visio, Report Builder, and PerformancePoint Dashboard designer.

- To simplify security, user authentication is handled by SharePoint Server 2010. Authentication of Services users is validated by the SharePoint Server 2010 authentication provider. Trusted locations can also limit access to content types and files.

- Publishing BI assets to SharePoint Server websites is a quick and secure way to share the right data, to the right people, at the right time, helping employees work faster and helping them make better decisions, faster.

Chapter 4
Excel Services

After completing this chapter, you will be able to

- Understand what Excel Services is, and what it is not.

- Understand the history of Excel Services and what important scenarios the product addressed with each release.

- Have a solid grasp of the high level areas of functionality Excel Services provides, from basic use all the way to extensibility.

- Be familiar with the most common administration concerns, including basic configuration, security, and basic external data configuration.

- Be able to apply advanced permission security to Excel files to allow tighter management and control.

- Create a workbook connected to external data that utilizes Excel business intelligence (BI) features.

- View and interact with a workbook in SharePoint by using Excel Services.

- Understand the different approaches for extensibility of Excel Services.

Excel Services Overview

Introducing Excel Services could be as simple as saying it's a server product that enables the refresh, recalculation, interactivity, editing, and display of Excel files in a browser-based way. Although a fairly short and accurate description, it might be misunderstood on a number of fronts. Let's clarify a little further exactly what Excel Services really is—and what its strengths are.

Over the years, we have found that it is sometimes worthwhile to explain what Excel Services is *not*, before helping people understand what it actually *is*.

Excel Services is *not*:

- A "toy" server product that was quickly put together and released as some kind of an interim solution or response to a competitive threat.

- Excel.exe packaged up and running on a server.

- An add-in, like Office Web Components (OWC) or some other ActiveX control, installed on your computer and running in the browser.

- A "thin" application, built on a webpage that converts Excel workbook files to HTML, that runs on your computer in a browser.

The preceding list contains some of the most common misconceptions about Excel Services. With those out of the way, we can get specific about what Excel Services *is*.

Excel Services is a full-fledged server product built and designed from the ground up to be scalable, manageable, performant, secure, robust, and extensible. It is tightly integrated into SharePoint and shares much of the functionality of SharePoint and of technology related to areas such as authentication, security, and manageability. Excel Services is a serious server product that is meant to be a long-term answer to a number of common problems with sharing and managing Excel workbook files.

Excel Services isn't just Excel.exe—architecturally. It is very different because it is a service designed to support many users scaled across many machines. However, from a usage standpoint, it is different as well; it is meant to be "Excel" in the server and cloud world. That doesn't mean simply duplicating all the Excel client functionality; it means that it extends the reach of Excel into the server and cloud. Excel Services is optimized around the kinds of Excel scenarios that are common in modern organizations, such as broadly sharing workbooks, parts of workbooks, and Excel-based BI insights across an organization in a way that can be tightly controlled, secured, and managed. Although there might be places where Excel Services functionality overlaps with Excel; Excel client and server are better together and naturally complement each other.

I won't go deeply into architecture because that's beyond the scope of this book, but it is worth taking the time to clarify that Excel Services is not like OWC. OWC ran as an add-in to the Internet Explorer browser and had to be installed on machines across an organization. This requirement carried with it all the security, upgrade, deployment, and manageability headaches that come with installing any client components broadly across many computers. Instead, Excel Services core components run on a server, either a single server or a group of servers. It is generally much easier to deploy and upgrade a few server machines than many client machines. People can use their browsers to view Excel workbooks and reports using Excel Services without having to install any client-side components. The browser rendering is completely thin, or "zero-footprint," because it uses only DHTML and JavaScript—no install required. And by "no install," we mean no install; it doesn't even require an Excel client to be installed on the user's machine.

Because the core Excel Services components are based on a server, the browser is rendering only the results of the Excel workbooks, refreshes, and calculations. The actual workbook file and all the intellectual property (formulas, and so on) are loaded on the back-end server, not in the client-side browser; so Excel Services isn't simply converting the entire file to HTML and in the process exposing the entire file and its contents. The results are rendered in the user's browser as HTML, but the Excel content underneath resides on the server. This makes it possible to do things such as show the *results* of formulas as HTML in the browser but keep the formulas themselves secure on the back-end server.

And make no mistake: Excel Services is loading native Excel workbook files. It isn't converting them or saving them as something else. These are real Excel files that an Excel client can open and edit.

Excel Services is actually a set of service applications that run on top of SharePoint. This simply means that you can get to the Excel Services functionality described in this chapter from inside SharePoint, and that functionality is tightly integrated into SharePoint for permissions, authentication, management, and so forth.

Brief History—the 2007 Release

Excel Services was first released as part of Microsoft Office SharePoint Server Enterprise Edition in 2007. The initial release of Excel Services was geared toward extending Excel-based BI solutions on the server and making managing Excel files easier.

BI Functionality

The Excel client added a lot of BI functionality in 2007, such as OLAP formulas, structured tables, conditional formatting for creating elements such as data bars and Key Performance Indicators (KPIs), better PivotTable functionality, and more. A significant part of BI revolves around sharing insights gained with your team, department, or organization. Excel Services was the answer to widely sharing those Excel-based BI reports through SharePoint. This is the reason why Excel Services generally did a great job at rendering new Excel file types geared toward BI. In 2007, Excel Services couldn't calculate or render many types of Excel files and objects, so the first release was clearly a subset of Excel functionality—and was really about exposing the BI features.

A Web Part, along with the ability to view parts of Excel workbook files in a Web Part (for example, showing a single chart), also shipped with SharePoint 2007. This made it possible to create dashboard experiences that integrated Excel content natively.

Sharing and Managing Workbooks

Sharing and managing Excel files was the other problem Excel Services tackled in 2007. Users could store their Excel files in SharePoint and assign permissions to them, so the files could be tightly managed and controlled.

When users needed to share Excel files more broadly, they no longer needed to copy and paste contents into email messages, send email attachments, or set up a terminal server where people could log on to view the files. They could simply send a link to the file in SharePoint, and people could view the Excel file by using Excel Services in a way that didn't alter the contents of the Excel file. With sufficient permissions, viewers could open the file directly in Excel to perform more advanced analysis or editing, or by restricting permissions, viewers could be limited to the browser-based view.

This new capability meant that workbook authors didn't have to worry about showing up at the Friday board meeting and have five other people show up with five different versions of the file—and five different versions of the numbers. The "one version of the truth" for the numbers could be contained in a single Excel file in a single place but could be viewed broadly by using Excel Services. Users didn't even have to have the Excel client installed to view the workbooks. And because Excel Services is just another service in SharePoint, it could be managed in a single place.

Extensibility

There was also a simple extensibility story for the 2007 release. There were two parts to it—a web service and user-defined functions.

Excel Web Services

Excel Web Services is a simple SOAP-based web service that allows customized programs to open, recalculate, and interact with workbooks from any application. This capability enables developers to use Excel Services for offloading Excel calculations to more powerful servers. Custom solutions could load those files on the server, set parameters, recalculate them, and get the results back using Excel Web Services.

User Defined Functions

Excel Services also had the ability to leverage User Defined Functions (UDFs). UDFs are simply custom managed-code solutions that can be installed on the server and then called from a workbook file just like any function. For example, you could write some custom C# code that returns all the items from a specific SharePoint list. You could then use that custom routine from a workbook on the server just like any other function. Instead of typing =SUM(A1, B1), you could type something like =MyCustomSharePointListFunction("http://URLtoMyList").

The 2010 Release

Excel Services had its capabilities expanded during the 2010 release wave of Office and SharePoint products.

Continued BI Support

In the previous release, there were a number of common features (for example query tables or comments) present in workbooks that were used as BI reports. The features may not have even been a core part of the report that authors wanted to share, but the presence of these features in the file prevented it from loading in Excel Services. Excel Services added support for more features that blocked files from loading in the previous release, making the server rendering option more relevant for a greater variety of workbook files. Excel Services also added support for the new BI functionalities that the Excel 2010 client introduced, such as sparklines, slicers, and PowerPivot support.

Editing and Excel Web Application

The 2010 release of Excel Services adds a powerful new capability: the ability to collabora-tively edit Excel files by using only a browser, which enables users to edit Excel files inside the SharePoint environment. Collaborative editing capability was shipped as part of the Office Web Applications.

So far, we have been using the term "Excel Services" generically to mean "the server product on SharePoint that has all the Excel-like functionality." But technically, there isn't an actual Excel Services product. There is an Excel Service Application that shipped as part of Microsoft Office SharePoint Server 2010, and there is an Excel Web Application that shipped as part of the Office Web Applications, which must be installed on SharePoint. These two products originate from the same team at Microsoft and have considerable overlap.

If you install them both, you see only one service application inside of SharePoint. That ser-vice application is a combination of capabilities from both of the installed services. For now, we use "Excel Services" to mean the combination of both services, and we address important differences between the two later in the chapter as appropriate.

Improved Extensibility

The 2010 release also revised the extensibility story, updating the existing SOAP-based web service to support the new editing functionality. The UDFs were still there and still supported, but the release also added a new object model: the ECMAScript object model.

This new object model (using JavaScript or JScript) gave developers the ability to build appli-cations that ran in the browser, using a language familiar to most web developers. This new object model can do many of the things the web service does, but it also allows the devel-oper to control basic properties of the workbook (such as whether the toolbar is visible in the user interface [UI]), as well as capture and respond to basic events. For example, you can easily write an application that enables a user to edit an Excel file in the browser and, based on what the user enters into certain cells or which cells are selected, trigger various processes (like SharePoint workflows) to kick off, have warnings shown, and so on. This is because the developer can hook into events such as the cell selection event or other events that can be useful for triggering key application behaviors.

Last, but certainly not least, the 2010 release added a REST-based API as well, which provides access to individual parts of the workbook, such as a specific chart, via a simple URL. The REST API makes it easy to embed Excel content in blogs, webpages, or even as refreshable images in applications such as Microsoft PowerPoint.

Excel Services as a Cloud-Based Service

Excel Services was introduced to the world as a hostable service during the 2010 release. All of SharePoint can be hosted on-premise and exposed as a service, and Excel Services supports that. Appendix A talks about hosted cloud-based services, so I won't discuss it in depth here. But Excel Services works as part of service-based SharePoint solutions.

Excel Services capabilities are also available on the Internet now, hosted by Microsoft. To try it, simply attach an Excel file to an email and send it to your Hotmail account or upload the file to your Windows Live SkyDrive account (*www.skydrive.com*), and then click the file to view or edit it. The fundamental technology being used there is Excel Services.

When to Use Excel Services

Generally speaking, you have many ways to build a solution with different BI products in the SharePoint ecosystem. This section is intended to give some guidance on when an Excel Services–based solution might be a better fit than some other products.

It's Already Excel

There was a question asked at the beginning of a presentation at a recent BI conference we attended:

Q: What's the number-one BI feature request across all BI applications, regardless of which company created those applications?

A: Export to Excel.

This answer contains a strong element of truth—many, many, BI solutions end up in or go through Excel at some point. Excel is a tool that business users understand and use to express core business logic. Excel has a rich history and many existing solutions at virtually every major business in the world. Excel doesn't require an "authoring" environment, developer tool, or developer environment—it's just Excel. Getting Excel out of a company's system is a tough challenge. "From my cold, dead hands" is an expression I have heard many companies' IT developers quote from conversations with their users when they discussed removing Excel from the ecosystem. Excel is a tool that people know, often love, and in which they have invested a lot of learning and solution time.

Depending on the needs of the users and requirements of the system, the path of least resistance is often to build it around Excel.

Excel: Fast to Create and Easy to Adopt

Continuing on the theme from the preceding section, people already know how to use Excel and likely have solutions already based in Excel. Prototyping a new BI-based solution is often faster when it's based on Excel Services than on some other tool. Why? Because it often means that most users don't need to learn anything new.

They don't need to learn a new suite of tools to "design a dashboard." A dashboard in Excel is usually the first sheet that has grid lines turned off, with the most important charts, data, and pivot table showing the most important grouping of the results. So business users of the BI system being designed already know how to create the BI content without new training time and expense. This means that the overall BI solution designer can focus on putting together the server pieces of the solution and leave the business logic and visuals to the existing Excel users.

> **Note** Sometimes a more formal dashboard solution is required, or the application needs some functionality that Excel Services doesn't support. Other chapters in this book, such as Chapter 7, "PerformancePoint Services," provide alternative options in those cases.

Because Excel Services acts much like Excel, after seeing that Excel Services provides the ability to manage Excel files, people are more likely to try it out, which makes it a great steppingstone to getting richer BI controls and solutions in place. Getting Excel files working on the server is typically quick and straightforward (often no harder than simply saving them in SharePoint). This makes it a great choice when you are taking initial baby steps toward introducing a deeper BI solution later, or when you are looking for a quick prototyping or proof-of-concept BI solution. It is no secret that people are more comfortable with what they know—that's one of the reasons PowerPivot uses Excel and Excel concepts as the front-end UI.

When users want to go beyond the capabilities of a workbook sheet, Excel Services provides a Web Part that supports more complex dashboards that can be deeply integrated into SharePoint. You can leverage this capability from within the SharePoint UI; no extra install or tool is needed.

It's a Great Ad-Hoc Tool

One of Excel's strengths is that it is a fantastic tool for doing quick analysis on the fly. You can easily add a new column to a table for a quick calculation, drill down on a pivot table to go deeper into the insight, or alter a slicer to change how the data is viewed. This kind of loose, ad-hoc data interactivity and exploration works equally well on Excel Services.

Other BI tools may not be as good at ad-hoc exploration. And if Excel Services doesn't support the full level of ad-hoc functionality that the user desires, the user can always just click Open In Excel and take the file into Excel client to do more. This works because Excel Services loads native Excel files; no conversions are required, and there's nothing special about those files—they can be opened on the client or server.

It Scales Excel Files to Many Users

Because Excel Services is a true server product, it can be scaled out to many machines or scaled up to use more resources on a single machine to meet the demands of many users viewing and interacting with workbooks in the system. For example, if you have some Excel-based BI reports that many people need to share, Excel Services is a natural choice. This is especially true in cases where the people who need to view the data might not all have an Excel client installed.

Configuration

This section discusses high-level security and configuration concerns. It is not meant to be an exhaustive list but focuses on the must-know concepts and most common "gotchas" that people have encountered when configuring the server.

Installation

You don't need to do anything special or extra to install Excel Services; it is part of the SharePoint installation. When you install the Microsoft Office SharePoint Enterprise Edition, Excel Services is installed. Similarly, when you run the configuration wizard at the end of the SharePoint installation, Excel Services is configured automatically.

The primary thing to point out for installation is that if you want the ability to create new Excel files or to edit Excel files by using only a browser, you also need to install the Office Web Applications on top of SharePoint. The installation and configuration of the Office Web Applications generally looks and behaves the same as the core SharePoint install—so there isn't anything new to learn from an install point of view. You should install and configure the Office Web Applications *after* installing and configuring the Microsoft Office SharePoint Enterprise Edition.

For the sake of simplicity and the purposes of this book, it is easiest to allow the post-setup configuration wizard to run to make sure your server and services are correctly configured.

Administration

You administer Excel Services just like any other service application in SharePoint—through an administration landing page where all the settings reside. Excel Services also supports PowerShell, and you can perform advanced administration through scripting. In a default configuration of Excel Services, the service should be secure, ready to use, and should support most workbooks without the administrator needing to do any further configuration.

To get to the administration landing page for Excel Services, on the Start menu, click Microsoft Office SharePoint Server | Central Administration. You'll see the Central Administration Console, the page from which you can manage all of SharePoint.

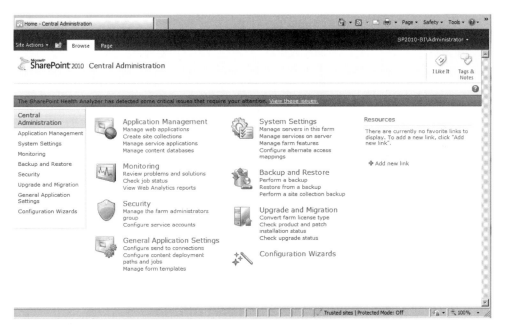

On the Central Administration Console, under Application Management, click Manage service applications. You'll see the Manage Service Applications page, as shown in the following illustration.

You can manage your service applications from the Manage Service Applications page. Each service application generally has both a service application and a service application proxy. The service application is the core engine that loads the files, handles security, manages sessions, and provides the core functionality. The proxy is a component that allows communication with the service application and allows for some advanced configuration options with respect to how the service application relates to the rest of the SharePoint farm. For more information and diagrams to help explain proxies, see *http://technet. microsoft.com/en-us/library/cc263199.aspx*. Of particular interest on that page are the topics "Services in SharePoint 2010 Products," at *http://go.microsoft.com/fwlink/?LinkID=167092*, and "Cross-farm Services in SharePoint 2010 Products," at *http://go.microsoft.com/ fwlink/?LinkID=167095*.

With some service applications, you manage the proxy separately from the service application itself. Excel Services is not one of those. You can perform all Excel Services management from the service application landing page; you don't need to manage the proxy separately.

Some service applications support running multiple instances of that service application in the farm or support running the proxy on one farm while hosting the service application on a different farm (also known as parent/child farms and inter-farm shared service applications), but Excel Services is designed to have only a single Excel Services application running in the farm. This is because Excel Services supports working with only the default Excel Services proxy of the default proxy group. You can have multiple groups defined per web application, but those scenarios are beyond the scope of this book. Sharing an Excel Services application across farms is also unsupported. For most enterprise deployments, a single Excel Services application running on the SharePoint farm is sufficient.

To get to the Excel Services administration landing page, on the Manage Excel Services Application shown in the following illustration, simply click the name of the Excel Service application you wish to manage.

From this page you can configure and manage the major pieces of Excel Services. Separate pages exist for each set of administrative task if you should need to change any settings to support a custom solution or adjust security settings to control resource usage or broaden capabilities.

File Security

Like any other files in SharePoint, Excel files are subject to SharePoint permissions and security. This remains true even after Excel Services is installed.

Server Security

The most important server-security concept that Excel Services takes advantage of is the notion of *trusted file locations*. Trusted file locations are simply directories from which Excel Services permits Excel files to be loaded. If an Excel file is not stored in a location in the list of trusted locations, Excel Services does not load it. By default, in Excel Services 2010, the entire SharePoint farm is considered to be a trusted location. That means that Excel Services can load any Excel file from any SharePoint location.

When a workbook is loaded on Excel Services, the server forces that workbook to respect settings that are defined for the trusted location from which it was loaded. Trusted locations have many available settings, so the server administrator can control the allowable operations as well as how many server resources workbooks can use.

For example, you can specify that workbooks loaded from *http://portal/teamsiteA* cannot be larger than 1 MB and can never be allowed to refresh against any data sources, but workbooks loaded from *http://portal/trustedTeamSiteB* can load much larger workbooks, up to 20 MB, and can query data sources.

> **Note** If workbooks are failing to load or if certain operations fail for those workbooks, check whether the workbooks are being loaded from a trusted location directory and whether the settings for that trusted location enable the types of operations you want to perform on those workbooks.

To see the trusted location list, go to the Excel Services Central Administration page and click Trusted Locations.

Select the trusted location you want to view and click the link to that location. As shown in the following illustration, you'll see a page that shows some of the settings and values that apply to the default trusted location.

- Session Management
- Workbook Properties
- Calculation Behavior
- External Data
- User-Defined Functions

External Data Configuration

One challenge for administrators is to get external data configured for use by Excel Services. Unfortunately, for deployments that aren't single-box evaluator style deployments, (where all components are installed on the same machine with a default configuration usually as a trial deployment), some amount of configuration is required to make external data connectivity work.

This section doesn't contain an exhaustive approach to all external data connectivity but does provide some simple guidance and links to detailed steps so that you can complete the high-level configuration needed to get going. Also, you can reuse much of the configuration work described here for other service applications, such as Visio Services, PerformancePoint Services, and even PowerPivot.

The simplest way to get data connectivity working on the server is to use a single account to connect to all the data sources or to save the credentials in the connection string. The downside of this is that there won't be any per-user security applied to the data. The single account used to get data for Excel Services is known as the "Unattended Account." Even if the credentials used to connect to the data source are in the connection string, for security purposes, Excel Services requires that you first have an Unattended Account configured. When the connection is made, Excel Services will use either the Unattended Account or the credentials stored in the connection string, depending on what is in the connection string.

The Unattended Account is simply a user account created for the purpose of read-only access to data sources. The account credentials (user name and password) must be stored in the Secure Store Service (SSS). (SSS is another service application, similar to Excel Services, that stores accounts securely.) The article at *http://technet.microsoft.com/en-us/library/ff191191. aspx*, "Configure Secure Store Service for Excel Services (SharePoint Server 2010)," contains instructions for configuring SSS and the Unattended Account for Excel Services.

Another option is to configure the Secure Store Service explicitly for credential retrieval. Basically, SSS stores credentials in a secure way that makes them available to service applications like Excel Services to use for things such as data refresh. An administrator must configure it and set permissions so the right user groups have access to the credentials. A workbook author must then know the key, or Application ID, to use in the workbook to ensure that the right set of credentials is requested when the user tries to refresh the data in the workbook. So it is better than the simple "one account for everyone to refresh data on the server" approach, does have more setup overhead, but usually isn't quite as hard to configure as the option we discuss next. For more information about Secure Store Service, see *http://technet.microsoft.com/en-us/library/ee806889.aspx*.

If you want per-user security, the best option is to configure Kerberos in your environment. Kerberos configuration can be complex—and you might not need it if your users need simple read-only access via a single account. See "Configuring Kerberos Authentication for Microsoft SharePoint 2010 Products," at *http://www.microsoft.com/downloads/en/details. aspx?FamilyID=1a794fb5-77d0-475c-8738-ea04d3de1147&displaylang=en*, for more information about Kerberos configuration.

To configure authentication in the workbook

In most deployments, the workbook author must explicitly mark which type of security option—Unattended Account (shown as "None" in the UI), SSS, or Kerberos (shown as Windows Authentication in the UI)—to use when Excel Services loads the file. If you are using a single-box deployment (and running your browser from that machine) or if you have configured Kerberos, the default settings are sufficient and you can skip this procedure.

Use the following procedure to get an existing workbook configured to use the Unattended Account.

1. Start the Excel client, and open the workbook for which you want to enable data refresh on the server.

2. On the Data tab, click Connections.

The Workbook Connections dialog box opens, as shown in the following illustration.

3. For *each* connection (only one is shown in the preceding image, but you can have more), select the connection and click Properties.

4. In the Connection Properties dialog box, click the Definition tab, as shown in the following illustration.

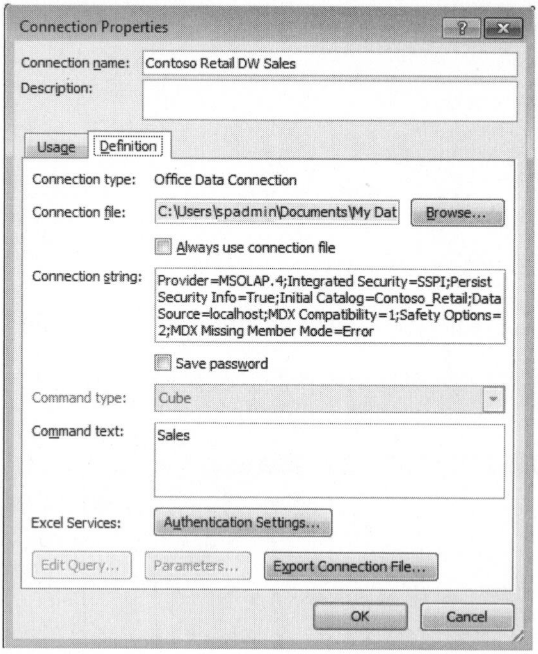

5. Click Authentication Settings to open the Excel Services Authentication Settings dialog box, shown in the following illustration, which enables you to specify how the data connection should authenticate (and thus how Excel Services can connect to the data sources when the workbook is loaded on the server).

6. In the Excel Services Authentication Settings dialog box, select the appropriate option based on how your server has been configured. The preceding screen shot shows the None option selected, which means the server will use the Unattended Account or will use any basic authentication credentials that might be stored in the connection string.

   You can set these options when the data connection is created. (For example, the Authentication Settings button for Excel Services is displayed in the last screen of the data connection wizard.)

Also, after you configure a connection this way, that connection can be shared and reused, so not every user in your organization needs to set the configuration. The best way to do this is to store the .odc connection file in a SharePoint Data Connection Library and let your users know that they can select preconfigured connections from there.

For more information about external data connectivity and configuration, see the following resources:

- A downloadable document showing more details on configuring Kerberos for Service Applications (like Excel Services) in SharePoint: *http://www.microsoft.com/downloads/ en/details.aspx?FamilyID=1a794fb5-77d0-475c-8738-ea04d3de1147&displaylang=en*

- A more basic webpage showing options for Configuring Kerberos in SharePoint 2010: *http://technet.microsoft.com/en-us/library/ee806870.aspx*

- Details about how to configure the Secure Store Service: *http://technet.microsoft.com/ en-us/library/ee806866.aspx*

- Details about configuring Secure Store Service for Excel Services and the Unattended Account: *http://technet.microsoft.com/en-us/library/ff191191.aspx*

Locking Down Excel Files

Because tight control over Excel files is a goal of many solutions, this section provides an overview of how to publish and secure server views of an Excel workbook.

Excel files can sometimes contain sensitive intellectual property (IP). For example, a workbook may use custom or proprietary formulas and logic to get a result. The result may often need to be shared, and the logic may need to be protected. This kind of overall solution is very difficult to achieve in Excel natively but can be done using Excel Services.

View Only Permissions

The secret to sharing the workbooks while protecting the IP is to apply the View Only permission for users who need to view the report but shouldn't be allowed to see any of the logic underneath. View Only permissions means that only a sanctioned application can be used to open files of a certain type. In SharePoint, Excel Services is registered as the file handler for the supported types of Excel files (.xlsx, .xlsb, .xlsm, .odc). Therefore, when View Only permissions are applied, only Excel Services can be used to open the Excel files. This means that users can't use the Excel client, can't select Save Target As, cannot download the file, and cannot open those files in any other way. The view provided by Excel Services does not expose any of the IP in the workbook.

> **Note** SharePoint grants the *highest* level of rights possessed when deciding whether you have permissions to complete an action. This means that when you apply View Only permissions to a user who is a member of another group, such as Readers (the default), that user gets the highest level of permission granted. In this case, even though you specified View Only permissions, because members of the Readers group have higher-level rights, that user can download and view the Excel file in the client, exposing the IP. The lesson here is that when you apply View Only permissions to users, make sure they aren't getting a higher level of access than intended because they are a member of some other group that can do more than just "view."

To apply View Only permissions

You can apply View Only permissions either by making the user a member of the Viewers group or by granting the permissions to a specific user directly. The permissions can be configured at many different levels in SharePoint: sites, lists, document libraries, or individual documents. The following procedure shows how you can explicitly apply View Only permissions to a user from a site.

1. View the site in your browser, click the drop-down Site Actions arrow, and then click Site Settings.

2. On the Site Settings page, under Users and Permissions, click Site permissions.

3. On the Permission Tools tab, click Grant Permissions. (You can also select an existing user or group, and then click Edit User Permissions.)

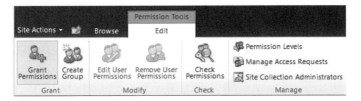

Clicking Grant Permissions opens the Grant Permissions dialog box.

4. In the Grant Permissions dialog box, enter the user or group for which you are setting permissions. Then expand the Add Users To A SharePoint Group (recommended) drop-down list, and select Viewers [View Only], as shown in the following illustration.

Grant Permissions   □ ✕

Select Users

You can enter user names, group names, or e-mail addresses. Separate them with semicolons.

Users/Groups:

Contoso/SPUser

Grant Permissions

Select the permissions you want these users to have. You can add users to a SharePoint group that has already been granted the appropriate permission levels, or you can grant the users specific permission levels.

Adding users to a SharePoint group is recommended, as this makes managing permissions easier across multiple sites.

Grant Permissions

⦿ Add users to a SharePoint group (recommended)

Viewers [View Only]   ▾

View permissions this group has on sites, lists, and items...

○ Grant users permission directly

OK   Cancel

> **Note** Alternatively, if you select the Grant Users Permission Directly option, you can se-lect the View Only permission level there.

5. Click OK to save your changes.

Now, when the specified users view an Excel file that has been assigned permissions in this way, they can fully interact with that file in the browser by using Excel Services, but they cannot otherwise open, access, or edit the file itself.

To publish an Excel file

View Only permissions are especially powerful when combined with the publish capabilities in Excel. The Excel client allows a user to choose which parts of the workbook are shown on the server. The entire file is always published, or saved, to the server because it is needed to enable full recalculation and refresh actions. But the workbook author can choose to display only certain parts of the file when it is rendered by the server. View Only restricted users have access only to these portions of the workbook in the UI and through the extensibility APIs, like the JSOM or Web Service.

The following procedure shows how to narrow down what is displayed in a workbook that is rendered on the server.

1. In the Excel client, click File, click Save & Send, and then click Save To SharePoint, as shown in the following illustration.

2. Click Publish Options (displayed at the top right section of the preceding illustration) to open the Publish Options dialog box.

The Show tab of the Publish Options dialog box controls what is shown on the server. Remember that Excel always saves the entire file; this dialog box controls only what gets displayed. By default, the entire workbook is displayed.

3. In the drop-down list, click Items In The Workbook to choose a range of sheets or to choose only specific items from the file. In the example below, only a chart and a pivot table have been selected for display.

4. Click OK to close the dialog box, and then complete the Save operation.

Only the selected chart and pivot table are available on the server. Notice that the UI that allows the user to open the file is trimmed as well.

Create the Workbook

Excel Services can be thought of as part of Excel—the part that extends the Excel-based BI story into the browser. This means that BI in Excel Services starts in Excel client. This section walks you through creating a simple workbook and then helps you save that workbook into SharePoint. This section does not provide an exhaustive list of all the BI features in Excel but does touch on a few that you can use to create an interesting report that can then be rendered in Excel Services.

To get the data in the workbook

The workbook used in the following procedure was created by connecting to the sample Contoso Retail DW database and connecting to the Sales cube.

1. To start the data connection wizard in Excel, click the Data tab, click From Other Sources, and then click From Analysis Services, as shown in the following illustration.

2. Complete the Data Connection Wizard to connect to the Contoso Retail DW database, click the Sales cube, and click Finish.

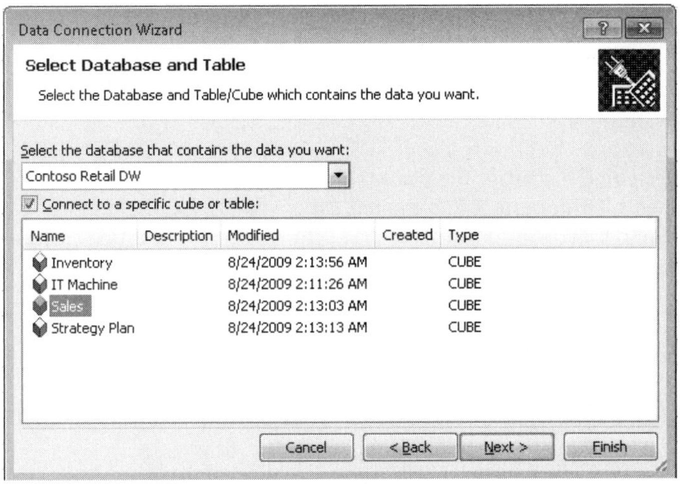

3. In the Import Data dialog box, shown in the following illustration, select PivotTable Report to create a new pivot table report in your sheet.

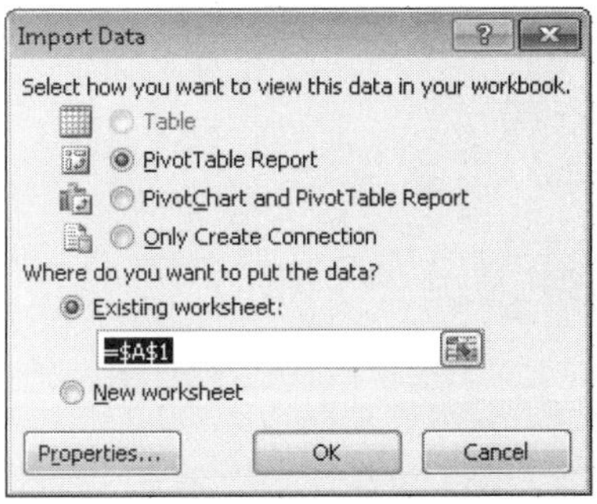

4. In the PivotTable Field List dialog box, shown in the following illustration, click Sales to filter the list of fields to display only those relevant for the Sales data.

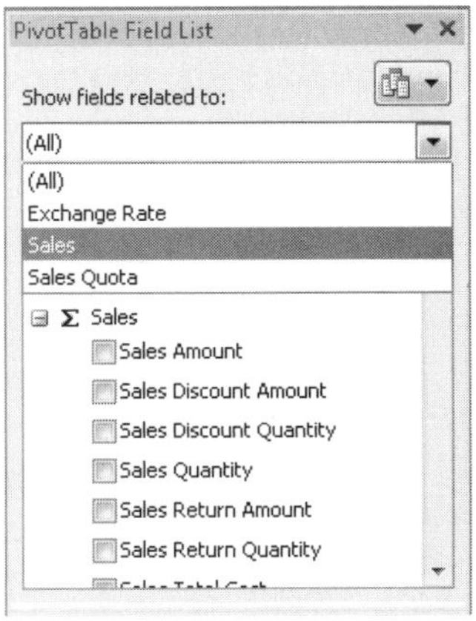

5. Scroll through the field list, selecting the check boxes next to the Sales Amount and Product fields. This adds the primary data to the spreadsheet that we will be working with.

> **Note** At this point, if you put the pivot table in cell A1, you should select the entire pivot table and then cut and paste it into the middle of your spreadsheet to leave yourself enough room to build a report around it. Feel free to adjust column widths as necessary so that you can read the data.

To add another PivotTable

Use the following procedure to add a second pivot table to the report so that you can compare product sales to the cost of making those sales.

1. On the Data tab, click Existing Connections.

2. Click the name of the Contoso connection you created earlier, and insert a new pivot table. Insert the pivot table to the right of the pivot table you created before. (We inserted this new table in column F, but you can always move these pivot tables around later if you need to.)

3. In the new PivotTable Field List dialog box, click Sales to show only data relevant to sales, and then click Sales Total Cost and Channel Name so that you can see the cost of sales from each sales channel.

As shown in the following illustration, you should now have two simple pivot tables showing data about sales, sales channels, products, and the cost of sales.

	B	C	D	E	F	G
1						
2						
3						
4						
5						
6						
7						
8						
9						
10	**Row Labels**		**Sales Amount**		**Row Labels**	**Sales Total Cost**
11	⊞ AUDIO		$150,703,104.28		Store	$2,946,272,277.52
12	⊞ TV & VIDEO		$1,348,482,541.08		Online	$1,113,997,399.07
13	⊞ COMPUTERS		$2,937,030,931.13		Catalog	$455,612,853.96
14	⊞ CAMERAS & CAMCODERS		$2,536,738,529.70		Reseller	$728,357,500.31
15	⊞ CELLPHONES		$884,480,287.07		**Grand Total**	**$5,244,240,030.86**
16	⊞ MUSIC, MOVIES & AUDIO BOOKS		$164,279,314.28			
17	⊞ GAMES & TOYS		$149,919,633.87			
18	⊞ HOME APPLIANCES		$3,915,829,318.64			
19	**Grand Total**		**$12,087,463,660.05**			
20						
21						
22						

4. Save the workbook.

You can use the following procedures to take advantage of some new Excel 2010 BI features.

To add conditional formatting

To make it easier to gain some insights into the data, the following procedure shows how you can add conditional formatting to help make the outliers in the data really pop.

1. Select the Sales Amount for each sales category on the Sales Amount pivot table. Don't select the grand total at the bottom though; you want the conditional formatting to apply only to the subtotals for each product category.

2. On the Home tab, click Conditional Formatting, click Color Scales, and then choose the color scale that appeals to you.

3. Repeat the previous steps for the Sales Total Cost pivot table, but this time use an icon set as shown in the illustration provided in Step 5 of this procedure. You might need to expand the column showing the Sales Total Cost after you apply the icon formatting so that the numbers display properly instead of showing hash marks (#####).

4. Right-click the Audio value in the Sales Amount pivot table, and select Expand\Collapse | Expand Entire Field from the pop-up menu to drill down one level on all product categories in the pivot table, exposing aggregated totals for all the products in each category.

5. Select all the products for the Audio group products, but do not select the total for the Audio category. (The total row is the row that has the color scale formatting applied to it.) Apply data bar formatting by clicking Conditional Formatting on the Home tab, clicking Data Bars, and then choosing a data bar color that appeals to you. Repeat this for each category in that pivot table.

You should now have a report with two pivot tables and some conditional formatting similar to the formatting shown in the following illustration.

Row Labels	Sales Amount		Row Labels	Sales Total Cost
⊟AUDIO	$150,703,104.28		Store	$2,946,272,277.52
⊞MP4&MP3	$64,628,514.00		Online	$1,113,997,399.07
⊞Recording Pen	$44,288,926.29		Catalog	$455,612,853.96
⊞Bluetooth Headphones	$41,785,663.99		Reseller	$728,357,500.31
⊟TV & VIDEO	$1,348,482,541.08		Grand Total	$5,244,240,030.86
⊞Televisions	$305,167,079.67			
⊞VCD & DVD	$36,600,418.77			
⊞Home Theater System	$702,158,027.41			
⊞Car Video	$304,557,015.23			
⊟COMPUTERS	$2,937,030,931.13			
⊞Laptops	$923,667,802.72			
⊞Desktops	$260,465,980.05			
⊞Monitors	$266,498,462.04			
⊞Projectors & Screens	$1,096,477,941.93			
⊞Printers, Scanners & Fax	$278,885,469.08			
⊞Computers Accessories	$111,035,275.31			
⊟CAMERAS & CAMCODERS	$2,536,738,529.70			
⊞Digital Cameras	$361,608,926.98			
⊞Digital SLR Cameras	$802,431,167.09			
⊞Camcoders	$1,320,998,679.93			
⊞Cameras & Camcoders Accessories	$51,699,755.70			

Adding Slicers

Slicers are a new feature that you can use in conjunction with pivot tables. They make filtering operations to display the correct subset of data much easier than it was in the past. Slicers look like toggle buttons that appear when the data they represent is being displayed in the tables they filter.

Slicers that don't contain data (because all their values might already be filtered out by some other filter) appear as disabled or empty. So not only is the slicer UI a more intuitive way to filter, it also provides visual clues that say something about the data.

Slicers also give users a great deal of control over the visual display of a report; they can resize and reposition the reports, can adjust the button sizes, and they can control the slicer color theme as well.

Slicers also become very useful in cases where you have different sets of data that need to be filtered by the same set of values. You can connect slicers to more than one pivot table, giving you the ability to "slice" the report.

To insert slicers

You can use the following procedure to add some simple slicers to the report you've been building in this chapter.

1. Select the Sales Amount pivot table by clicking any cell in the pivot table. (For example, in the illustration shown in Step 3, the Bluetooth Headphones cell is selected.)

2. On the Insert ribbon, click Slicers to see a UI very similar to the pivot table field list.

3. Scroll down to select the calendar year and the product subcategory name, as shown in the following illustration, and then click OK.

Two new slicers have been inserted into the workbook. Now you can add some formatting.

To format the slicers

1. Click and hold on the title of the slicer to drag the Product Subcategory Name to the right of your pivot tables. Then drag the Calendar Year to a position above your pivot tables.

2. Select the Product Subcategory Name slicer, and click the Slicer Tools tab. In the Buttons group, change the Columns value to **3**, the Height value to **0.2"**, and the Width value to **.92"**. Then, in the Size group, change the Height value to **4.15"** and the Width value to **3.01"**.

3. Repeat the process in Step 2 for the Calendar Year slicer, but this time, in the Buttons group, set the Columns value to **3**, the Height value to **0.2"**, and the Width value to **1.05"**. Then, in the Size group, set the slicer Height value to **1.1"** and the Width value to **3.4"**.

4. In the Slicer Styles group, select the light green style (or any other style that appeals to you).

You should now have a report that looks something like the following illustration.

At this point, spend some time playing around by selecting the slicer buttons. You should see your pivot table update. Notice how some buttons look inactive at certain points. If you click one of these inactive buttons, your pivot table goes blank because there is no data for those buttons. Also notice that you can select (or Ctrl+Click) multiple buttons at the same time. Finally, notice that you can clear the slicer by clicking the Clear icon at the top of the slicer.

To connect the slicers to another PivotTable

Now let's connect your slicer to the other pivot table. The Sales Total Cost pivot table shows different data, but the fields that the slicers are filtering apply to that set of data as well.

1. To connect the Product Subcategory Name slicer to that pivot table, select the slicer and then on the Slicer Tools tab, in the Slicer group, click PivotTable Connections.

2. When the PivotTable Connections dialog box opens, make sure each check box next to each pivot table is selected as shown in the following illustration, and click OK.

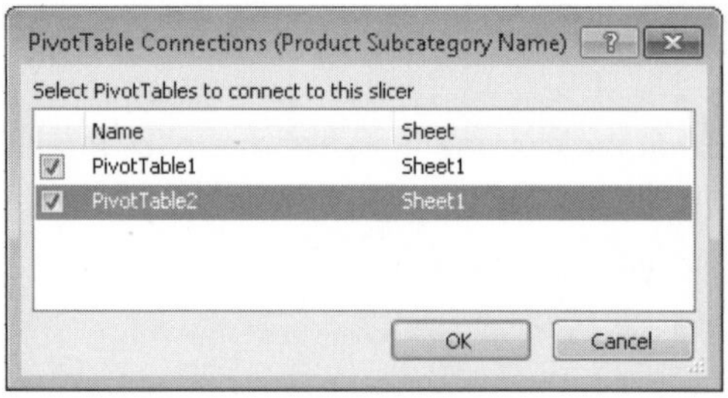

3. Repeat the preceding steps for the Calendar Year slicer.

Now when you click the slicers, you should see both pivot tables being updated.

To add a chart

What report would be complete without a chart? Let's add a chart to show the split of Sales Cost.

1. Highlight values from the Sales Total Cost pivot table (don't select the Grand Total row though), and on the Insert tab, click Pie to choose and insert a 2-D split pie chart, as shown in the following illustration.

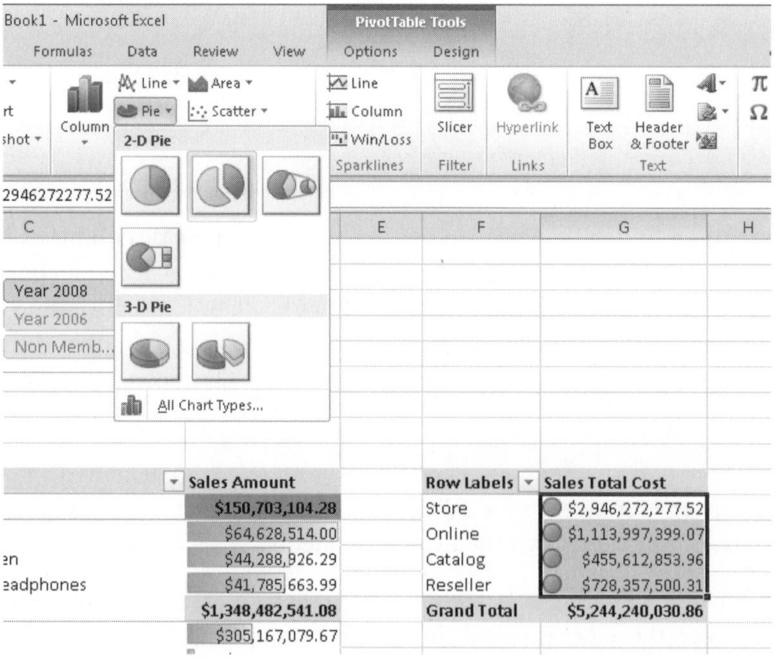

2. To format the chart so that it looks a little better in the report, drag the chart to position as needed, and then grab the corner of the chart to resize it so that it fits above your Sales Total Cost pivot table. You can optionally choose a chart style you like from the chart ribbon as well.

3. Click the Chart Analyze tab, and then in the Field group, click Hide All.

4. Finally, click the word Total in the chart, and then type in **Total Sales Cost**.

The chart in the workbook should now resemble the following illustration.

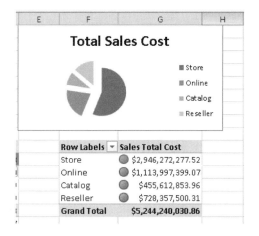

Clean Up the Report

If you want to make things fit together a bit more tightly in the report, resize columns B and E to make them smaller and spend some time lining up edges of pivot tables, resizing charts, slicers, and so on.

If you don't like how the pivot table columns resize and adjust the look of your report when you drill down or filter on your pivot table, you can turn the resize behavior off. To do this, right-click your Sales Amount pivot table and click PivotTable Options on the pop-up menu. When the PivotTable Options dialog box opens, clear Autofit Column Widths On Update check box and click OK.

The report, with the preceding minor adjustments to size and position completed, should resemble the following illustration. (Notice that the Sales Amount pivot table has most of its fields collapsed.)

Sparkline Overview

Sparklines are a great new BI feature in Excel 2010 that you can use for showing large amounts of graphical data in a way that can be summarized in a single cell.

To add some data and insert a PivotTable

You can use the following procedure to add some simple sparklines to the sample report. However, before you can add sparklines, you need to add some data in the spreadsheet that you can summarize. To do this, you can insert another pivot table from the existing data.

1. Select cell K3 as the designated location for the new pivot table. Then, just as you did to insert your first pivot table, on the Data tab, click Existing Connections, and under Connections In This Workbook, click the Contoso Retail DW Sales connection, and then click Open.

2. When the Import Data dialog box opens, click OK to accept the default of creating a PivotTable Report.

Column Labels ▾			
⊞ Year 2007	⊞ Year 2008	⊞ Year 2009	Grand Total
Sales Total Cost $1,888,459,186.75	$1,731,140,050.76	$1,624,640,793.35	$5,244,240,030.86

You should now have a new pivot table in the workbook.

3. In the PivotTable Field List dialog box, click Sales to limit the fields to data relevant only to sales. Then select the Sales Total Cost check box for the measure, and select the Calendar YWD check box in the Date field, as shown in the illustration in Step 4 of this procedure.

4. Referring to the following illustrations, drag the Calendar YWD value from the Column Labels box into the Row Labels box so that the calendar dates are displayed on the rows.

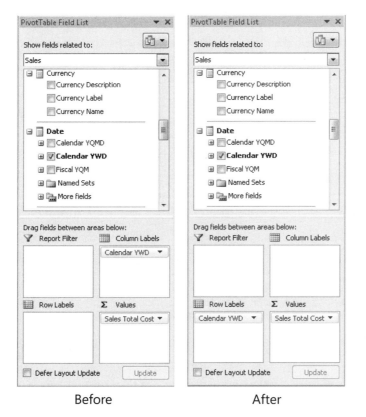

Before   After

You should now have a new pivot table in the workbook that resembles the following illustration.

K	L
Row Labels ▼	**Sales Total Cost**
⊞ Year 2007	$1,888,459,186.75
⊞ Year 2008	$1,731,140,050.76
⊞ Year 2009	$1,624,640,793.35
Grand Total	**$5,244,240,030.86**

To insert the sparklines

1. Select the cell for Year 2007 in the pivot table, right-click it, and select Expand\Collapse | Expand Entire Field.

   The pivot table should expand to show the totals for each week of each of the three years.

2. Select each of the weeks for the year 2007 (but do not select the grand total for 2007). On the Insert tab, in the Sparklines group, click Column, as shown in the following illustration, to open the Create Sparklines dialog box.

   In the Create Sparklines dialog box, the Data Range text box is populated with the data you selected from the pivot table, as shown in the following illustration.

   Create Sparklines

   Choose the data that you want

   Data Range: L5:L57

   Choose where you want the sparklines to be placed

   Location Range:

   OK   Cancel

3. Click the Edit Reference button on the right side of the Location Range text box to collapse the dialog box and enable you to select a cell where you want to place the finished sparkline. Select cell C7. This populates the dialog as shown in the following illustration.

4. Click the Ref Edit button on the right side of the textbox shown in the preceding illustration to expand the Create Sparklines dialog box once more, and then click OK to insert the sparkline.

A default blue sparkline representing the trend of data for the year 2007 is inserted into the cell you selected, as shown in the following illustration.

Connect the Slicer to the Sparklines

To be truly interactive, the sparkline should update when the report is sliced using the slicers. It doesn't make sense for the date slicer to affect the sparkline because the sparkline is always for the year 2007. But when the products are sliced, the sparkline should change. Because the sparkline is based on a pivot table, you can simply connect the Product SubCategory Name slicer to the pivot table on which the sparkline is based.

To connect the slicer to the pivot table, follow the steps in the earlier procedure titled "To connect the slicers to another PivotTable," except perform them for the Product SubCategory slicer against the Sales Total Cost pivot table on which the slicer is based.

Repeat this process for all of your sparklines.

Try clicking the slicer, and notice how the pivot tables—and now the sparklines as well—update with new data as you slice the report.

To enhance the look of the sparklines

You don't have to settle for the default sparkline appearance. You can use the following procedure to change the default look by dressing up the sparkline a bit.

1. Click the Design ribbon under Sparkline Tools. This ribbon contains many options for formatting or adjusting other properties for the sparkline.

2. Choose a faded red style from the styles gallery. Then in the Show group of the spark-line tools ribbon, select the High Point and Low Point check boxes to highlight the high and low points of the trend. The sparkline should now resemble the following illustration.

> **Note** In the Slicer Styles group on the Sparkline Tools Design tab, you can optionally also click Marker to change the color of the marker to a darker, more pleasing shade of red.

3. To make it more obvious what year this trend belongs to, select the cell containing the sparkline and type in **2007**. Then adjust the size of the text, the color of the text, left-align it, and apply any other text formatting as you please. The sparkline now resembles the following illustration.

4. Follow the preceding steps to create sparklines for 2008 and 2009 below your existing sparkline. I chose different colors for each year, so my finished set of sparklines displays as shown in the following illustration.

To hide the PivotTable that the sparklines are summarizing

The last step in getting the sparklines in your report is to hide the pivot table from which they summarize data. The pivot table is large, and the numbers it shows aren't particularly interesting. The only interesting data from that pivot table is the trend—and you have captured those trends using only three cells with the sparklines!

> **Note** By default, if you hide rows that a sparkline is summarizing, that sparkline ends up showing no data. To keep the sparkline showing the trend data, you need to change this setting.

1. Select the sparkline you want to adjust. (You can adjust them only one at a time.)

2. On the Sparkline Tools Design tab, click Edit Data in the Sparkline group, and click Hidden & Empty Cells, as shown in the following illustration, to open the Hidden And Empty Cell Settings dialog box.

3. In the Hidden And Empty Cell Settings dialog box, shown in the following illustration, select the Show Data In Hidden Rows And Columns check box and click OK.

4. Repeat Steps 1 through 3 for each sparkline.

5. Select the columns K and L that contain the pivot table you created. Right-click the column headers, and select Hide to hide the pivot table so that it is not visible as part of your report.

At this point, you have a nice report that you can save to SharePoint.

To finish and save to SharePoint

Before you save the report, you can use the following procedure to make the file look a little nicer by turning off the display of gridlines and headings.

1. On the View tab in the ribbon, clear the Gridlines And Headings check box. This turns off row and column headings, making the report look much cleaner.

2. Go ahead and resize, adjust, change colors, and generally clean up your report to get it looking exactly the way you want. (We deleted Sheet2 and Sheet3 because they weren't used, renamed Sheet1 to Report, and applied a faded green style to each of our pivot tables.)

3. The finished report will be interactive via the slicers and drill-down buttons on the pivot table, and you should see the complete report updating when you interact with it. The finished report should resemble the following illustration.

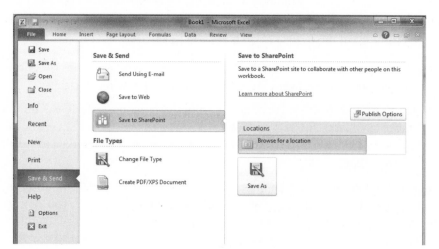

Now the file should look more like a report that might be proudly shown across an organization.

Note To load the file to Excel Services, you must first save it to SharePoint. You can follow the steps outlined in the section titled "Locking Down Excel Files," earlier in this chapter, or you can simply save the file to SharePoint.

4. To save the file to SharePoint, click File, and then click Save & Send. Click Save To SharePoint, and then select a location or click Save As.

Viewing and Editing Workbooks in Excel Services

This section provides important information about viewing and editing your Excel Services workbooks, as well as displaying your workbooks in a SharePoint dashboard.

Viewing Workbooks

The file from the preceding section should now be saved in SharePoint. To use Excel Services, simply navigate to the document library where you saved the file and click the file. This renders the file in the browser by using Excel Services, as shown in the following illustration.

Notice that the report's visual fidelity is maintained even though this version of the file is rendered in your browser. Excel Services also has complete *calc fidelity*, meaning that a workbook calculated in the Excel client yields the same numbers when calculated on the server.

> **Note** In some workbooks, some formulas are deactivated on the server for security reasons because they can expose information about the server environment.

Also notice that the workbook is interactive. For example, try drilling down on the pivot table: The data refreshes on the server just as it would on the client. Also try using one of the slicers. You'll see that the entire report is sliced just as it would be sliced in the Excel client.

Excel Services provides a setting to control whether a default click on a document opens the Excel file in the thick client (the Excel client) or Excel Services. To access that setting, from the SharePoint document library in the browser, on the Library tab, click Library Settings. On the next page, under General Settings, click Advanced Settings. In the Opening Documents In The Browser section, you can choose whether the document library follows the default server policy, opens using a web browser, or opens using the Excel client.

Opening Documents in the Browser

Specify whether browser-enabled documents should be opened in the client or browser by default when a user clicks on them. If the client application is unavailable, the document will always be opened in the browser.

Default open behavior for browser-enabled documents:

○ Open in the client application
○ Open in the browser
● Use the server default (Open in the browser)

Editing Workbooks

You can try editing this or any other Excel file that you can view on Excel Services.

> **Note** Editing works only if you have installed the Office Web Applications product on SharePoint.

Because this file uses external data refresh, it is editable on Excel Services only if you first check the file out. This is true of all Excel files that perform a data refresh because all editing is collaborative on the server. Any user with permissions to edit the file can join at any time. When editing collaboratively, all users share the same session—and hence all users would share the same set of credentials, which can present a security issue in some environments. To prevent cases where other users might be using your credentials to perform a data refresh, Excel Services requires that you first check the file out to prevent others from joining the edit session.

When you check this file out from the document library and then view it with Excel Services, you can click the Edit In Browser tab. The editing capabilities are basic in Excel Services; you can add formulas (by typing the = sign in a cell and then typing the formula name), add text, format cells, add hyperlinks, add tables, and more. The editing is a subset of the most basic spreadsheet editing functionality and can be useful in many cases where you have a single spreadsheet that many users need to enter data into.

To see collaboration in action, simply open another instance of your browser, go to the SharePoint document library, and chose to edit the file in the browser. In this case, you are now "collaborating" with yourself.

Excel Services and Dashboards

SharePoint provides the ability to combine insights from Excel workbooks to be consumed side by side with other data in SharePoint. The most common way to do this is to configure a Web Part page in SharePoint. This gives a quick and easy way to get Excel based data into a dashboard format that many BI users are familiar with. See Chapter 8, "Bringing It All Together," for a more complete discussion and step-by-step guidance.

Extending Excel Services

When designing a BI solution, you inevitably run into places where the functionality that came with the product isn't sufficient to do something customized to your particular needs. This is where *extensibility* comes in; it involves extending the product to meet a custom set of scenarios.

This section provides a high-level overview of the extensibility mechanisms available for Excel Services, but it is not intended to be a one-stop shop for details about any specific extensibility mechanism. Instead, it provides descriptions of each approach, when you might want to use that approach, and provides some pointers to online references where you can get more information.

The four primary ways to extend Excel Services are as follows:

- User Defined Functions
- Excel Web Services
- Javascript Object Model
- REST

The following subsections provide an overview of each.

User Defined Functions

UDFs are simply managed-code assemblies written to perform a specific task and deployed to the server. These managed assemblies can be called from a workbook just like any other Excel function. So they can take a set of parameters from other cells in the workbook, and they can return a single value or an array of values.

UDFs are particularly useful when you are using custom-coded routines to calculate a particular set of values in a particular way. They are also great mechanisms to use for performing other tasks in the system or in another system. Some UDF examples I have seen include: refreshing data from a SharePoint list; writing some custom data values into a data store that are specific to the user viewing the workbook; retrieving values from a custom data store; performing complex mathematical computations; and parsing data from the web, returning a list of values based on the custom web query.

UDFs aren't a replacement for full VBA solutions or macros. For example, they don't provide any type of object model against a workbook on the server.

To learn more about UDFs, see "Excel Services User-Defined Functions" at *http://msdn. microsoft.com/en-us/library/ms493934.aspx*.

Excel Web Services

Excel Services provides a SOAP-based web service that allows programmatic access to workbook files loaded on the server. The web service isn't only for use on the web—you can call it from any application that knows how to call a web service, including custom-built client-side applications and other web-service aware Microsoft applications, such as InfoPath.

The web service is a great way to access values from a workbook when you don't need to display the Excel UI. It enables you to do things such as set values, recalculate the workbook, refresh the data, and retrieve the entire workbook or just values from certain cells. If the Office Web Applications are installed and Excel Services editing capabilities are enabled, you can also persist values in the workbook.

To learn more about Excel Web Services, see "Excel Web Services" at *http://msdn.microsoft. com/en-us/library/ms572330.aspx*.

ECMAScript (JavaScript, JScript) Object Model

The Excel Services ECMAScript object model (JSOM) is similar to Excel Web Services in many ways: it supports loading workbooks, setting values, recalculating and refreshing workbooks, and the ability to retrieve specific values from the workbook. It also supports a number of things that the SOAP-based web service doesn't, such as displaying the UI and an event model.

ECMAScript code is designed to be run on a page inside a browser as part of a solution where the user is interacting with the core Excel Services UI. It provides events, so you can programmatically react to things that the user does. For example, when performing some simple data validation, if a user types in a value that is below 100 in cell A1, you might want to show a pop-up window stating, "The value is too low. Enter a value greater than 100." Events include such activities as "a cell is being edited" or "a value in a cell has changed." These events are fired by Excel Services, and your solution can take action on them.

Some events allow you to know which cells have been selected. This makes it possible to navigate the Excel Services UI to a different location in the workbook or even to have a second window on the page that shows Excel Services UI based on the selection. Solutions with VBA buttons on the first Excel sheet are fairly common. When users click a button on the first sheet, they might be taken to a different part of the report. Unfortunately, such solutions don't work on Excel Services, because VBA isn't supported. But you can re-create such solutions by using the JSOM on a webpage.

To learn more about the Excel Services ECMAScript, see "Excel Services ECMAScript (JavaScript, JScript)," at *http://msdn.microsoft.com/en-us/library/ee556354.aspx*.

Excel Services REST

REST stands for Representational State Transfer. It is commonly used to retrieve an XML description of a webpage by using only the URL to the webpage. For Excel Services it means that, given a URL to a workbook file, you can access the entire file or parts of the file from any client that knows how to traverse a URL and request content.

This powerful concept allows users to build useful solutions without actually writing any code. The "code" in this case is just a carefully crafted URL. The URL specifies the path to the workbook. Then the REST query portion of that URL specifies any values that should be set into certain cells in a workbook, as well as what object or values should be retrieved.

REST supports retrieving many types of objects from a workbook (charts, cell values, tables, and so on) and enables you to specify what format they should be in (xml html, or an image).

Using REST, you can easily embed a chart or table of data based on Excel logic into a blog, webpage, or any other application that can traverse a URL. And the file itself isn't embedded—the file is stored safely in SharePoint. Instead, Excel Services loads the file, recalculates it to get the latest numbers, and returns only the result to be embedded in the webpage. So as the file updates, the blog or page gets the latest numbers or image as the page is reloaded.

REST is also a great way to quickly and easily retrieve data from the workbook in xml format for further processing as part of a more advanced solution.

The same concept works for anything that can traverse a URL and bring back data from it, including applications such as Microsoft Word, PowerPoint, or InfoPath. Have you ever wondered how to get an Excel chart into a PowerPoint deck and make it refreshable—without having to copy the file or embed the full file into PowerPoint? REST is the answer. Leave the file in SharePoint, and insert an image into PowerPoint. Then, in PowerPoint, specify that the image is from a link, provide the REST URL to the chart, and enjoy an image that gets refreshed every time a user opens the PowerPoint file.

To learn more about the Excel Services REST, see "Excel Services REST API," at *http://msdn. microsoft.com/en-us/library/ee556413.aspx.*

Summary

Many existing BI solutions are already in Excel, and by adding SharePoint plus Excel Services to the mix you can gain the extra level of control and functionality needed to fully leverage Excel based BI solutions. Excel Services with SharePoint provides management, security, support for the new Excel-based BI functionality, and a way to broadly share and interact with spreadsheets. Excel Services doesn't require any client-side install but still allows users to recalculate, refresh, interact with, and even edit spreadsheets. (You need to install the Excel Web App as part of the Office Web Applications for edit capabilities.) Excel Services, in the tradition of Excel, also provides a platform for building more advanced solutions via one of the four extensibility mechanisms (UDFs, web services, JSOM, and REST).

In this chapter you had an overview of all of Excel Services along with some step-by-step guidance to help get you started with the product. The following table contains a quick summary of options and steps for common tasks, along with pointers to the relevant sections in this chapter for more detail.

To	Do this
Adjust settings to customize or troubleshoot your Excel Services configuration	Launch the Central Administration page and navigate to the Administration page for your Excel Services service application:
	■ See the Global Settings page for core settings that are service-wide.
	■ See the Trusted File Locations page to change settings that are specific to individual workbooks (like file size).
	■ See the Trusted File Locations page to adjust most administration settings related to external data.
	■ For more information, see the sections, "Administration," on page 95, "File Security," on page 97, "Server Security," on page 97, and "External Data Configuration," on page 99.

To	Do this
Tightly lock down Excel files so that the IP in the workbook is protected while still allowing the workbook to be shared broadly	Configure View Only permissions on the file in SharePoint. For more information, see the section, "Locking Down Excel Files," on page 103.
Connect a workbook to external data from Excel client and create a pivot table	Use the Data Connection Wizard to connect to data as well as create a pivot table. For BI, this is usually against an OLAP source such as Analysis Services. For more information, see the procedure, "To configure authentication in the workbook," on page 100.
Connect multiple pivot tables together so that they can be filtered in an easy and intuitive way	Add Slicers to the workbook and hook them up to your pivot tables. For more information, see "Adding Slicers," on page 113.
Help users more easily find trends, outliers, and generally make sense of the data	This really boils down to making a great report in Excel and utilizing the BI features that are appropriate for the kind of data you are visualizing. Options include: ■ Use Charts to show patterns and relationships. See the procedure "To add a chart," in the section "Adding Slicers." ■ Use Slicers to allow more intuitive filtering of pivot tables. For more information, see "Adding Slicers." ■ Add Conditional Formatting to help call out outliers, or create a simple KPI icon for status. For more information, see the procedure "To add conditional formatting," on page 04xx. ■ Add Sparklines to visualize trends in small spaces. For more information, see "Sparkline Overview," on page 118.
Share workbooks broadly without requiring Excel	Upload or publish the workbooks into SharePoint. Simply click the file in SharePoint, and use Excel Services to view and interact with the workbook in the browser. For more information, see "Viewing and Editing Workbooks in Excel Services," on page 125.
Allow editing for workbooks in situations where employees are on the go, are away from their installed Excel version, or otherwise need to make collaborative or simple edits.	Use the editing capabilities added by installing the Excel Web App as part of the Office Web Apps on SharePoint. This enables editing of workbooks in the browser. For more information, see "Editing Workbooks," on page 126.

To	Do this
Extend the capabilities of Excel Services to address custom needs or enable custom scenarios	Depending on what you want to do, many options for customizing your scenario are available, including the following: ■ Use UDFs to perform custom calculations or processing from inside a workbook. ■ Use Excel Web Services to gain programmatic access to the workbook to leverage the server-side workbook's logic and calculations. This is a good choice in cases where your application doesn't need the core Excel Services UI. ■ Use ECMAScript (JSOM) to build solutions that are surfaced on the webpage as part of the UI. This is a good choice if the user interacts with the UI or if you need to take actions based on events that occur. ■ Use REST when you need simple and quick access to visualizations for viewing them as HTML, results from a cell or range of cells in a workbook, or want to get an XML representation of the file or part of the file. REST is a great choice for embedding Excel objects and results in a webpage and for getting information from a workbook when you don't want to write code (because it requires you only to craft a URL). ■ For more information, see "Extending Excel Services," on page 127.

Chapter 5
PowerPivot for Excel and SharePoint

After completing this chapter, you will be able to

- Understand PowerPivot for Excel and PowerPivot for SharePoint.

- Understand how PowerPivot extends Excel functionality with Data Analysis Expressions.

- Create PowerPivot workbooks in Excel 2010.

- Publish PowerPivot workbooks to SharePoint 2010.

- Set up a periodic data refresh to a PowerPivot-enabled workbook in SharePoint 2010.

Introduction

As explained in Chapter 1, "Business Intelligence in SharePoint," you can understand business intelligence (BI) as activities and practices that use fact-based support systems to improve the business decision-making process. Traditionally, those fact-based support systems have often been data-driven analytics and reporting tools developed by database administrators (DBAs) and developers, such as standard reports, scorecards, and applications.

Clearly, the DBAs and developers from an IT department cannot handle all that demand. An IT department has only so many resources and must focus on the most important projects. It's likely that IT has been able to satisfy only a small fraction of the BI demand.

So, what happens with all that demand that does not make it onto IT's plate? Usually, those projects get done without involving IT at all. The users cobble up solutions themselves—and they can do a good job if they use the right tools. In other words, they are already performing self-service BI. Self-service BI is a way for business users to easily access the data that they need to create the necessary reports and analysis themselves, without involving IT personnel at their company.

While many tools exist that business or information workers can reach for to help meet their BI needs, it's Microsoft Excel that they use most often. A large number of today's business decisions are based on information stored in Excel workbooks. Unfortunately, this popular approach has a few caveats:

- It's fairly common to share those workbooks by email or in a file share. This can potentially raise security issues.

- It's hard to ensure that everybody working with a given workbook is using the same version, because access to such files is rarely monitored or controlled.

- Refreshing existing workbooks with new data can be a lot of work—and potentially, it's work that should be done often.

- Many times the data sources for those workbooks can be used without IT's knowledge.

As a consequence, a natural—and inevitable—tension exists between users, who want to get things done quickly, and the IT department, which wants control. There is nothing wrong with either side's approach; that's just how things are.

To address the needs from the business users, while simultaneously keeping the needs of the IT department in mind, Microsoft developed PowerPivot for Excel and PowerPivot for SharePoint. Together, these applications represent Microsoft's implementation of self-service Business Intelligence.

PowerPivot may not solve all the problems, but it is paradigm shift that gives powerful BI capabilities to business analysts that they can develop themselves. Here are a few such capabilities that PowerPivot brings to the table:

- Adding more powerful tools for the users in Excel Tasks that used to take hours now take only minutes (or even seconds), and some tasks that were simply impossible are now possible. For example, PowerPivot makes it possible to work with millions of rows in an Excel workbook.

- Scheduled, automatic report refresh You can configure the workbooks to refresh automatically and periodically without human intervention.

- Transparency for IT After a workbook has been published to a SharePoint location, everything happens within the realm of IT. That way, IT controls the security of the workbooks through SharePoint, can control which data sources are being used by the PowerPivot workbooks, and can learn which workbooks are actually being used and by whom, and so on.

PowerPivot for Excel is an add-in for Microsoft Excel 2010. It includes a modified version of the SQL Server Analysis Services engine. It plugs this powerful and fast data-crunching engine into Excel, greatly enhancing the capabilities of the most-used client available. Instead of dimensional modeling, users work with tables. Instead of Multidimensional Expressions (MDX) queries, users work with Data Analysis Expressions (DAX), a language that resembles Excel's Formulas language.

 Note MDX is a powerful and complex query language for OLAP databases.

Similarly, PowerPivot for SharePoint integrates the SQL Server Analysis Services 2008 R2 engine with SharePoint 2010. PowerPivot for SharePoint gives users the ability to securely share, manage, and refresh workbooks stored in SharePoint, while giving IT the control necessary for managing security and learning about workbook usage.

A Brief History of PowerPivot

PowerPivot's history started with two internal Microsoft papers by Amir Netz in 2006, who was then an Architect in the SQL Server Analysis Team.

The first paper introduced the concept of a BI "sandbox," which was conceived as a product that would allow BI applications to be created in a much easier way—in a controlled environment that would include relational databases, multidimensional databases, and a reporting tool. While the paper helped to shape PowerPivot from concept to product, many of the original ideas changed. For example, in the original paper, Microsoft Access was the client application, not Excel, but nevertheless, many of Netz's ideas formed the essence of PowerPivot.

The second paper was about an in-memory BI engine. The business idea was to take advantage of the market trends in computer hardware (such as reduced RAM prices and increased adoption of multi-core processors) that would allow this in-memory engine to be feasible. In fact, the in-memory engine would make some of the ideas in the first paper possible.

Eventually, Microsoft created a small incubation team to explore the ideas in the papers. This incubation team spent the SQL Server 2008 R2 development cycle writing specifications, plans, code, and tests for the product that eventually became PowerPivot. PowerPivot for Excel 2010 and PowerPivot for SharePoint, currently in their first version, were released in May 2010 as part of the Microsoft SQL Server 2008 R2 release.

When Do I Use PowerPivot for Excel?

If you are considering using Excel 2010 to crunch data, you should use PowerPivot. It is a free download. PowerPivot for Excel enhances Excel's capabilities in many different ways:

- It provides the ability to work with complex data in a relational way, using tables.

- It uses the in-memory Analysis Services Engine, the VertiPaq engine, to work with huge amounts of data without the limitations of Excel.

- It offers many ways to acquire data. You can gather data from many different data sources—from relational databases such as SQL Server, Oracle, Teradata, cubes in SQL Server Analysis Services, text files, and data feeds, and you can even copy and paste! This data is then embedded into the workbook.

- It provides an easy way to work with the data embedded in the workbook by using DAX, which is a powerful expression language to define calculations. DAX is designed to be similar to Excel formulas, for ease of use, but adds greater processing power that can work with large amounts of data.

> **Note** Appendix B, "DAX Function Reference," provides a list of DAX functions, along with brief explanations of each.

When Do I Use PowerPivot for SharePoint?

After you have created PowerPivot workbooks by using your desktop Excel application, you'll probably want to:

- Share them with other users in a secure and reliable way

- Refresh them periodically and automatically

- Make sure that all the workbook's users see its most current version

- Turn your workbook into a web-based BI application, viewing and interacting with it in the browser

- Empower the IT professionals with tools to assist with the management of the PowerPivot workbooks

PowerPivot for SharePoint is designed to meet the requirements of all the preceding scenarios, giving you a way to share, refresh, and update workbooks in a secure way that adheres to IT security policies while enabling users to interact with the content of the workbooks from their browsers.

Getting Started

PowerPivot for Excel 2010 is a managed Excel add-in that is part of the SQL Server 2008 R2 release. Microsoft offers it as a free download, available at *http://www.powerpivot.com/download.aspx*.

Installing PowerPivot for Excel

Starting with the 2010 release, Excel comes in two versions: a 32-bit version and a new 64-bit version. PowerPivot also comes in 32-bit and 64-bit versions—and your versions should match. So if you are using the 32-bit version of Excel, you should install the 32-bit version of PowerPivot, and if you are using the 64-bit version of Excel, install the 64-bit version of PowerPivot.

Note If you are working with large amounts of data, you should use the 64-bit version. The 32-bit version is limited to 2 GB of memory for Excel processes, and because PowerPivot runs within the Excel process, it would actually have somewhat less than 2 GB of available memory. The memory limit of the 64-bit version of both Excel and PowerPivot is essentially all the memory available on your computer.

To get started with PowerPivot and the examples in this chapter, perform the steps in the following procedure.

To get started with PowerPivot

1. Install Excel 2010 from the Office suite along with the Office Shared Features. The Office Shared Features include Visual Studio Tools for Office (VSTO) 4.0, which is a prerequisite for using PowerPivot for Excel.

2. Download and install PowerPivot for Excel, available at *http://go.microsoft.com/fwlink/?LinkId=207852*.

3. Install SQL Server 2008 R2. You can use an existing SQL Server 2008 or 2008 R2 instance.

Note This is only needed to use the PowerPivot for SharePoint examples.

4. For the examples in this chapter, you will use the relational database from the "Microsoft Contoso BI Demo Dataset Retail Industry." You can download the Contoso sample database (ContosoBIDemoBAK.exe) from *http://go.microsoft.com/fwlink/?LinkId=214637*. After downloading the file, run it to extract the relational backup file.

5. Open SQL Server Management Studio and connect to your SQL Server 2008 instance, and then restore the Contoso relational backup database that you downloaded and extracted in the preceding step.

After you have installed both Microsoft Excel 2010 and PowerPivot for Excel, you'll see a new PowerPivot tab on the Excel ribbon, as shown in the following illustration.

On the PowerPivot tab, click PowerPivot Window. A new window opens with the PowerPivot ribbon, as shown in the following illustration. Using the PowerPivot window, you can import data from various sources, manage relationships, filter, and create calculated columns with DAX.

Installing PowerPivot for SharePoint

PowerPivot for SharePoint must be installed by an IT professional because the installation requires administrative access to servers. Installing PowerPivot for SharePoint is potentially a very complex task, depending on the configuration of your SharePoint farm. Fortunately, some good white papers have been published, which describe the setup process in detail. These include:

- "PowerPivot for SharePoint—Single Server Installation" (*http://msdn.microsoft.com/en-us/library/ff963565.aspx*)

- "PowerPivot for SharePoint—Existing Farm Installation" (*http://msdn.microsoft.com/en-us/library/gg144594.aspx*)

Creating a PowerPivot Workbook

When you have successfully installed both Microsoft Excel 2010 and PowerPivot for Excel and have the Contoso relational database ready for use, you are ready to create a BI application with PowerPivot. The first step is to import the data.

Importing data

There are many places from which you might want to import data, including the following:

- A relational database (SQL Server, Oracle, Teradata, DB2, and so on)
- A cube (SQL Server Analysis Services database)
- A Reporting Services report
- A data feed
- Text files
- Windows Azure Marketplace DataMarket
- Data stored in your clipboard

The following sections explore some of these methods in more detail.

Importing from a Relational Database

To import data from a relational database, you need to identify the database, make a connection to it, and select the data you want. You can practice these steps in the following procedure.

To import database data

1. On the Home tab of the PowerPivot window, click From Database, as shown in the following illustration, and then click From SQL Server.

2. The Table Import Wizard starts. Fill in the Server Name field with the server name and instance of the SQL Server you want to access (or select a database from the drop-down list).

3. From the Database Name drop-down list, select the ContosoRetailDW database you installed earlier, as shown in the following illustration, and then click Next.

4. In the next wizard screen, to import data from the selected relational database, you can choose to either select from a list of tables and views or write a custom SQL query to retrieve the data. For this exercise, select the Select From A List Of Tables And Views To Choose The Data To Import option, as shown in the following illustration.

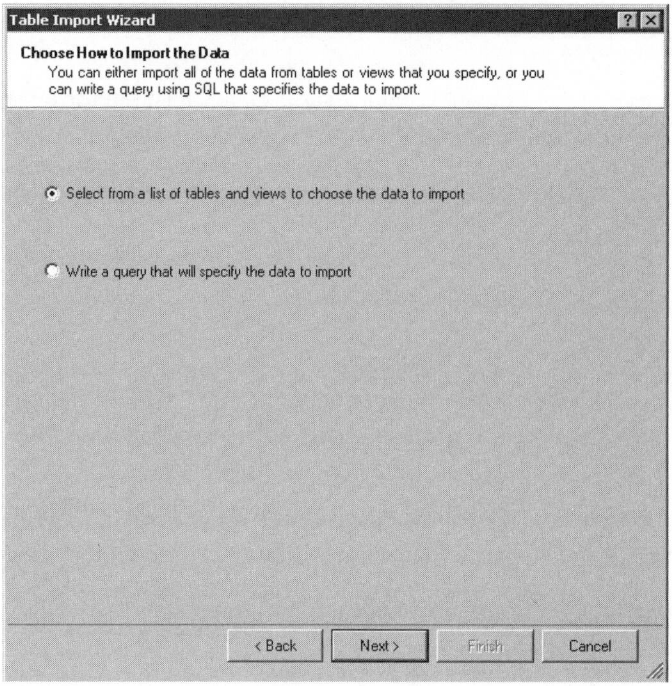

5. The Select Tables And Views page shows a list of tables. Select the check boxes next to the DimChannel, DimDate, DimGeography, DimProduct, DimProductCategory, DimProductSubcategory, DimPromotion, DimStore, FactInventory, and FactSales tables. You can see some of these tables selected in the following illustration.

6. On the Select Tables And Views page, you can also click either Select Related Tables
or Preview & Filter. Clicking Select Related Tables selects tables that have relationships
with the table or tables you have already selected; clicking Preview & Filter displays the
first 50 rows of the currently selected table, looking similar to the following illustration. This view can be useful when you want to verify that a selected table is indeed the
table you want to import. Selecting or deselecting the check boxes in the header row
lets you select or exclude columns from this view.

7. Close the Preview page shown in the preceding figure, if you opened it, and then, in the Select Tables And Views dialog box, click Finish.

At this point, PowerPivot for Excel sends a command to the VertiPaq engine to create the PowerPivot data store, which is an Analysis Services in-memory database, retrieving the data you specified from the relational SQL Server data source you selected.

After the import operation starts, you can see the quantity of rows imported as the VertiPaq engine processes the tables. PowerPivot for Excel also tries to import any existing relationships between the tables being imported.

8. When the operation completes, on the Import Summary dialog box, click Close.

Notice that the PowerPivot window fills with the data you imported, as shown in the following illustration. The tables are organized as separate tabs, each accessible from the bottom of the window just like a typical Excel worksheet.

Choose one of the sheets—that is, one of the tables—to see all its columns and rows. At the bottom of the PowerPivot for Excel window is a Records field, which shows you how many rows that particular table has loaded. The FactSales table, for example, has more than three million rows—and all that data is available. You can scroll through it seamlessly, thanks to the

VertiPaq engine, which uses a columnar technology to achieve high compression rates and processing power. When you scroll, apply filters, or perform calculations, PowerPivot for Excel sends queries in the background (known as tabular queries) to the VertiPaq engine, which retrieves the results amazingly fast.

Importing from Windows Azure Marketplace DataMarket

Released in October 2010, Windows Azure Marketplace DataMarket (referenced hereafter as Azure DataMarket, for simplicity) is a service with which developers and information workers can easily discover, purchase, and manage premium data subscriptions (some of these data subscriptions are free; some are not) that reside in the Windows Azure platform. By bringing data with a wide range of content from authoritative commercial and public sources together into a single location, Azure DataMarket is perfect for PowerPivot users who want to enrich their applications in innovative ways.

To accommodate this new service from Microsoft, PowerPivot for Excel was updated from its first version—partly to provide users with a better experience when using Azure DataMarket and partly to optimize connections to the Azure DataMarket data feeds. The changes implemented are relatively small but should make a significant difference for those of you who plan to work with data from Azure DataMarket data feeds.

> **Note** Even if you do not have the updated version of PowerPivot installed, you can still connect and use the Azure DataMarket data feeds by using the standard data feed user interface. It might just take a little more effort to use the feeds that way.

Before you can start using Azure DataMarket, you must have a registered account. You can register your Windows Live ID account for free here: *https://datamarket.azure.com/register/*.

To import data from Azure DataMarket, you can perform the steps in the next exercise.

To import data from Azure DataMarket

1. On the Home tab of the PowerPivot for Excel window, click From Azure DataMarket, as shown in the following illustration.

2. On the Connect To An Azure DataMarket Dataset page of the Table Import Wizard, fill in the Azure DataMarket Dataset URL field with the address for the dataset that you want to import data from. In the Security Settings box, copy your account key into the Account Key field. (Your account key is available at the My Data page, in the Account Keys section at the Azure DataMarket website, when you subscribe to a dataset.) For illustrational purposes, we will import data from the 2006–2008 Crime in the United States (Data.gov) dataset at *https://api.datamarket.azure.com/Data.ashx/data.gov/Crimes/*, as shown in the following illustration. The Crime dataset subscription is free of charge.

Alternatively, from the Azure DataMarket Dataset webpage, you can elect to open a query in PowerPivot (from a drop-down menu). A dialog box appears that asks you to open or save the query. If you choose to save, PowerPivot saves an Atom file at a location you specify. The Atom file contains the query information; you can use it in the Azure DataMarket Dataset URL field in the Table Import Wizard by clicking Browse and navigating to the file's location.

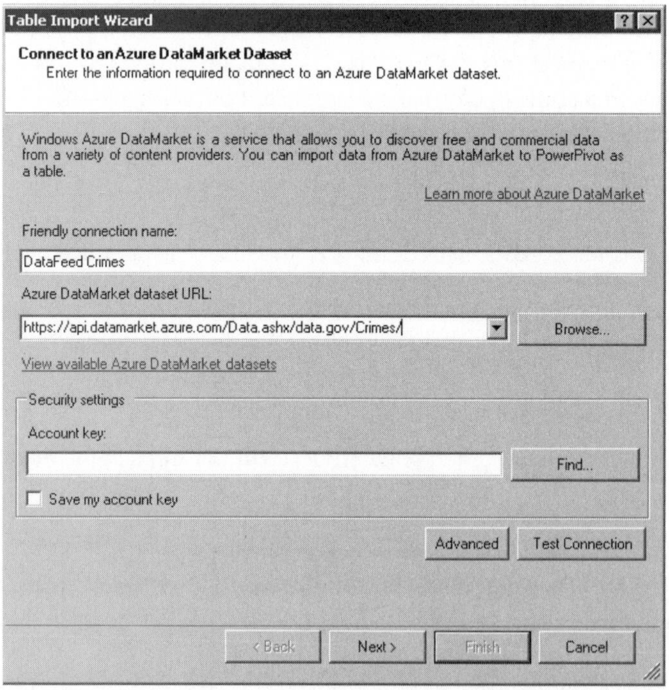

Note For security reasons, the Account Key field in the previous illustration was inten-
tionally left blank.

3. PowerPivot imports the data from the Crime dataset and makes it available on a new
tab in the PowerPivot window, as shown in the following illustration.

ROWID	State	City	Year	Population	ViolentCrime	MurderAndNonEgligentManslaughter	ForcibleRape	Rob
154828	Washington	Medina	2008	3626	1		0	0
123970	Washington	Colville	2007	5055	3		0	1
124065	Washington	Raymond	2007	2976	5		0	1
132239	Washington	Clarkston	2006	7430	12		0	1
132256	Washington	Eatonville	2006	2368	6		0	1
132335	Washington	Prosser	2006	5228	5		0	1
132346	Washington	Ridgefield	2006	2918	1		0	1
154834	Washington	Morton	2008	1091	7		0	1
154886	Washington	Snoqualmie	2008	9103	3		0	1
123965	Washington	Chewelah	2007	2334	2		0	1
154751	Washington	Black Diam...	2008	3979	14		0	1
132313	Washington	Moxee	2006	1435	1		0	1
132372	Washington	Tenino	2006	1611	1		0	1
154790	Washington	Everson	2008	2159	5		0	1
124026	Washington	Medical Lake	2007	4493	2		0	1
124072	Washington	Ritzville	2007	1714	2		0	1
132238	Washington	Chewelah	2006	2324	14		0	1
132277	Washington	Ilwaco	2006	998	2		0	1
132286	Washington	La Center	2006	1905	4		0	1
132309	Washington	Morton	2006	1102	1		0	1
154775	Washington	Coulee Dam	2008	1057	3		0	1
123971	Washington	Connell	2007	2987	2		0	1
154874	Washington	Roy	2008	810	9		0	1

Record: 1 of 25,683

Pasting from the Clipboard

You can also import data into PowerPivot for Excel by pasting it from the clipboard.
PowerPivot can use any data that is in a tabular format, which includes tables copied from
a webpage. When you click Paste on the Home tab of the PowerPivot window, the Paste
Preview dialog box opens, as shown in the following illustration. Paste Preview lets you view
the data that will be copied as a new table. While still in Paste Preview, you can choose to use
the values of first row as the columns headers.

Enhancing and Analyzing the Data

After importing some data, you can start to enhance the data and get it ready for analysis. This section explores a few basic PowerPivot for Excel 2010 features, such as creating relationships and calculations with DAX.

Note The subjects of DAX and data analysis with PowerPivot are large topics and deserve their own book. A full explanation is out of scope for this book, but you can find a more complete and in-depth view of DAX and PowerPivot for Excel features in the book *PowerPivot for Excel 2010: Give Your Data Meaning* (Redmond: Microsoft Press, 2010), by Marco Russo and Alberto Ferrari.

PowerPivot for Excel was designed to look and work as much like Excel as possible, so if you're familiar with Excel, you will find actions such as sorting and filtering data and moving and renaming columns in the PowerPivot windows both natural and intuitive. You might also notice some differences. For example, the Design tab in the PowerPivot window provides more operations that you can perform on the table, such as refreshing the data in the table (or all tables), and hiding, adding or deleting columns, as shown in the following illustration. You can also create and manage relationships between tables, as discussed in the next section.

Relationships

A relationship is an association or a connection between two tables. When you create a relationship between two tables, you are defining a way to navigate from one table to another by connecting a single record in one table to one or more records in another table. Relationships are a fundamental concept of relational databases—but not a concept available in Excel. This is one of the key differences between PowerPivot workbooks and regular Excel workbooks: Excel does not offer a mechanism to relate different tables.

Depending on the data source used to acquire your data, PowerPivot can automatically get relationships (and related tables) for you. For example, if you connect to a relational database such as a SQL Server, PowerPivot can import related tables for you from that database. When PowerPivot cannot retrieve table relationships automatically (as when importing data from a Data Feed or a text file), PowerPivot for Excel provides ways for you to define them.

You can create a relationship between two tables as follows: Select the column in the table that contains the "many" side, and then right-click and select Create Relationship from the context menu. Also, you can define a relationship by selecting the column you want to use and clicking Create Relationship (see the preceding illustration) in the Relationships group on the Design tab of the PowerPivot window, as shown in the following illustration. This example creates a relationship between tables imported from Azure DataMarket on the web and data imported from a relational database.

Calculations with DAX

DAX formulas are designed to be as similar as possible to Excel formulas. Just as in Excel, all DAX formulas begin with an assignment operator, such as an equals sign (=), but DAX works with tables (as in a database) rather than with cells arranged in a tabular fashion. The main difference between Excel formulas and DAX is that DAX never uses cell coordinates (B2, C3, and so on). Also, DAX does not work with cell ranges. To work with ranges, you can use DAX functions to apply filters to narrow down the data you are interested in.

Here is a simple example of a DAX formula:

```
=FactSales[SalesAmount]-FactSales[TotalCost]
```

This calculation defines the Margin column in the sample workbook by subtracting the TotalCost column from the SalesAmount column, which yields a profit-margin value.

PowerPivot evaluates the DAX expression for each row of the FactSales table and populates the FactSales[Margin] column with the result, as shown in the following illustration.

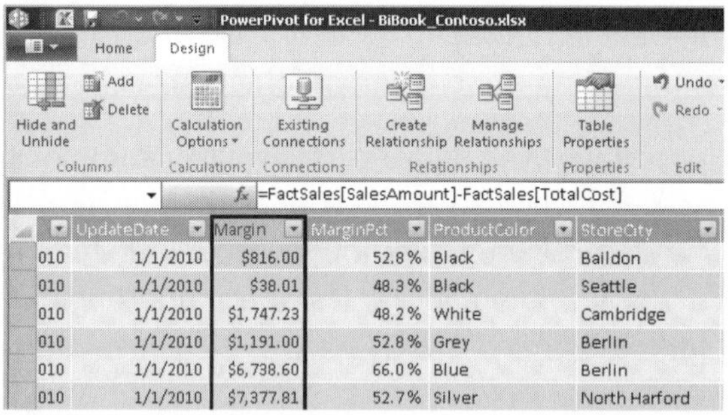

Here's a slightly more complex DAX formula:

```
=SUMX(RELATEDTABLE(FactSales),FactSales[SalesAmount])
```

In the preceding formula, the DAX expression calculates a value for each row from the *DimProduct* table by scanning the rows in the *FactSales* for the current row, retrieving the *SalesAmount*, and performing a summation of the *SalesAmount*. In other words, this DAX formula filters the *FactSales* table that corrensponds to the product of the current row at *DimProduct* table and aggregates the *SalesAmount* value, as shown in the following illustration.

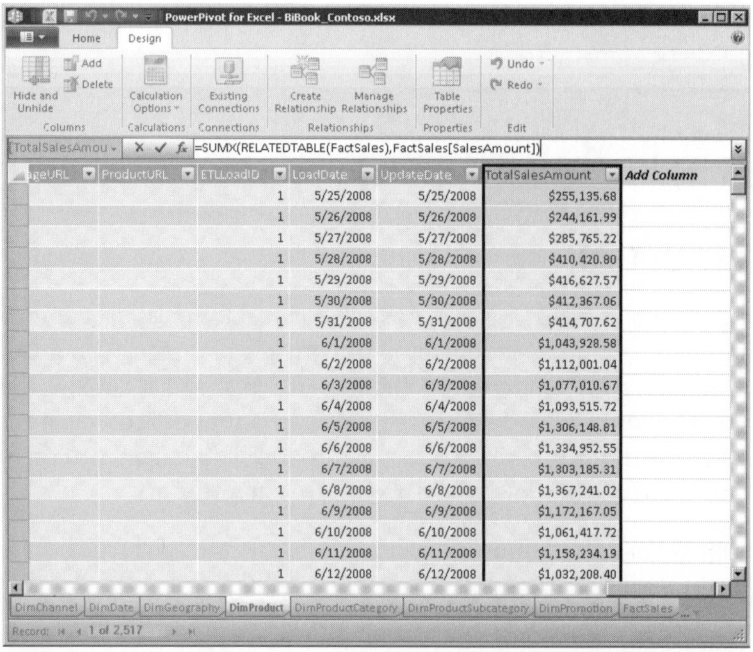

Appendix B, "DAX Function Reference," provides a list of all available DAX functions along with a short description of each. For more information about DAX, see the "Data Analysis Expressions in PowerPivot for Excel 2010" white paper and sample workbook available for download at *http://www.microsoft.com/downloads/en/details.aspx?displaylang=en&FamilyID= 1ae63bfb-c303-44e3-ae44-7413d499495d*.

PivotTables and PivotCharts with PowerPivot

You can consider PivotTables and PivotCharts as the two features that make Excel an excellent BI client tool. Using these features, you can analyze large amounts of data in a quick and easy way—and PowerPivot takes advantage of both features. PowerPivot provides different ways to insert various combinations of PivotTables and PivotCharts into a workbook. You can access these features from the PowerPivot window or from the PowerPivot tab on the Excel ribbon as shown, respectively, in the following illustrations.

The options in those two menus provide easy and convenient ways to insert a single PivotTable, a single PivotChart, or a combination of PivotTables and PivotCharts into a PowerPivot workbook.

A single PivotTable is the most basic configuration. The following illustration shows a new PowerPivot PivotTable before adding any fields. Notice that, for the PowerPivot PivotTable and for the PowerPivot PivotCharts (in the succeeding illustration), the PowerPivot field list is shown instead of the standard Excel field list.

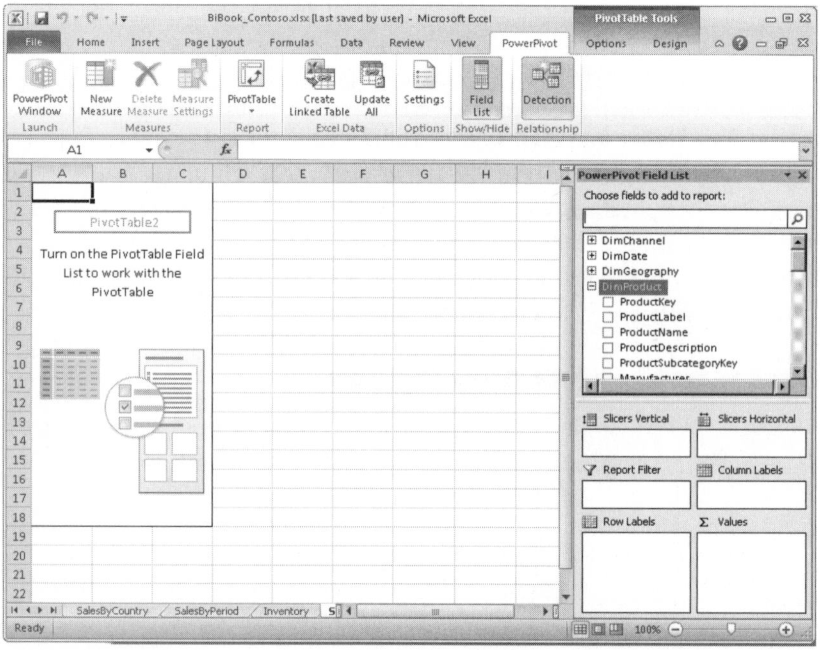

Selecting PivotChart inserts a single PivotChart in your workbook, as shown in the following illustration. PowerPivot also creates a PivotTable on a separate sheet that contains the data that the PivotChart uses. This additional sheet's name follows a standard naming convention: "Data for Sheet <x> Chart<y>." For this example, we inserted a PivotChart named Chart1 in the Sheet2 sheet, which created a new sheet named "Data for Sheet2 Chart1." (See the following illustration.) This naming scheme can help you browse from the PivotTable that contains the support data back to the PivotChart (as long as you neither rename the PivotChart's sheet nor move the PivotChart to a different sheet).

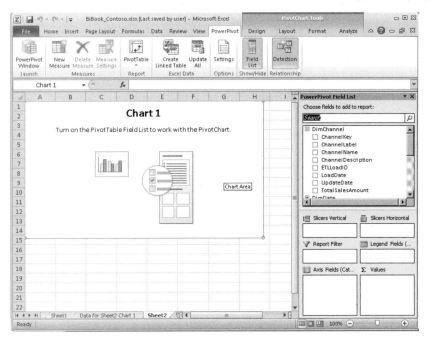

The following illustration shows a PowerPivot PivotChart displaying Total Sales By Country from the Contoso database.

Publishing to SharePoint

After creating a PowerPivot workbook by using PowerPivot for Excel, you'll likely want to share it with others in your department or organization. Your workbook becomes much more useful when others can use it.

To publish your workbook

1. In Excel, click the File tab on the Excel ribbon.

2. Click Save & Send, as shown in the following illustration.

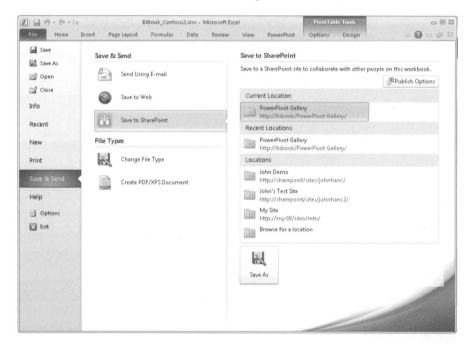

3. In the Save & Send section, click Save To SharePoint.

If you are publishing to a SharePoint site that has PowerPivot for SharePoint installed, you should publish it to the PowerPivot Gallery. The PowerPivot Gallery is a special PowerPivot-enabled SharePoint document library with additional functionality that goes above and beyond the features available in standard SharePoint 2010 document libraries.

PowerPivot Gallery

PowerPivot Gallery is a visually rich SharePoint document library installed with PowerPivot for SharePoint. Its enhanced visual presentation aids in interpreting the data in each sheet of PowerPivot workbooks in the Gallery, as shown in the following illustration.

Clicking a specific sheet in a PowerPivot workbook opens the workbook in the browser, where you can analyze it further, as shown in the following illustration.

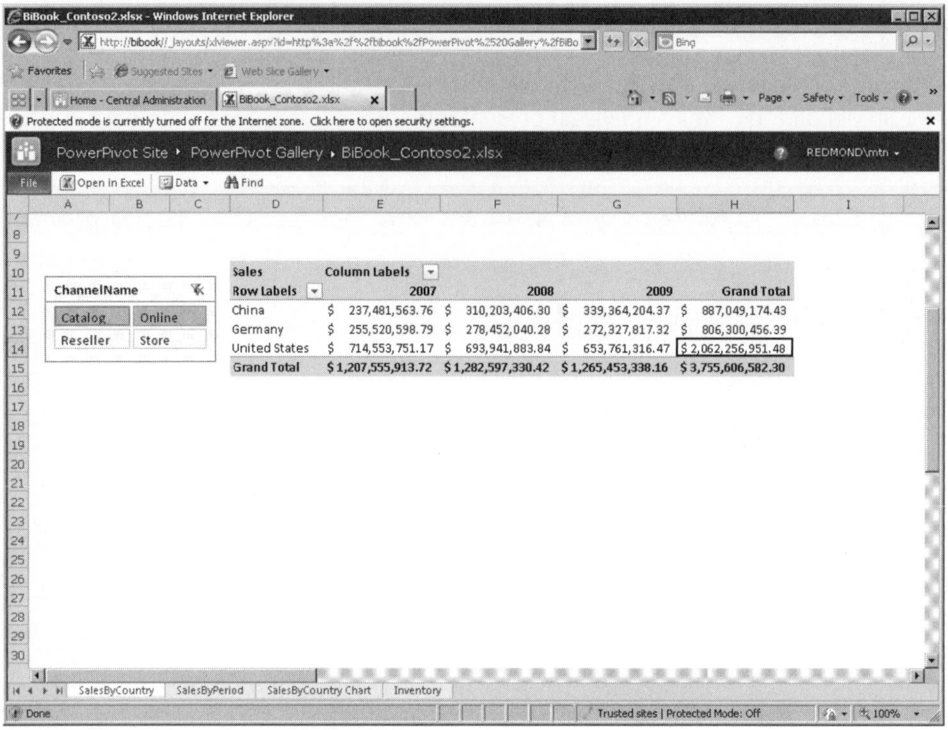

Scheduling Data Refreshes

PowerPivot for SharePoint provides a data-refresh feature that can automatically retrieve updated data from the external data sources you used to build the workbook originally. Any PowerPivot workbook owner can schedule data refresh for workbooks saved to the PowerPivot Gallery or to any other PowerPivot-enabled SharePoint document library. The following illustration shows the drop-down menu that opens the data-refresh schedule page.

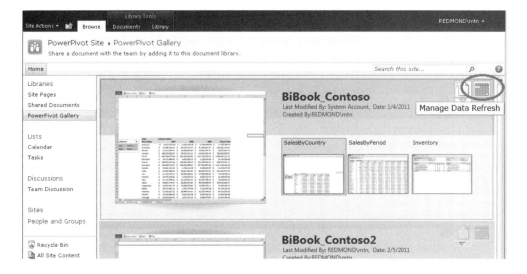

PowerPivot Gallery offers another way to get to the data-refresh feature: To schedule a data refresh through the PowerPivot Gallery, SharePoint users who have Contributor permission can click the Calendar icon shown for each workbook in a PowerPivot Gallery.

Note When a user does not have sufficient privileges on the workbook, the Calendar icon is not available on the page.

The following illustration shows the icon that opens the data-refresh schedule definition page.

The following illustration shows the initial view of the schedule definition page. To start setting up a data-refresh schedule, click Enable. This makes the page active so that you can fill in the values you want to use.

The Manage Data Refresh page has six sections, as described in the following table.

Section	General description
Data Refresh	Enable or disable a data-refresh schedule.
Schedule Details	Define the frequency and timing details of a data refresh.
Earliest Start Time	Specify the earliest start time for a data refresh.
E-mail Notifications	Specify email addresses of the users to be notified in the event of data-refresh failures.
Credentials	Provide the required credentials for refreshing data on your behalf.
Data Sources	Select which data sources should be automatically refreshed. You can also use this section to create custom schedules that vary for each data source or to specify credentials for connecting to the data source.

Data Refresh

To enable or disable a data-refresh schedule, select or clear the Enable check box on the Manage Data Refresh page. When Enable is selected, you can edit all parts of the data-refresh schedule. When Enable is not selected, the page is read-only and you're essentially freezing the data, meaning that after you click OK, subsequent data-refresh operations for that workbook cannot occur.

Schedule Details

In the Schedule Details section, you can specify the frequency and timing details of the data refresh by choosing one of the following options:

- Daily

- Weekly

- Monthly

- Once

Using the Daily option, you can schedule a data refresh to occur every n day(s), every weekday, or on specific days of the week.

If you select the Also Refresh As Soon As Possible check box, data gets refreshed as soon as the server can process it. This refresh occurs in addition to the periodic data-refresh schedule and is available for periodic schedules only (that is, daily, weekly, and monthly schedules). Select this check box when you want to verify that the data refresh runs properly. For example, you might not know whether data credentials are configured correctly. This option provides a way to test the data refresh before its scheduled execution time. In short, checking the Also Refresh As Soon As Possible option refreshes the workbook as soon as possible once; subsequently, the workbook refreshes following your periodic schedule specification.

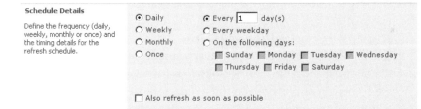

The Weekly option is for scheduling data refresh on a weekly basis, such as every n week(s) or on specific days of the week.

You can use the Monthly option data-refresh schedule to run either on a specific day of the month or on the first, second, third, or last specific day of the week every n month(s).

Schedule Details

Define the frequency (daily, weekly, monthly or once) and the timing details for the refresh schedule.

- ○ Daily
- ○ Weekly
- ● Monthly
- ○ Once

- ○ Day `1` of every `1` month(s)
- ● The `second ▼` `Monday ▼` of every `3` month(s)

☐ Also refresh as soon as possible

The Once option schedules a one-time data-refresh operation that runs as soon as the server can process the request. After the data refresh completes, the system disables this schedule. Notice that the Also Refresh As Soon As Possible check box is not available for this option.

Schedule Details

Define the frequency (daily, weekly, monthly or once) and the timing details for the refresh schedule.

- ○ Daily
- ○ Weekly
- ○ Monthly
- ● Once

Earliest Start Time

In the Earliest Start Time section, you specify details about when you prefer data refresh to occur. You can enter a specific time before which data refresh should not start, or you can choose to refresh data after business hours. This page does not determine the time at which the data refresh actually starts; instead, the schedule is queued and processed based on available resources. For example, if the server is busy with on-demand queries (which take precedence over data refresh jobs), the server waits to refresh your data until those queries have been processed. You can also choose to run a data-refresh operation after business hours. The administrator of the PowerPivot Service Application for your organization determines the definition of "business hours."

Earliest Start Time

Specify the earliest start time that the data refresh will begin

- ● After business hours
- ○ Specific earliest start time:
  `12 ▼` : `00 ▼` ● am ○ pm

E-mail Notifications

In this section of the page, you can specify email addresses for individuals or groups who should be notified when a data refresh fails. You can receive notifications of successful data-refresh operations through the regular SharePoint alerting system for email notification. (The basis of the alert would be a new file added to the target document library.)

E-mail Notifications

Specify e-mail address of the
users to be notified in the
event of data refresh
failures.

REDMOND\mtn ;

Credentials

PowerPivot for SharePoint uses the SharePoint Secure Store Service to store any credentials
used in data refresh. In the Credentials section of the schedule page, the schedule owner can
specify the Windows credentials that are used to refresh data on his or her behalf. Any data
source that uses trusted or integrated security is refreshed using these credentials. For the
data refresh to succeed, the selected credentials should have access to the data sources for
this workbook. You can choose from one of the following options:

- Use an account preconfigured by the administrator (the service application's unattended data-refresh account).

- Use a specific Windows user name and password.

- Use a predefined Secure Store Service target application ID that stores the Windows
  credentials you want to use.

Both the PowerPivot unattended data-refresh account and the predefined Secure Store
Service target application ID must be set up by a SharePoint administrator in Central
Administration. Because these credentials are shared among all users, this option is typically used where additional credentials are required for data access. A good example is
when all the data sources use SQL Server authentication (that is, the actual user names and
passwords are on each data source). In this case, the unattended execution account can be
a low permission service account. Due to the way data refresh uses Windows accounts, it is
normally not a good idea to have the unattended execution account be someone's primary
user account, because anyone can impersonate that user if he or she accesses data by using
a trusted connection.

Credentials

Provide the credentials that
will be used to refresh data
on your behalf.

- ⦿ Use the data refresh account configured by the administrator
- ○ Connect using the following Windows user credentials
- ○ Connect using the credentials saved in Secure Store Service (SSS) to log on to the data source. Enter
  the ID used to look up the credentials in the SSS ID box

A schedule owner can also choose to type the Windows user credentials to be used on the
data refresh. These credentials are securely stored in SharePoint's Secure Store Service.

Credentials

Provide the credentials that
will be used to refresh data
on your behalf.

- ○ Use the data refresh account configured by the administrator
- ⦿ Connect using the following Windows user credentials

  User Name: [   ]

  Password: [   ]

  Confirm Password: [   ]

- ○ Connect using the credentials saved in Secure Store Service (SSS) to log on to the data source. Enter
  the ID used to look up the credentials in the SSS ID box

The third option lets a schedule owner specify credentials previously saved in a Secure Store Service Target Application. To use this option, you must enter the Target Application ID used to look up the credentials in the Secure Store Service. The Target Application ID specified must be a group entry, and both the interactive user and the PowerPivot System service account must have read access.

Credentials

Provide the credentials that will be used to refresh data on your behalf.

- ○ Use the data refresh account configured by the administrator
- ○ Connect using the following Windows user credentials
- ● Connect using the credentials saved in Secure Store Service (SSS) to log on to the data source. Enter the ID used to look up the credentials in the SSS ID box

  ID: [   ]

Note Setting up and maintaining Secure Store Service is outside the scope of this book. For more information about Secure Store Service, see the following TechNet and MSDN articles:

- "Configure the Secure Store Service (SharePoint Server 2010)" at *http://technet.microsoft.com/en-us/library/ee806866.aspx*

- "PowerPivot for SharePoint – Existing Farm Installation" at *http://msdn.microsoft.com/en-us/library/gg144594.aspx*

Data Sources

A workbook can have many data sources that have different characteristics. As shown in the following illustration, you can choose to create a data-refresh schedule using different options for each data source.

Data Sources

Select which data sources should be automatically refreshed.

View: Collapse All | Expand All

☐ All data sources

Refresh	Data Source	
☑	BiBook	▾
☐	DataFeed ServiceQuery	▾
☐	DataFeed GetIndicators	▾
☐	DataFeed ServiceQuery2	▾
☑	DataFeed Crimes 2	▾

The schedule definition page provides options for choosing the data sources to be refreshed and when to refresh them. It also provides fields for specifying database credentials or other non-Windows credentials used on the database connection. You must select at least one data source to save the schedule. The data source's credentials are not used for impersonation but are instead included on the connection string as UserName and Password. These credentials override those used on the connection string for the original data import.

As shown in the following illustration, different settings are available for each data source. You can specify a custom schedule data source, or you can use the general schedule specified for the workbook.

> **Note** The only modifiable elements in the connection string are the UserName and Password elements. To edit any of the other elements—for example, to change the source server name—you must download the workbook to your desktop, edit it using the PowerPivot Excel add-in, and then republish it to SharePoint.

Monitoring with PowerPivot for SharePoint

The PowerPivot Management Dashboard provides administrators responsible for the server side of PowerPivot with the capabilities they need to understand usage patterns of the PowerPivot workbooks in SharePoint and to take appropriate actions. For example, the growing size of a particular workbook may indicate the need to acquire more memory. You can access the PowerPivot Management Dashboard by browsing to SharePoint's Central Administration and then clicking General Application Settings, as shown in the following illustration.

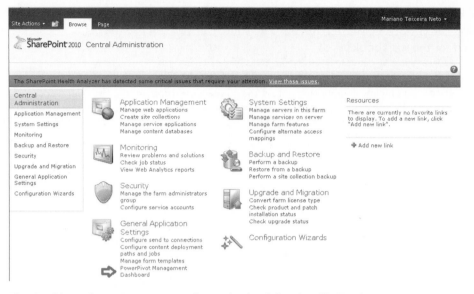

The Dashboard page appears as shown in the following illustration.

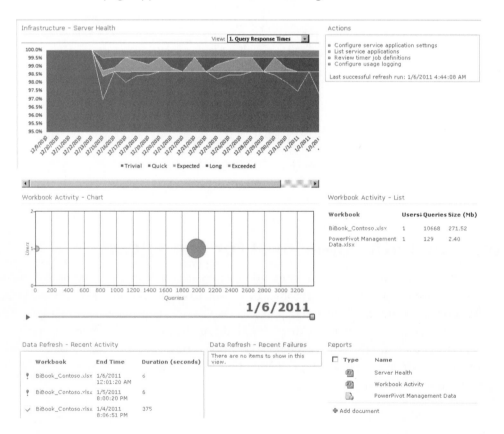

The PowerPivot Management Dashboard can be broken down into the main areas (Web Parts) described in the following table.

Web Part	Description
Infrastructure—Server Health	Provides information about infrastructure; it shows the CPU and memory usage for the PowerPivot Analysis Services service. It also contains a histogram of overall query response for the PowerPivot service application.
Workbook Activity	Provides a high-level representation of the number of users, the number of queries sent to a workbook, and the size of the workbook over time.
Actions	Allows an administrator to configure PowerPivot-specific settings within a SharePoint farm.
Data Refresh	Provides a breakdown of the recent activities and recent failures for PowerPivot data refresh in SharePoint.
Reports	Enables administrators to view source Excel workbooks and databases used by the PowerPivot Management Dashboard.

Infrastructure—Server Health

This section of the PowerPivot Management Dashboard provides indicators of the server's health. It does so through the following indicators:

- Query Response Times
- Average Instance CPU
- Average Instance Memory
- Activity
- Performance

Query Response Times

As shown in the following illustration, the Query Response Times view is the default view of the Server Health Web Part. The purpose of this chart is to provide a quick overview so that you can determine whether the majority of the queries are running as expected or whether they are running too slowly.

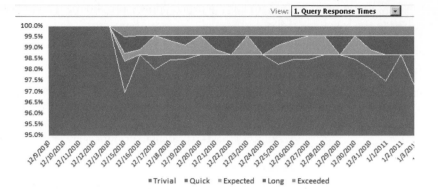

When query response time increases, you will want to determine which queries are running slowly, and why.

The following table summarizes the default query response time definitions. These definitions can be modified by selecting Central Administration | General Application Settings | PowerPivot | Configure Service Application Settings.

Category	Definition (in milliseconds)
Trivial	0 < time < 500
Quick	500 < time < 1000
Expected	1000 < time < 3000
Long	3000 < time < 10000
Exceeded	>= 10000

Average Instance CPU

Switching to the Average Instance CPU view in the Server Health Web Part shows the CPU load on the SharePoint Application Server that has PowerPivot installed, as shown in the following illustration.

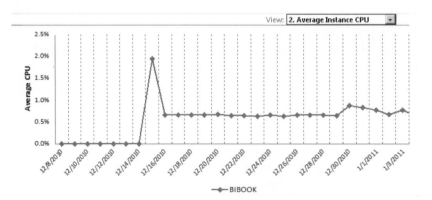

The preceding illustration shows that for this SharePoint Application Server, CPU load is not an issue because, on average, it's using less than one percent of the CPU's capacity.

Average Instance Memory

Memory can become a concern for your environment because the PowerPivot VertiPaq engine loads the workbook in memory. As the number of users and the size of their workbooks grow, they require an increasing portion of the server's memory. Taking a quick look at the Average Instance Memory view, you can easily see when more memory is being used over time, as shown in the following illustration.

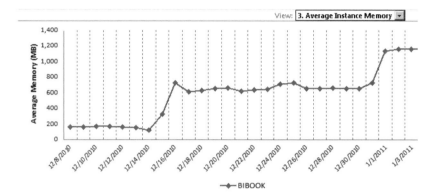

Activity and Performance

Although you can toggle between the Infrastructure—Server Health Activity and Performance views, you can get an even better view of this data by using the Workbook Activity and Server Health reports directly. To do that, click in either the Workbook Activity or the Server Health workbook located in the Reports area of the PowerPivot Management Dashboard. (See the second illustration in the section "Monitoring with PowerPivot for SharePoint.")

Workbook Activity

This area contains two parts: a Chart section and a List section.

Chart

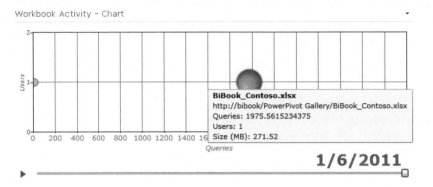

This Chart Web Part is a Silverlight control that displays a bubble chart. The chart's axes represent the number of users and the number of queries sent to a workbook. A sliding bar indicates the date. As you move the pointer over each bubble, the name of the corresponding workbook and the number of users connected to that workbook display, along with the number of queries sent to the workbook. Also, as you move the date sliding bar, the bubble size indicates how the workbook has grown over time.

List

The Workbook Activity - List section provides a quick way to view the current activity attributes (workbook name, number of queries, users, and size) of the server, as shown in the following illustration.

Workbook Activity - List

Workbook	Users↓	Queries	Size (Mb)
BiBook_Contoso.xlsx	1	10668	271.52
PowerPivot Management Data.xlsx	1	129	2.40

Data Refresh

The PowerPivot data-refresh mechanism performs many activities in the background. In the PowerPivot Management Dashboard, you will find a section dedicated to reporting the recent data-refresh–related activities in the environment

Recent Activity

As the name suggests, this Web Part shows recent data-refresh activity in the environment. It reports the most recent PowerPivot workbook data refreshes, along with the time each refresh completed and its duration, as shown in the following illustration.

Data Refresh – Recent Activity

	Workbook	End Time	Duration (seconds)
❗	BiBook_Contoso.xlsx	1/6/2011 12:01:20 AM	6
❗	BiBook_Contoso.xlsx	1/5/2011 8:00:20 PM	6
✓	BiBook_Contoso.xlsx	1/4/2011 8:06:51 PM	375
✓	BiBook_Contoso.xlsx	1/3/2011 8:06:32 PM	376
✓	BiBook_Contoso.xlsx	1/2/2011 8:07:43 PM	413
✓	BiBook_Contoso.xlsx	1/1/2011 8:06:42 PM	393
✓	BiBook_Contoso.xlsx	12/31/2010 8:06:36 PM	375
✓	BiBook_Contoso.xlsx	12/30/2010 8:08:05 PM	429
✓	BiBook_Contoso.xlsx	12/29/2010 8:05:43 PM	334
✓	BiBook_Contoso.xlsx	12/28/2010 8:05:37 PM	336

1 2 3

Clicking a workbook in the Recent Activity report redirects you to that workbook's data-refresh history page, where you can find details about the failure. The following illustration shows the data-refresh history page for the BiBool_Contoso.xlsx workbook.

Recent Failures

This Web Part focuses on reporting recent data-refresh failures. With this information in hand, you can go back to the Recent Activity Web Part and start investigating the underlying reasons for why a particular data refresh failed.

Reports

Reports

☐ Type	Name
📄	Server Health
📄	Workbook Activity
📄	PowerPivot Management Data

➕ Add document

As shown in the preceding illustration, the Reports Web Part contains the Excel workbooks that are the source for the PowerPivot Management Dashboard charts. Clicking a workbook opens that workbook in the browser, and you can identify the charts shown in the PowerPivot Management Dashboard.

Summary

This chapter briefly introduces you to PowerPivot for Excel and PowerPivot for SharePoint. It provides guidance on creating a PowerPivot workbook, importing data from various data sources, and mashing them up using DAX. This chapter also demonstrates how to publish a PowerPivot workbook to SharePoint and how to schedule data refreshes, and it explains how IT professionals can manage PowerPivot for SharePoint by using the PowerPivot Management Dashboard. To learn more about PowerPivot, you can look for books dedicated to PowerPivot for Excel and to PowerPivot for SharePoint. You can also find more information by referencing the following resources:

- The official MSDN blog at *http://blogs.msdn.com/powerpivot*.

- Rob Collie's blog at *http://www.powerpivotpro.com* (for PowerPivot for Excel). Rob Collie was a Program Manager in the Analysis Services team that worked on PowerPivot for Excel.

- Dave Wickert's blog at *http://www.powerpivotgeek.com* (for PowerPivot for SharePoint). Dave Wickert is a Program Manager on the Analysis Services team, working on PowerPivot for SharePoint.

Chapter 6
Visio and Visio Services

After completing this chapter, you will be able to

- Understand the historical background for Visio.

- Discover what's new in Visio 2010 and Visio Services.

- Determine when and where you should use Visio Services.

- Understand the architecture of Visio Services.

- Understand Visio 2010 as an authoring tool for connecting to data in a database.

- Know the available data source options.

- Understand how to configure Visio Services, including security.

- Know how to publish Visio diagrams to SharePoint Server 2010.

Introduction

You can realize valuable insights by combining the well-established vector diagramming tools in Microsoft Visio with Microsoft SharePoint to create data-driven visualizations that display appropriate objects, context, and metrics. These data-driven visuals become agents both for front-line employees who take action and for managers at all levels, thus contributing to better decisions.

Consider the impact you can have by creating data-driven diagrams that provide interactive processes, context, business structures, flowcharts, metrics, store layouts, interactive and dynamic organizational charts, heat maps, status on IT networks, and more.

SharePoint 2010 includes Visio as a service application called Visio Services. You no longer need to install an ActiveX control to view Visio drawings in a browser. Visio Services is a SharePoint service application that provides all the records management features that Excel Services has to offer.

This chapter describes client data-driven diagram features and also shows how to set up Visio Services so that you can publish Visio diagrams and Visio 2010 Web Drawings to SharePoint.

A Brief History of Visio

Visio goes back a long way. A company called Axon Corporation was founded in 1990 (when Microsoft Windows 3.0 was widely adopted) to develop and market mainstream business graphics software products for personal computers. The idea of presenting more than tables of words and numbers proved popular, and the company continued to develop methods for drawing on computers.

The company was purchased by Microsoft in 2000. Microsoft integrated some of the Visio Enterprise Network Tools, adding support for network and directory services diagramming to Visio. Microsoft continues to update Visio. For example, you can now track physical and virtual hardware by using the downloadable add-ins discussed later in this chapter.

Visio, in its simplest form, is a diagraming application that uses vector graphics for drawing, for data diagraming, for schematic diagrams, and for creating measured (scaled) drawings. The available editions are Standard, Professional, and Premium; you need either Professional or Premium to connect visual objects to data sources.

The business intelligence (BI) features were largely highlighted in Visio 2003. One example is how users began to build shapes and add context with color to give business users "strategy maps." Visio 2007 added the capability to use PivotDiagrams to show data from numerous sources with automatic refresh.

What Does Visio Give You?

You might already be familiar with all that Visio can do; it's now a substantial product that has evolved over two decades. There are over 60 different drawing templates available in Visio 2010, split into 8 categories.

Visio 2010 includes new features such as SharePoint integration and Business Process Modeling Notation, and it has been updated to use the Fluent user interface (the ribbons) introduced in Office and other Microsoft applications.

As you review Visio 2010 as a tool for pushing the envelope for making decisions easier with visuals, consider the available functionality in the following list. It provides only a glimpse of what you can do in Visio:

> **Note** The availability of some functionality in the list depends on the version you own.

- AutoConnect functionality
- Autodesk AutoCAD capabilities
- Brainstorming diagrams

- Business process diagrams
- Clip art integration
- Context-sensitive Help and links to task-specific templates
- Flowcharts
- Microsoft Office Outlook 2010 integration
- Microsoft Office Project integration with Visio Gantt charts and timelines
- Microsoft Office SharePoint Server integration through Document Workspaces
- Microsoft Visual Studio programming support (including Microsoft .NET)
- Multilanguage and complete Unicode support
- Organization charts
- PDF and XPS file support
- Review mode
- Save as webpage feature with navigation controls
- Shape customization
- Shape data reporting
- Microsoft Tablet PC support (including digital ink)
- Theme support
- Timelines and calendars
- Wizards for generating diagrams from existing data
- Workflow shapes (3-D)
- XML Web services integration
- Building, space, and floor plans
- Data-driven solution support (including data-related APIs)
- Data Link functionality
- Database modeling diagrams with reverse engineering of any Open Database Connectivity–compliant data source
- Directory services diagrams
- Engineering diagrams (electrical, chemical, and more)
- ITIL diagrams
- Logical network diagrams
- Network rack diagrams

- PivotDiagrams

- Sample diagrams

- Software diagramming and reverse engineering

- Value stream maps

- Website mapping and documentation (including auto-generation of website maps)

You can find a complete list of functionality and a version comparison chart at *http://office. microsoft.com/en-us/visio/visio-edition-comparison-FX101838162.aspx*. The major features fall into the following categories:

- Key templates and shapes to jump-start your diagramming

- Key features for intuitive navigation and easy diagramming

- Dynamic, data-driven diagrams

- Sharing with anyone, even those who don't have Visio installed

- Integration with other products

- Customization and extensibility

BI in Visio 2007 and Visio 2010

Microsoft Office Visio Professional 2007 and Microsoft Visio 2010 (Professional and Premium) help you analyze how a process or other area is actually performing by connecting relevant data for the business user to the shapes in your diagram. Visio will let you connect diagrams to multiple data sources, including Excel, Access, SQL Server, and SharePoint Foundation List. The BI features discussed in this section apply both to Visio 2007 to Visio 2010.

PivotDiagram

Visio 2007 introduced the PivotDiagram, which is a collection of shapes arranged in a tree structure that helps you to analyze and summarize business data that can be refreshed in a visual format.

The PivotDiagram begins as a single shape, called a *top node*, which contains information imported from a worksheet, table, view, or cube. You can break the top node into subnodes to view your data in various ways. In Visio 2010, the PivotDiagram tab on the ribbon gives you more options, as shown in the following illustration.

> **Note** If you want a visual representation of each row in a worksheet, table, or view but you don't need to analyze or summarize the data, use the Link Data To Shapes feature on the Data tab. For more information, see "Enhance your data with data graphics," at *http://office.microsoft. com/en-gb/visio-help/enhance-your-data-with-data-graphics-HA010048784.aspx.*

Because there is no better way to explain than to show, we include an example of how to create a PivotDiagram later in this chapter. For now, see the following example from the article "Create a PivotDiagram," found at *http://office.microsoft.com/en-us/visio-help/create-a-pivotdiagram-HA010357089.aspx?CTT=1.*

Parts of a PivotDiagram

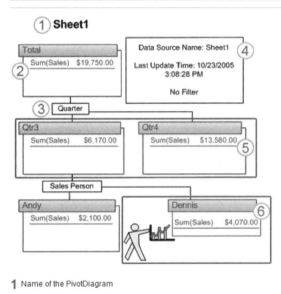

1 Name of the PivotDiagram

2 Top node of the PivotDiagram

3 Breakdown shape

4 Data legend

5 The Qtr3 and Qtr4 shapes together are a level

6 Node with a shape applied to add impact

As you can see from the preceding illustration, you can show a hierarchal visual of your data.

You can insert a PivotDiagram into any Microsoft Office Visio 2010 Professional or Premium drawing together with other information, such as a chart or graph.

To insert a PivotDiagram into your drawing

1. Click the File tab.

2. Click New, Business, and then double-click PivotDiagram, as shown in the following illustration.

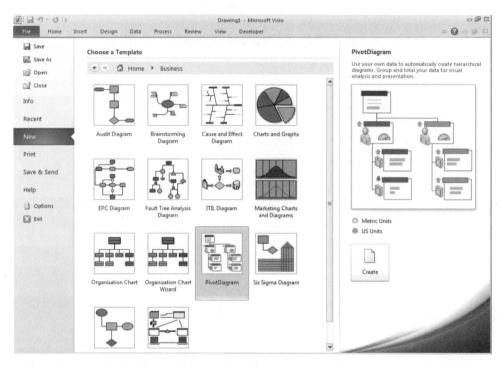

3. Follow the steps in the Data Selector Wizard, or you can select Previously Created Connection if an .odc file was already created. We created an .odc file connected to Contoso Sales data in Chapter 4, "Excel Services."

After you click Finish, the following shapes appear on the drawing page:

- ❑ A data legend containing information about the data source
- ❑ A text box for the name of the PivotDiagram
- ❑ The top node, which contains the imported data set

PivotDiagram also appears in the ribbon.

4. Click the top node on the drawing page, and in the PivotDiagram window, under Add Category, click the category (usually a column in your data source) by which you want to group your data.

You can use filters to show which nodes appear in different levels. If your data source is a SQL Server Analysis Services cube, perform the following steps.

To filter data display for different levels

1. Right-click the item that you want to filter, and click Configure Dimension.

3. Click Configure Level in the Configure Dimension dialog box.

4. Locate operations in the leftmost column under Filter and under Show data, and type the values into the rightmost column to specify the data that you want to work with.

You can customize data in PivotDiagram nodes by showing or hiding data, by using the summary function to show Average, Min, Max, or Count, and by limiting the number of nodes that display in the levels.

Visio Data Selector Wizard

The Visio Data Selector Wizard enables you to connect to data in Excel, Office Access, SQL Server databases, SQL Analysis Services, and other data sources. As you can see in the following illustration, you can also select a previously created connection, which would be an Office Data Connection (ODC) file.

Data Graphic

A data graphic is a set of enhancements that you can apply to shapes to show data that the shapes contain. A data graphic presents your data as a combination of textual and visual elements, such as flags and progress bars.

You can create your own data graphic. On the Data tab, shown in the following illustration, you can select Data Graphics, where you can see the data graphic as an available object to enhance. Other objects and images can be applied even when they are not created in Visio.

Design	Data	Process	Review	View	Developer	PivotDiagram

☐ Shape Data Window
☐ External Data Window

Data Graphics ▾   Insert Legend ▾

No Data Graphic

Available Data Graphics

Sales

📇 Create New Data Graphic...

✎ Edit Data Graphic...

✓ Apply after Linking Data to Shapes

466675054. 36

Data Source Name: Contoso_Retail - Sales

Last Update Time: 3/30/2011 11:54:19 AM

No Filter

The New Data Graphic dialog box shows the item you have created that is linked to data.

New Data Graphic

📄 New Item...   ✎ Edit Item...   ✕ Delete   ▲ ▼

Data Field	Displayed as	Position

Click 'New Item' to display data on shapes.

Default position

Horizontal: ☐ Far Right ▾

Vertical: ▣ Middle ▾

Display options

☐ Show border around items at default position

☐ Hide shape text when data graphic is applied

[?]   Apply   OK   Cancel

After you create a new item, it appears in the New Data Graphic dialog box.

You can add text, data bars, icons, and color-coding to enhance your data graphic. To learn how to accomplish these tasks, see "Enhance your data with data graphics" at *http:// office.microsoft.com/en-us/visio-help/enhance-your-data-with-data-graphics-HA010379394. aspx?CTT=1.*

As you add to the data graphic, you can see how the visual shows data-driven images to help viewers make decisions by showing data and visual status.

1 The function of the process ("Test") is shown as a unique fill color.

2 The cost of the process ("$50,000.00") is shown as a data bar.

3 The status of the process ("Not Started") is show as a question mark icon.

4 The owner ("Phyllis Harris") and end date ("9/30/2009") of the process are shown as text callouts.

Visio Viewer

Before we tell you about publishing Visio diagrams to SharePoint, you should know that you can still view Visio diagrams by using Visio Viewer even if you do not have Visio installed. Visio Viewer is a free download and is implemented as an ActiveX control that loads and renders Visio drawings inside Internet Explorer. You can download Visio Viewer for Visio 2010 and Visio 2007 from the download page at *http://www.microsoft.com/downloads/en/details. aspx?displaylang=en&FamilyID=f9ed50b0-c7df-4fb8-89f8-db2932e624f7.*

> ⚠️ **Important** Visio Viewer 2002 and Visio Viewer 2003 have been discontinued. If you use Visio Viewer 2007, ensure that you have the latest upgrades—or upgrade to the Visio 2010 Viewer. The Visio 2010 Viewer has all the functionality of the previous viewers and includes all the security fixes.

What's New in Visio 2010 and Visio Services

This section describes new features for creating BI solutions in Visio 2010.

Diagram Validation in Visio 2010

Visio 2010 Premium introduces mechanisms for validating diagrams to reinforce graphical and semantic correctness, such as a company's standardized method for business process modeling notation. Diagram Validation provides you with one-click access to review diagramming standards and discover common errors. End users validate their diagrams against a custom rule set by clicking the Process tab, and then in the Diagram Validation group, clicking Check Diagram. The rule set can reinforce Visio elements that are required for corporate diagrams. Visio 2010 also ships with pre-created rule sets. It's expected that third-party companies will help by creating customized rule sets.

By default, four templates include rule sets for:

- Business Process Modeling Notation (BPMN) diagram
- Basic Flowchart diagram
- Cross Functional Flowchart diagram
- Microsoft SharePoint Workflow diagram

By standardizing rule sets for process and flowchart diagrams, we suggest that decision making becomes even more simple. Business users can think more about the data and visual, and less about what methods that were used to create the process and flowchart diagrams. Next to each file in the Process Diagram Repository is a column named "Category," which displays the validation status of each document, as shown in the following illustration.

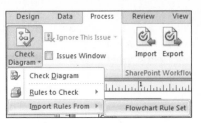

> 📝 **Note** David Parker's new book, *Microsoft Visio 2010 Business Process Diagramming and Validation*, explains Visio diagram validation and the APIs behind it, and helps you build tools to make it all easier.

SharePoint 2010 Visio Services

The ability to share Visio diagrams in SharePoint Server 2010 is new in Visio 2010. Similar to Excel, Visio acts as an end-user authoring tool, so anyone that knows how to use Visio can contribute to a shared view of the diagram. The SharePoint Server engine behind this capability is called Visio Services.

The concept and advantages behind enabling Excel Services to replicate the same client functionality as an Excel Spreadsheet in a service also applies to Visio Services. By using SharePoint Visio Services, diagram authors can take advantage of a variety of document management features in SharePoint, such as diagram access control using permissions, diagram change-tracking by using versioning, and the ability to attach diagrams to SharePoint workflows.

> 📝 **Note** Visio Professional 2010 or Visio Premium 2010 is required for publishing to SharePoint Server. Microsoft Visio Standard 2010 and previous versions of Visio cannot publish to the server.

Scenarios include:

- Viewing diagrams in the browser without having to install Visio on each client machine. This means that users can view diagrams in any modern browser (Internet Explorer, Firefox, Safari, and so on), on any platform, without installing Visio, the Viewer, or the Drawing Control.

- Refreshing data-driven diagrams in the browser. Visio Services has adopted the Visio data connectivity features for browsers. Before Visio Services renders a data-driven diagram, it retrieves the diagram's linked data from the established external data source and updates diagram visual characteristics, such as color. Visio Services supports refresh-on-open functionality, user-triggered refresh, and automatic periodic refresh.

- Integrating diagrams into SharePoint applications such as Web Part solutions and collaborative solutions where multiple lists and Web Parts are packaged together. You can also integrate line-of-business data into SharePoint sites as well as customize user-interface elements and business processes.

Visio Diagram Repository

Visio Services takes full advantage of SharePoint 2010 support for document management needs. For example, organizations and departments can manage collections of process diagrams that were historically stored on network file shares. Examples of end-user requests that led to using SharePoint 2010 for document storage include:

- I want to view updates to specific process diagrams.

- I want to edit the most recent version of a process diagram.

Administrators and managers have also made requests concerning Visio file management, such as:

- I want to monitor compliance of my organization's diagrams against internal standards.

- I want to quickly locate all processes that involve a particular department or category.

The Visio Process Repository is a new SharePoint site template that leverages SharePoint's collaboration features. This includes check-in and check-out, versioning, and workflow. The Visio Repository integrates with several of the new process management features in Visio and is built on top of SharePoint Server 2010, so you can take advantage of other SharePoint features, such as automatic email notifications (when documents change) and the revision history for any given document.

The Process Diagrams document library, shown in the following illustration, comes pre-populated with several templates that you can use to create new process diagrams. These aren't just templates—they are SharePoint content types, which help define attributes of a document. To learn more, see "Introduction to Content Types" at *http://msdn.microsoft.com/ en-us/library/ms472236.aspx*.

You can store other diagram types in a Visio Process Repository. To learn how to publish a diagram to a Visio Process Library, in Chapter 8, "Bringing It All Together," see the procedure "To publish to SharePoint."

Process Diagrams Document Library

When you create a Visio Process Repository, it creates a Process Diagrams document library for you. Two specialized columns exist for this library:

- **Keywords**   This column displays the swim-lane headings of each cross-functional flowchart in the document library.

- **Category**   This column displays the validation status of each document, when used with the Diagram Validation feature in Visio 2010. The feature makes it easier for administrators and managers to monitor whether the processes in the repository meet their organization's standards.

You can see the Keywords and Category columns in the following illustration.

Downloadable Add-Ins for Visio and Visio Services

In addition to the many built-in templates and add-ins, you can find several downloadable add-ins to help you get up and running right away.

Another site that shows what you can do with Visio 2010 and Visio Services with content and templates dedicated to BI is *http://visiotoolbox.com/2010/.* To get to the add-ins, click the Downloads And Trials tab, and then click the Templates link to see how the following add-ins can assist you in connecting to live data. Here's a brief description of each add-in:

- **Visio 2010 Add-In for System Center Operations Manager 2007 R2**   Helps you monitor and manage your IT network in a Visio diagram that you can share with others via their browser in Microsoft SharePoint 2010.

- **Visio 2010 add-in for Disk Space Monitoring**   Provides a graphical view of free space available in the servers on a network. This add-in has a client and a server component.

- **Visio 2010 add-in for Exchange Server 2007**   Makes it easy for Exchange administrators to manage, monitor, and administer user mailbox and user distribution group details. Instead of viewing single user data, administrators can create data-linked Visio diagrams that display Exchange Server 2007 data at a glance—such as sites, servers, and so on—and dramatically increase productivity.

- **Visio 2010 add-in for Rack Server Virtualization**   Helps you monitor and manage the virtualization of racks and servers in your data centers. Using this add-in, you can get a consolidated view of the physical servers and racks in the data center and compare the power consumption and space-saving before and after consolidation.

- **Visio 2010 add-in for System Center**   Provides a comprehensive list of alerts from System Center Operations Manager 2007 as well as system information, user group information, and update information from System Center Configuration Manager 2007 in a single consolidated view. This add-in has both a client and a server component.

- **Visio 2010 add-in for WBS Modeler**   A Visio 2010 add-in for WBS Modeler that improves the project planning process by giving you the opportunity to generate project plans from a work breakdown structure (WBS), by using a graphical representation of elements. The WBS Modeler can be used either to visualize and edit an existing project plan or to create a new project plan in Visio Professional 2010 or Visio Premium 2010. You can then export the plan to Microsoft Project 2007 or Microsoft Project 2010 to carry out the next planning steps. The application enables effective integration of Visio with Microsoft Project and provides an approach to visually and graphically create, edit, and modify project plans by using Visio.

When Do I Use Visio and Visio Services for BI?

As you can see, Visio 2010 adds a lot to the diagram author's "toolbox" for creating rich, data-driven diagrams. SharePoint Server 2010 introduces the ability to share these diagrams using Visio Services. The strength that Visio Services brings to BI lies primarily in the designer's creativity for delivering visualization that can connect to SharePoint lists, Excel workbooks, SQL Server data, custom data adapters, and a variety of other data, depending on the data provider that is available.

You can use Visio 2010 as an authoring tool and share information in SharePoint Visio Services in the following areas:

- When you want to share Visio diagrams in a browser by using SharePoint Server 2010, without asking users to download a client.

- When you want to provide insights to users with a visual diagram connected to trusted data (see Chapter 3, "Getting to Trusted Data") or other data sources, such as a SharePoint list or an Excel spreadsheet.

- When the Visio diagram can help place information in context and give more meaning to objects in the diagram, a process, metrics, an organizational chart, and so on.

- To build a visual representation of your business structures that bind to data. For example, you might want users to visualize progress of projects when connected to Microsoft Project Server.

The following section contains two studies that show how companies have implemented Visio 2010 and Visio Services and how the following benefits are realized:

- Empower authors to more quickly create diagrams and show results in visuals to users.

- Reduce costs by providing users with visuals that give transparency to processes and help them make fast, cost-saving decisions.

- Show performance, or what is being measured, graphically so that trouble areas are easily spotted.

Case Study: Global Crossing

The Global Crossing case study is derived from case studies located at *http://www.microsoft.com/casestudies/Case_Study_Detail.aspx?casestudyid=4000007172*. We encourage you to navigate available case studies to discover how tools are being used and whether a company, industry, or departmental profile matches yours.

Global Crossing offers a range of data, voice, and security products to Fortune 500 companies, as well as to carriers, mobile operators, and Internet service providers.

Global Crossing's product development uses process flows to help their internal decision-makers visualize new products and services. As part of a sales proposal, sales engineers must quickly show customers a visual representation of complex network diagrams so that they can make better decisions about solutions. A picture is worth a thousand words when breaking down the complexity of a network.

Visio 2010 and Visio Services now provide the following features to help Global Crossing streamline their process for innovating and generating more business:

- The ribbon is new to Visio 2010. It helps users easily locate commands in the toolbar, getting to a diagram faster and with more polish and flair.

- The Link Data To Shapes and Automatic Link wizards allow sales engineers to quickly and easily link Visio shapes to Microsoft Excel spreadsheets that include detailed specifications.

- Diagram validation provides users one-click access to review diagramming standards and uncover common errors. Daria Levin, Product Development Manager at Global Crossing, says, "When you have a standard methodology for documenting process flows across the organization, this validation tool is a great way to keep everyone more consistent."

Case Study: Virgin Mobile India

Virgin Mobile is another good Microsoft case study (*http://www.microsoft.com/casestudies/ Case_Study_Detail.aspx?CaseStudyID=4000007186*) from which to gain insights as to where to use Visio and Visio Services.

Virgin Mobile grows successful businesses in sectors ranging from mobile telephony to transportation, travel, financial services, leisure, music, holidays, publishing, and retailing. Virgin Mobile has created more than 200 branded companies worldwide with approximately 50,000 employees, in 29 countries. Its revenues around the world in 2008 exceeded £11 billion (approximately $17 billion in U.S. currency).

Virgin Mobile India has its own call center operations in India with 60 employees, which management considers a key competitive differentiator. The India call center management relies on a number of daily and weekly stand-alone graphical Interactive Voice Response (IVR) and Queue reports to review trends, analyze performance, and support decision making. Their performance report development processes were previously very manual in nature, requiring data extraction from multiple data sources, which in turn needed to be manipulated and converted into a visual form for presentation. The process was very time-consuming and error-prone, limiting the reports' value to call center management.

To design a solution, Virgin Mobile India's operations division started with five key contact-center performance reports, which addressed metrics such as call volume, number of agents, call resolution, call abandonment, and variance. With their key performance indicators required for the solution identified, the team set out to design a visual performance dashboard using Visio 2010.

According to the project manager, Rajesh Negi, "There were many reasons why we chose Visio. I think the clincher for us was being able to visually represent all the information we wanted so that it would be easier for users to actually see the data. Any issues will catch your eye very quickly, because you can review performance graphically."

Virgin Mobile India expects to realize a number of significant benefits from their Visio 2010 solution, including 2,880 annual labor hours saved, a 5 percent improvement in the percentage of calls answered, and an increase in customer satisfaction.

Configuration (Visio Services)

The authors believe the documentation for setting up Visio Services on TechNet is reliable and simple to follow. For this reason, this chapter omits the setup information and instead provides conceptual information about security and high-level steps that point you to relevant documentation. Additionally, the following instructions are simplified because we ran the Configuration Wizard to establish default service applications for our server. When you do this, the Configuration Wizard creates and starts a Visio Services service application that's ready to use, but it does not configure security. For references and information about setting up SharePoint Server 2010, see the section titled "SharePoint 2010 Installation and Configuration" in Appendix A, "Virtual Machine Setup and SharePoint Configuration."

Security (Visio Services)

Security for Visio Web Drawings (.vdw files) includes security for those that are connected to data and those that are not connected to data.

> **Note** Security can also be applied to the data source itself, limiting user access.

You can limit access to files in a document library by setting library rules for the access control list (ACL).

Before connecting to a data source, you must determine the data source you want to connect to. Visio Web Drawings can connect to the following supported types of data sources:

- Microsoft Office Excel workbook
- Microsoft Office Access database
- Microsoft SharePoint Foundation Services list
- Microsoft SQL Server database
- Other OLE DB or ODBC data source
- A previously created connection

File Security

Visio files are like other files in SharePoint; they're subject to SharePoint permissions and security. You can find several sources from which to learn more about permissions and security for SharePoint groups, users, and sites and site content. For more information, see "Managing permissions and security," at *http://office.microsoft.com/en-us/windows-sharepoint-services-help/CH010064986.aspx*.

Server Security

The Visio Graphics Service gives you control for processing and displaying Visio Web Drawings. Visio Web Drawings use the following methods for specifying how to connect to data:

- Embedded connection information
- External connection information using an ODC file. In the following section, we will investigate methods for connecting to information.

Connecting to SharePoint Lists and Visio Services

If the Visio Web Drawings are not connected to data, published Visio Web Drawings (.vdw files) must be stored in SharePoint document libraries for viewing. SharePoint Server 2010 maintains permissions for the files that are contained in the document library, and you can limit access by setting the library rules to a particular drawing.

If the Visio Web Drawings are connected to data such as Excel workbooks (hosted on the same farm) or databases in SQL Server, you can control access to data sources by defining the data providers that are trusted and by configuring them in the list of trusted data providers. To learn more about how to create a Visio Graphics Service trusted data provider, see "Configuring Visio Graphics Service trusted data providers (SharePoint Server 2010)" at *http://technet.microsoft.com/en-us/library/ee524056.aspx*.

Remember that if you want to view Visio drawings that are connected to either SharePoint lists or Excel Services (on the same farm as the drawing), you must have access to both the drawing and the SharePoint list, and to the Excel workbook, to have access.

Connecting to SQL Server databases by using the Secure Store Service—together with Excel Services or with Visio Services—to access data sources through SQL Server Authentication, requires that you configure the following:

- A Secure Store Service target application containing the SQL Server credentials with access to the data source

- The Unattended Service Account

- A required connection, if using Visio Services, to the Secure Store Service target application through an ODC file that can be created and managed in Microsoft Excel 2010

> **Note** If the external data source that you want to access is not on your local computer, you might need to contact the database administrator for a password, user permission, or other connection information.

It's out of the scope of this chapter to show you how to set up the Secure Store Service and a target application, but we give you a link in Appendix A that shows you how to create an ODC file and store it in a Data Connection Library.

You control access to data sources by defining the data providers as trusted and including them in the list of trusted data providers. Data providers are drivers that client applications (such as Visio) use to connect to specific data sources.

You can view the list of available data providers or add a new provider by going to Central Administration, clicking Manage Service Applications, and clicking Trusted Data Providers, as shown in the following illustration.

After clicking Trusted Data Providers, you see the user interface shown in the following illustration.

You must now determine how the user will be authenticated (identified) by the server that hosts the data. The next step is for the user to receive authorization or permission to access data on the server.

> **Note** As noted in the TechNet article, "Configuring a SharePoint Server 2010 farm for business intelligence by using NTLM," at *http://technet.microsoft.com/en-us/library/gg266385.aspx*, authentication methods between the three built-in BI SharePoint service applications can have different names with similar purpose and functionality. For example, in PerformancePoint Services, Per User Identity refers to Integrated Windows authentication.

Consider the following methods and definitions for securing authentication:

- **Integrated Windows Authentication**   Use to enable Windows-based clients to seamlessly authenticate with the data source without having to manually provide credentials (username/password).

> **Note** You cannot use the preceding method to connect with remote data sources unless Kerberos authentication is configured.

- **Secure Store Service** (requires additional configuration)   Use this authentication method to configure the Visio Graphics Service so that it maps the user's credentials to an independent credential that has access to the database.

> **Note** The preceding method can be used only when Visio Web drawings use an ODC file to specify the connection.

- **Unattended Service Account** (requires additional configuration)   Use this authentication method when no other authentication method is specified and when you want to create an authentication method for all users through a single account. This is the default authentication method if an ODC file used for the Visio Web Drawing does not already specify another authentication method.

> **Important** Visio Services can access external data sources by using a delegated Windows identity—but the external data sources must reside within the same domain as the SharePoint Server 2010 farm or the Visio Services Application and must be configured to use the Secure Store Service. If you're not using the Secure Store Service and if external data sources do not reside within the same domain, authentication of the external data sources fails.

When to Use an .odc File

The ODC file lets you update external data connection properties in one place. Any Excel 2010 workbook or Visio 2010 diagram that uses the ODC file for its data connection uses the updated connection properties. You can also open the ODC file directly, which can also open an Excel workbook that already contains the external data connection.

A Data Connection Library in Microsoft SharePoint Server 2010 is a library that contains two kinds of data connections by default: an ODC file, and a Universal Data Connection (UDC) file (used for Microsoft InfoPath 2010 files). You would want to use an .odc for the following reasons:

- To save to the same SharePoint site location so that the data in the Visio Web drawing can be refreshed.

- To manage and update external data connection properties in one place, in a SharePoint list.

You can also have a direct connection to the data source. You might want to do this when you move your Visio file from a different farm and still want to maintain data source connectivity.

Planning and Architecture (Visio Services)

The following illustration shows an overview of the process for publishing Visio diagrams that connect to SharePoint Products and display in a browser.

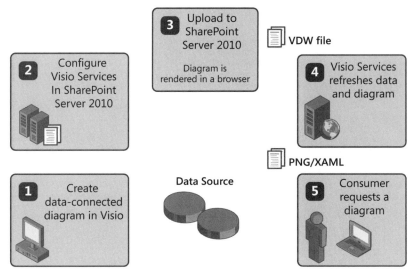

When creating a data-connected diagram in Visio, you perform the following steps:

1. Connect to a data source.

2. Link shapes to data.

3. Display linked data graphically.

4. Refresh linked data that has changed in the data source to update linked shapes to resolve any subsequent conflicts that might arise.

Creating the Visio Diagram

The Premium version of Visio comes with templates that contain images that you can connect to data sources. For example, the following image displays a Project Management diagram that shows organization and team performance with a PivotDiagram. You can break down data from Excel across different performance dimensions to create a presentation-ready report.

You might ask how you can tell whether the sample is a PivotDiagram. The answer is: on the Help menu, click Sample Diagrams, and in the Samples window, click the sample. A description of the sample appears below its picture on the right side of the window.

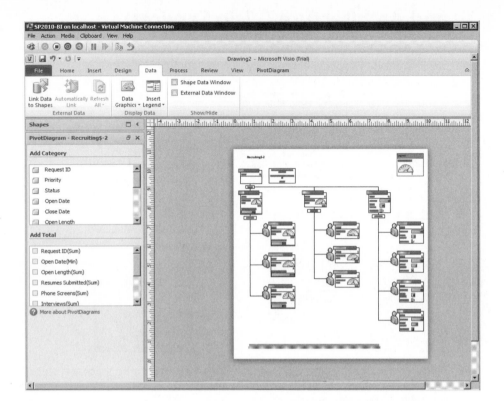

Connecting to External Data and Display Data on the Shapes

The .odc file enables you to update external data connection properties in one place. Any Excel 2010 workbook or Visio 2010 diagram that uses the .odc file for its data connection uses the updated connection properties. You can also open the .odc file directly, which can also open an Excel workbook that already contains the external data connection.

A Data Connection Library in Microsoft SharePoint Server 2010 is a library that contains two kinds of data connections by default: an Office Data Connection (ODC) file, and a Universal Data Connection (UDC) file (used for Microsoft InfoPath 2010 files). It might be easier for you to create the ODC file first in Excel, as follows:

1. Create the ODC file in Excel 2010.

2. Publish it to SharePoint Server 2010.

3. Connect to it as a data source from Visio 2010 when you create a new data-connected diagram.

Important Use Excel 2010 to edit an ODC file, to change the data query, to edit authentication information, to specify a target application, or to modify other settings.

You can use the following procedure to create an ODC file to use for connecting from Visio.

To create an ODC file in Excel

1. Open Excel 2010, click the Data tab, and then click Connections.

The Existing Connections folder appears so that you can see what is already available. It is empty in the image because you haven't created any ODC files yet.

2. Click Browse For More, and then in the Select Data Source dialog box, shown in the following illustration, click New Source.

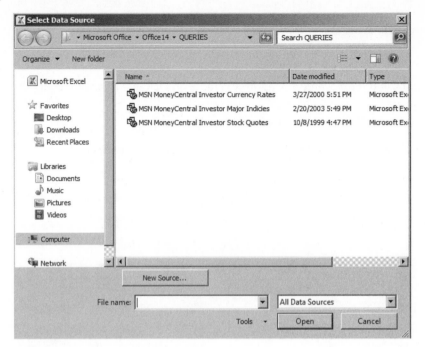

3. In the list box, select Microsoft SQL Server Analysis Services, and then click Next.

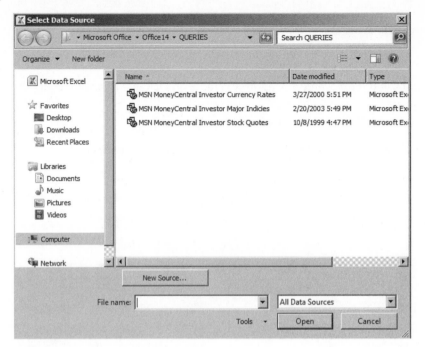

4. In the Server Name field, type **SP2010-BI**, and then click Next.

5. Select the Contoso_Retail database, and then click the Sales cube.

> **Note** A perspective is a simplified view of a cube that narrows the objects that are relevant to sales.

6. Select Always Attempt To Use This File To Refresh Data, and then click Finish.

Data Connection Wizard [?] [X]

Save Data Connection File and Finish

Enter a name and description for your new Data Connection file, and press Finish to save.

File Name:

SP2010-BI Contoso_Retail Sales.odc | Browse...

☐ Save password in file

Description:

(To help others understand what your data connection points to)

Friendly Name:

SP2010-BI Contoso_Retail Sales

Search Keywords:

☑ Always attempt to use this file to refresh data

Excel Services: | Authentication Settings... |

| Cancel | < Back | Next > | Finish |

To connect to data by using the Data Selector Wizard

1. On the Data tab of the Visio ribbon, click Link Data To Shapes.

2. On the Data Selector page, select the data type you want to connect to.

Data Selector [X]

What data do you want to use?

○ Microsoft Excel workbook

○ Microsoft Access database

○ Microsoft SharePoint Foundation list

◉ Microsoft SQL Server database

○ Other OLEDB or ODBC data source

○ Previously created connection

| [?] | Cancel | < Back | Next > | Finish |

Note The "Select Custom Range" button in the Data Selector Wizard (the Link Data To Shapes button on the Data tab) doesn't work for XLSX files. Excel does not start when you click the button. To work around this, save the Excel data source workbook as an XLS file.

3. Type the database server name, and then select your authentication method.

Note In this example, we previously granted SPAdmin permissions in SQL Server Windows Authentication and provided access to the data ContosoRetailDW database. This does not give the Visio user access to any Visio Web diagrams published to SharePoint Server via Visio Services. For this, you must configure authentication for Visio Services.

4. On the Select Database And Table page, select the ContosoRetailDW database, and then select DimEmployee.

5. Select the data connection (*.odc) file.

Note If you want to create a data-refreshable Visio Web Drawing (*.vdw) for use with Visio Services on SharePoint, the data connection file (*.odc) must be located on the same SharePoint site as the Visio Web Drawing.

An ODC file that has a connection string and data query for your dataset can be created in Excel and exported to a data connection library. You can then connect to it from the Visio 2010 Data Selector. To do this, see the article "Using Secure Store with SQL Server Authentication," at *http://technet.microsoft.com/en-us/library/gg298949.aspx.*

6. Select the columns and rows you want to include.

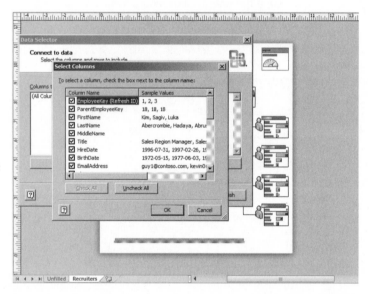

7. Drag the selected rows onto the page to link the data to the existing shapes.

	EmployeeKey	ParentEmployeeKey	FirstName	LastName	MiddleName	Title	HireDate	BirthDate	EmailAdd
	3	18	Luka	Abrus		Sales Regio...	1997-12-12	1964-12-13	roberto0@
	4	18	Kirk	Nason	J.	Sales Regio...	1998-01-05	1965-01-23	KirkNason
	5	18	Humberto	Acevedo		Sales Regio...	1998-01-05	1965-01-23	Humberto
	6	1	Yoichiro	Okada		Sales State ...	1998-01-11	1949-08-29	thierry0@
	7	2	Pilar	Ackerman		Sales State ...	1998-01-20	1965-04-19	PilarAcke
	8	3	Aaron	Painter	M.	Sales State ...	1998-01-20	1965-04-19	AaronPai
	9	4	Terry	Adams		Sales State ...	1998-01-26	1946-02-16	jolynn0@
	10	5	David	Probst		Sales State ...	1998-02-06	1946-07-06	ruth0@co
	11	1	Manoj	Agarwal		Sales State ...	1998-02-06	1942-10-29	gail0@co
	12	2	Michael	Raheem		Sales State ...	1998-02-07	1946-04-27	barry0@c
	13	3	David	Ahs		Sales State ...	1998-02-24	1949-04-11	jossef0@
	14	8	Miguel	Saenz		Sales Store ...	1998-03-03	1961-09-01	terri0@co
	15	9	Kim	Akers		Sales Store ...	1998-03-05	1946-10-01	sidney0@

Notice that the External Data pane at the bottom of the figure contains the employee data that results from selecting data from the Contoso database through the wizard.

To create a SharePoint Data Connection Library

1. Browse to a SharePoint Server 2010 site on which you have at least Design permissions. If you are on the root site, create a new site before you perform the next step.

2. On the Site Actions tab, click More Options.

3. On the Create page, click Library (under Filter By), and then click Data Connection Library.

If you have installed Silverlight, creating the Data Connection Library is simpler, and the Create dialog box resembles the following illustration.

4. On the right side of the Create page, type a name for the library, and then click Create.

SharePoint creates the Data Connection Library, shown in the following illustration.

5. Copy the URL of the new data connection library.

After you have planned the authentication method and configured security for Visio Services, you can also connect your diagram to data by using the Data Selector Wizard available in Visio. This wizard can be used for SQL Server but is not available for SQL Server Analysis Services data.

Publishing a Visio Diagram

Visio Web Drawings can have hyperlinks, multiple pages, and other features—such as a standard Visio drawing—including the ability to connect to external data sources.

Instead of saving your file as a drawing, you save it as a Visio Web Drawing in a SharePoint document library. The Visio Web Drawing (*.vdw) is a new Visio file type that allows diagrams to be rendered and edited in the browser by using Visio Services in SharePoint 2010.

To publish a diagram as a Web Drawing

1. Click the File tab.

2. Click Save & Send.

3. Under Save to SharePoint, select the site where you want to publish the diagram. You can also select Browse For A Location to select a site, or you can type the location where you want to publish the diagram.

4. Under File Types, select Web Drawing.

5. Click Save As to open the Save As dialog box.

6. Select the Automatically View Files In Browser check box if you want to view the drawing after you click Save.

7. Click Options to open the Publish Settings dialog box, and configure which pages and data sources to publish. Items you do not select will be hidden or disconnected.

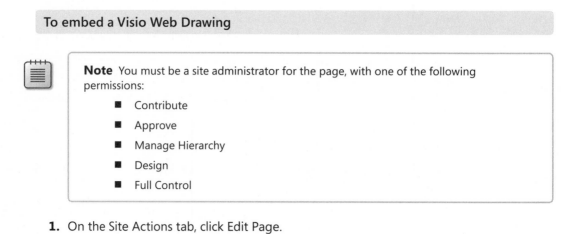

8. Check to see that the Save As Type option is set to Web Drawing, and then click Save.

Visio Drawing Web Parts

Visio Services allows you to embed Visio Web Drawings in other SharePoint pages. Using the Visio Web Access Web Part, you can embed either static or data-driven Visio Web Drawings in SharePoint pages.

To embed a Visio Web Drawing

Note You must be a site administrator for the page, with one of the following permissions:

- Contribute
- Approve
- Manage Hierarchy
- Design
- Full Control

1. On the Site Actions tab, click Edit Page.

2. Click Add A Web Part.

3. On the Page tab, select Business Data under Categories, select Visio Web Access under Web Parts, and then click Add to open the Select A Web Drawing Page, shown in Step 4.

4. On the Select A Web Drawing page, click Click Here To Open The Tool Pane to assign an existing Web Drawing to display in the Web Part. The Visio Web Access Web Part tool pane appears.

5. Type the URL to the Visio Web Drawing in the text box, or click Browse to navigate to the SharePoint folder where the drawing is located. After the URL is in the input field, at the bottom of the configuration panel, click Apply.

```
◄ Visio Web Access                    ✕
  ⊟  Web Drawing Display

  Web Drawing URL
  ┌─────────────────────────────┐ ┌──┐
  │http://sp2010-bi/sites/VisioRep│ │  │
  └─────────────────────────────┘ └──┘

  ☑  Override the Web Drawing's
  default initial view using the web
  part's current page, pan and zoom

  ☐  Force raster rendering

  Automatic Refresh Interval (in
  minutes)
  ┌─────────────────────────────┐
  │                             0│
  └─────────────────────────────┘

  Expose the following shape data
  items to web part connections
  ┌─────────────────────────────┐
  │                             │
  └─────────────────────────────┘

  ⊟  Toolbar and User Interface

  ☑  Show Refresh

  ☑  Show Open in Visio

  ☑  Show Page Navigation

  ☐  Show Zoom
```

You can either customize the Visio Web Access Web Part with the features below the Web Drawing URL or click OK or Apply to see your Visio Web Drawing embedded in the page.

Extending Visio Services

There are ways you can extend what Visio 2010 and Visio Services can do for you. For example, you can add a Visio Web Access Web Part to a SharePoint Server 2010 Web Parts page. We show an example of this in Chapter 8, "Bringing It All Together", under the section "To Embed the Web Drawing as a Web Part."

You can interact with the drawing programmatically by using the Visio Services ECMAScript API. To learn more, see "Customizing Visio Web Drawings in the Visio Web Access Web Part," at *http://msdn.microsoft.com/en-us/library/ff394649.aspx*.

To extend your ability to connect your Visio drawing to other data sources, you can write custom data providers to connect to any data source. Custom data providers need to be implemented as .NET assemblies that accept connection strings and return data as ADO.NET data sets.

Summary

This chapter covered the following:

- Why you should use Visio 2010 and Visio Services in SharePoint 2010.
- How to create a PivotDiagram and Data Graphic.
- How to connect a Visio drawing to data.
- How to publish your Visio diagram either as a Visio drawing or as an embedded Web Part.

As we suggest in the beginning of the chapter, consider the impact you can have by creating data-driven diagrams that provide interactive processes, context, creating business structures, flow-charts, showing metrics, store layouts, interactive and dynamic organizational charts, heat maps, giving status on IT networks, and more.

> **Note** Visio Services supports OLEDB and ODBC data sources. The driver for the data source must be installed on every application server that is running Visio Services, and it must be a trusted data provider. When using the Visio client to create the Visio Web Drawing that contains the data connection to the data source, the machine used must also have the driver installed.

The following table provides quick references for using Visio Services with SharePoint.

To	Do this
Connect SharePoint to live data	Use one of the available add-ins. For more information, see the "Downloadable Add-Ins for Visio and Visio Services" section on page 183.
Use Visio Services...	<ul><li>For diagrams connected to trusted data</li><li>To place information in context and give meaning to objects in the diagram</li><li>To provide shapes that help identify trends and exceptions</li><li>To build visual representations of business structures that bind to data</li></ul>

Chapter 7
PerformancePoint Services

After completing this chapter, you will be able to

- Understand the historical background for PerformancePoint Server 2007 and Services (SharePoint 2010).

- Know the components and other features that make up a PerformancePoint Dashboard, including KPIs, scorecards, reports, and more.

- Learn what is new in PerformancePoint Services 2010 in SharePoint Server 2010.

- Understand when and why you will want to use PerformancePoint Services.

- Understand configuration and security setup for PerformancePoint Services.

- Create a simple PerformancePoint dashboard with a KPI, scorecard, filter, and report.

Introduction

In Chapter 1, "Business Intelligence in SharePoint," you saw the basic pattern for creating key performance indicators (KPIs), which are derived from a company vision, a company strategy, and measurable objectives. PerformancePoint Services in SharePoint Server 2010 is one of the newest business intelligence (BI) tools complementing SharePoint Server 2010. It's a monitoring and analytics service that helps organizations monitor and analyze their business by providing tools for building dashboards, scorecards, and KPIs. When set up properly and with access to trusted data (see Chapter 3, "Getting to Trusted Data") and other data sources and reports, these PerformancePoint components (and others) help you answer the following questions across an organization:

- What has happened? (monitoring)

- What is happening? (monitoring)

- Why is it happening? (analysis)

By answering these questions, you and your employees can better predict what will happen—and make informed business decisions that align with company-wide objectives and strategy.

This chapter provides an introduction to PerformancePoint Services by helping you create many of the components that it offers, using the tools it provides.

This chapter works in concert with Chapter 8, "Bringing It All Together," which shows you how to publish a PerformancePoint Web Part. In some ways, the PerformancePoint Dashboard becomes a "Microsoft BI aggregator," by providing methods to make connections to most of the other BI tools discussed in this book.

History of PerformancePoint Services

In 2005, Microsoft Office Business Scorecard Manager 2005 was released as a product to help organizations build, manage, and use scorecards and KPIs—and then enable the organization to use all these components to perform analysis.

The successor to Business Scorecard Manager, PerformancePoint Server 2007, became part of the Office 2007 system of products and is positioned to be a complete performance management application. PerformancePoint 2007 lets you monitor the progress of KPIs, which are shared as key goals or drivers of the business. The analysis capability of PerformancePoint 2007 lets you see the data behind the KPI with several options. The Planning application lets you plan, budget, and forecast with business modeling tools.

Microsoft Office PerformancePoint Server was re-engineered in April 2009. It is available as part of the non-free versions of SharePoint Server 2010 and is expected to be influential in the marketplace because of its well-engineered BI options and features.

Overview of PerformancePoint Services Components

Before discussing the improvements made in PerformancePoint Services 2010 (in comparison with PerformancePoint 2007), we want to give you a quick tour of the basic elements: data sources, dashboards, scorecards, KPIs, indicators, and reports. Later in the chapter, you'll see more detail about each element.

PerformancePoint stores these elements as content types in SharePoint document libraries and lists. PerformancePoint elements stored in lists comprise dashboards, scorecards, reports, filters, KPIs, and indicators, while the elements stored in document libraries are data sources.

The following sections provide a more detailed look at the PerformancePoint elements.

Data Sources

Data sources are of paramount importance to data-driven applications, which is why we covered the topic early on in Chapter 3. In PerformancePoint, data sources are elements that store the connection information required to access the data that serves as the underlying source for KPIs, analytic charts, and grids. Data sources can also drive dashboard filters.

You should know that an Analysis Services cube is a "preferred data source," because that data source type extends what you can do in a PerformancePoint Services dashboard. For example, you can slice and drill down to uncover the underlying data that results in a high-level value. You cannot do this with tabular data. But because this is a dashboard authoring tool, you have several data source options available.

> **Important** In Dashboard Designer, when you create a data source for an Excel workbook, you actually import that workbook as the data source. PerformancePoint stores an internal copy of the Excel file, so any modifications you make to it are independent of the original file.

Following are the different data sources that you can use:

- Multidimensional
    - Analysis Services (2005, 2008, and 2008 R2)
    - SQL Server R2 PowerPivot for Excel Services
- Tabular
    - Excel workbook (2007 or 2010)
    - Excel Services (2007 or 2010)
    - SharePoint list (2007 or 2010)
    - SQL Server (2005, 2008, and 2008 R2)
    - Custom data source

Indicators

PerformancePoint is all about providing visualizations that help decision makers. Indicators are the images that represent the approximate value of a key performance indicator (KPI) in a scorecard. Typical indicators consist of icons. An example might be a traffic light icon that confers meaning, such as the following:

- **Green**   On target
- **Amber**   Needs attention
- **Red**   Off target

You can also create custom indicators.

KPIs

KPIs are actually the original reason that Microsoft sold a scorecard product (Business Scorecard Manager). Although KPIs can be displayed in stand-alone Web Parts in SharePoint, they become more meaningful in the context of a scorecard. In their simplest form, they are made up of actual, target, and threshold numbers. KPIs in PerformancePoint can be complex, driven by multiple data sources, with multiple thresholds that correspond to multiple levels of achievement or targets. You can also migrate KPIs from a SQL Server Analysis Services cube. You'll learn more about KPIs later in this chapter in the hands-on practice.

Recall from Chapter 1 that two of the key elements that make up a KPI are a company strategy and an objective. An example might be:

- **Strategy**   Improve satisfaction for customers that own mountain bikes.
- **Objective**   Increase repeat business from mountain bike customers by 20 percent.

The KPI is the number of quarterly repeat sales from customers who purchase mountain bikes.

The KPI target is a numeric goal or metric, which as described in the preceding objective, aims to increase repeat business in that segment by 20 percent. The next step is to incorporate a data source to compare the desired target with the actual performance, to see where the business is in terms of achieving the objective.

Scorecards

A scorecard collects KPIs and objectives to provide a comprehensive view of the health of a department or organization by comparing and evaluating the strategy.

KPIs and related data sources and indicators are the foundation from which scorecards are created. As part of PerformancePoint Services, scorecards can also contain dimensional data elements that provide a hierarchical breakout of the KPIs, which are in turn based on the hierarchical data elements discussed in Chapter 3—in a cube.

The important point is that Dashboard Designer provides a feature-rich drag-and-drop interface for designing layout and for previewing scorecards, making the process quick and intuitive.

Reports

In PerformancePoint Services, a report is a reusable element that can take several forms and provide access to interactive and static data through a variety of avenues. Most of the report types offered by PerformancePoint can stand on their own and are not bound to a scorecard or KPI, so they provide something extra to a dashboard. The report types that exist in PerformancePoint are:

- **Analytic chart**   This report type displays interactive charts from specified data.

- **Analytic grid**   This report type displays figures as a set of rows and columns.

- **Excel Services**   This report type enables you to reference an Excel spreadsheet, published in Excel Services, so that you can view it in a dashboard.

- **KPI Details**   A simple report type that displays the properties of a selected KPI metric in a scorecard. The KPI Details report works as a Web Part that links to a scorecard or individual KPI to show relevant metadata to the end user in SharePoint Server. You can add this Web Part to PerformancePoint dashboards or to any SharePoint Server page.

> **Note**   You must first create a scorecard.

- **ProClarity Analytics Server Page**   This report type maintains backward compatibility with existing reports created using ProClarity Professional and published to ProClarity Server.

- **Reporting Services**   This report type lets you publish an SSRS report in a dashboard.

- **Strategy map**   This report type uses a Visio diagram as a template for displaying KPIs in a rich, graphical format. A strategy map report lets you display color-coded KPI indicators. You can also show numeric and textual data on a map. The underlying Visio diagram is linked to a scorecard to show at-a-glance organizational performance measures. When you put the four perspectives discussed in Chapter 1 together with a scorecard and strategy map, you get a Balanced Scorecard that captures the four main areas of BCS: Finance, Operations, Sales, and Human Resources (sometimes referred to as FOSH metrics).

- **Web page**   This is a jack-of-all-trades report type. It's a standard ASPX webpage, so you can display data in HTML format. Parameters selected in the connections between other components are passed to a connected component in the `Request.Params` collection to allow an ASPX page to show arbitrary data. Use this report type to show legacy reports that cannot otherwise be integrated into a dashboard.

Context Menu Features

Each of the following features requires that you configure the KPI row to be set to Source Data.

A Decomposition Tree is a visual method to let you see how underlying data is connected to a particular value. To use it, you click to drill down in a hierarchical fashion from a parent value to its associated child nodes, broken down by dimension. To open the Decomposition Tree, simply click an individual value, such as a point in a line chart or a cell in a grid or scorecard, and then select Decomposition Tree in the context menu. The Decomposition Tree opens in a new window where users can drill down and view the derived dimensional data from the SSAS cube.

> **Note**   A Decomposition Tree is available in a PerformancePoint dashboard only after it has been deployed to SharePoint Server 2010. Users must also have Microsoft Silverlight 2 or Silverlight 3 installed on their computers.

Show details is a feature or report view that gives you detailed row-level information for a specific KPI or report derived from Analysis Services. You access this feature by browsing an analytical chart, grid, or scorecard. Static information is displayed for the data, organized in table format. You can use this feature when you see an interesting value and want to see more data that contributes to that value.

Each report type can be configured to provide visualizations and connect to different data sources. For example, you might need to configure filters and parameters, which are interfaces to help you determine what will drive the report behavior.

Dashboards

A dashboard is a collection of one or more scorecard or report elements arranged in a set of webpages, hosted by SharePoint Server and displayed in a web browser. Users who want to view and work with dynamic report or scorecard data do so through the dashboard. The dashboard synchronizes PerformancePoint components so that they work together to control how business data is aggregated and displayed to users. Filters help determine what data gets displayed and the context in which report and scorecard data reach the customer.

The following diagram shows the different elements and how they come together to make a PerformancePoint dashboard.

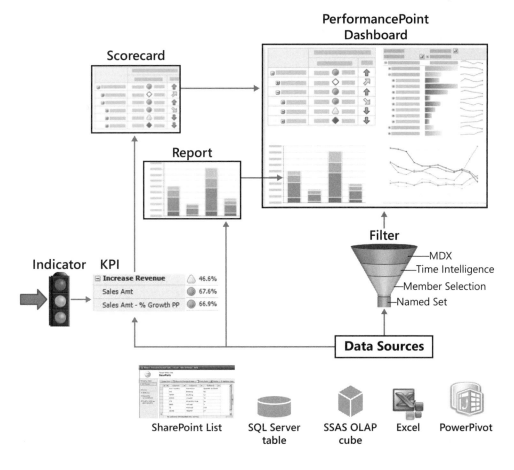

Filters

A filter is a Web Part object that allows dashboard users to select a subset of the data rendered on a dashboard. You can apply value-based filters, such as "Top 10" or "is more than," to analytic reports, but you do not create these value-based filters with Dashboard Designer; the filters are automatically available to users when you deploy a dashboard.

When you create a reusable dashboard filter, you must save it to SharePoint Server. Including value-based filters in a dashboard, you give dashboard users the ability to focus on more specific information.

Parts of Dashboard Designer

The following illustration provides a quick overview of the major features in the Dashboard Designer authoring environment.

1. Use the Workspace Browser to view, open, and save dashboard items and to deploy a dashboard to SharePoint. The Workspace Browser includes two categories: Data Connections and PerformancePoint Content. When you click an item in either category, that item's content appears in the center pane. For example, if you click Data Connections, you see data connection details in the center pane. The ribbon's Edit and Create tabs and the Details pane change dynamically to reflect the item selected in the Workspace Browser.

2. You use the center pane to view and edit data connections and dashboard content. Depending on where the focus is in the Workspace Browser, different tabs are available for the center pane. For example, if you select a Pie Chart, three tabs appear: Design, Query, and Properties. You can also preview dashboard items in the center pane.

3. The ribbon helps simplify viewing, editing, and publishing dashboards and dashboard items.

    a. The Home tab provides toolbar commands to view, open, and dashboard items.

   b. The Edit tab dynamically displays only those toolbar items relevant to the dashboard items selected in the Workspace Browser. For example, the Edit tab displays
   no items until you create a filter via the Editor tab.

   c. The Create tab dynamically displays toolbar items relevant to the item you want
   to create, such as a KPI, scorecard, dashboard, and so forth.

Not numbered in the preceding illustration, the Details pane appears when you select a
dashboard item that shows information about that item. Also, the File tab lets you view
change settings, Save options, and the default location for workspace files. The Workspace
File is a new feature that helps you navigate and locate files saved to your desktop. You can
create and save a workspace file on your computer to view and manage your own reusable dashboard objects. This saves you time because you avoid having to browse through a
long list of dashboard objects that others may have saved to SharePoint lists and document
libraries.

The Dashboards document library contains only live dashboards that have been deployed.

Other Dashboard Designer Features

The following sections provide a brief glance at some other Dashboard Designer features.

Dashboard Content in SharePoint Folders

- The Data Connections content library is a container for data sources that you can reuse
  in dashboard objects. The data connection contains information and security details for
  each data source.

- The PerformancePoint Content list is a SharePoint list that contains scorecards, reports,
  filters, unpublished dashboards, and other dashboard items that you can organize into
  folders.

- The Dashboards library contains published dashboards that have been deployed from
  Dashboard Designer.

Dashboard Item History

You can enable version control on SharePoint lists and document libraries that contain your
dashboard items. When enabled, if unwanted changes occur, you can revert back to a previous version.

What's New in PerformancePoint Services

SharePoint Services is a service application integrated with SharePoint Server 2010. As such, when you purchase SharePoint Server 2010, you also get the functionality of what was once its own server product (without the cost of another server product). Additionally, the benefits of document management, back-up and restore, and other SharePoint-specific benefits apply to PerformancePoint assets. The benefits discussed in the following sections describe some enhancements over the previous version, PerformancePoint Server 2007. These include SharePoint features such as a simplified security model, workflow, and more.

Improvements for Dashboard Authors and Users

You can now save dashboard items to SharePoint Server 2010 lists and document libraries, which was not possible in 2007. That means you can take advantage of SharePoint permissions to control who can view or edit your dashboard items, as well as take advantage of the ability to view a version history of dashboard items.

Following are new features for authors and viewers of PerformancePoint dashboards:

- **Improved sophisticated KPIs** You can now create scorecards that have multiple actuals in the KPIs. This means that you can have more than one metric for each KPI on the same row. You can also create scorecards that include advanced KPIs based on calculated metrics for your dashboard. The new KPI Details report provides additional information about scorecard KPIs. You can show types of metrics that are used for KPIs, how scores are calculated, and what thresholds drive individual scores.

- **Improved report types** The analytic chart and grid offer a pie chart as the view type that resembles an analytic line or bar chart. Users can click a wedge to see the next level of detail or drill into data to view a different dimension derived from an Analysis Services cube. You can now enable your dashboard users to open a Decomposition Tree report from a report or a scorecard.

- **Time Intelligence** In scorecards and reports, you can use Time Intelligence to show dynamic time periods, such as year-to-date, quarter-to-date, and month-to-date data, along with year-to-date results objectives or other metrics.

> **Note** The exact functionality depends on how you configure the data source and Time Intelligence.

- **Improved filters** You can create reusable filters that can be shared across multiple dashboards and can link to more SharePoint Web Parts.

You can now apply value-based filters, such as "Top 10" or "is more than," to analytic reports. These filters are automatically available when you deploy a dashboard and don't need to be configured in advance. For example, to see the Top 10 geographical regions in a report, you would simply right-click the report and select Top 10. The report automatically updates to display those records.

Improvements for IT Professionals

The following sections describe the new PerformancePoint features for IT professionals.

Platform Integration with SharePoint Products and Technologies

Built on the SharePoint 2010 platform, PerformancePoint provides you with a more robust deployment, scalability, and performance-model story. In SharePoint Server 2010, services are no longer contained within a Shared Service Provider (SSP). Instead, the infrastructure for hosting services is integrated, with more flexible configuration of service offerings. The service application framework is a common service model that gives you a more consistent server management experience. Here's a short list of new features:

- From the SharePoint Central Administration website, you can now perform bulk security operations.

- Services are now installed by default; in SharePoint 2007, you had to set up SSP separately.

- You can restore a site collection, site content, or list content to a previous version or point in time.

- All websites in a farm can share a single set of services.

- You can now configure and dedicate only the services you need on a physical or logical server, rather than the entire list of services.

- You can include and link PerformancePoint Services Web Parts with other SharePoint Server Web Parts on the same page.

Security

You can now use SharePoint Server 2010 to manage user credentials and to secure access to dashboard content and its underlying data sources with user authentication. The SharePoint Server 2010 authentication provider handles authentication of PerformancePoint Services users.

You can use trusted locations to limit access to PerformancePoint Services content types to specific sites and data connections. Dashboards and dashboard items are stored and secured within SharePoint lists, giving you a single security and repository framework. Remember that data source connection information is stored in document libraries, while PerformancePoint content types are stored in lists. Published dashboards are stored in a separate Dashboard document library.

Improvements for Developers

Each report, data source, or filter is stored as serialized XML in the list or library. You should use PerformancePoint Services APIs only to modify content types. Dashboard Designer cannot be extended. PerformancePoint Web Parts (scorecards, reports, and filters) use Microsoft SharePoint Foundation 2010 connection interfaces, which enable PerformancePoint Web Parts to send or receive values from SharePoint Web Parts that have compatible connectivity elements.

Note For more information about extending PerformancePoint Services, see the document "What's New: PerformancePoint Services" on MSDN at *http://msdn.microsoft.com/en-us/library/ ee557869(office.14).aspx.*

Retired Features

PerformancePoint Services no longer supports Trend Charts, PivotTable reports, PivotChart reports, ODBC data sources, Analysis Services 2000, ActiveX Data Objects, or 32-bit server architecture.

When to Use PerformancePoint Services

Use PerformancePoint Services for creating dashboards, scorecards, and KPIs that help deliver a view of performance visually in the form of KPIs, scorecards, and various types of often dynamic reports. Consider the example of an IT operations scorecard in Chapter 1. The scorecard measures database space and other metrics gathered from Systems Center Operation manager. The dashboard is a point of entry for drilldown analysis to drive agility and alignment across an organization. PerformancePoint Services gives users integrated analytics for monitoring, analyzing, and reporting.

The following areas describe where you can use PerformancePoint Services and Dashboard Designer as an authoring tool when you want to:

- Create rich dashboards that convey the right information, aggregating content from multiple sources and displaying it in a web browser in an understandable and collaborative environment. Scorecard and report interactivity lets you analyze up-to-the-minute information and work with the data quickly and easily to identify key opportunities and trends.

- Implement a Balanced Scorecard methodology to measure finance, operations, sales, and human resources. These are sometimes called FOSH metrics.

- Perform root cause analyses, using analytics to examine data while viewing only the most pertinent information by using the new Decomposition Tree.

Available Case Studies

Although this book covers which tool to use, as described in Chapter 2, "Choosing the Right BI Tool," we suggest you try to map your particular industry or department's challenges and search for relevant information about how others have resolved those challenges. The TechNet "Business Intelligence Scenarios" page at *http://technet.microsoft.com/en-us/bi/default.aspx* highlights example scenarios that might be applicable to your own situation.

The next section provides a brief case study that shows how one company, Tenaska, a Capital Management branch of an energy company, has implemented PerformancePoint Services and describes some of the benefits the company realized. First, you should know that this is an early example. Case studies and scenario-solutions will continue to appear as companies share specific challenge-scenarios and show how they've initiated new and better solutions by using SharePoint 2010 and other Microsoft technologies.

Additionally, a targeted search on *http://www.microsoft.com/casestudies/Case_Study_Search_Results.aspx*, using the term "PerformancePoint" in the Search field, results in case studies like that of Tenaska.

> **Tip** You can also review industry and departmental case studies for PerformancePoint 2007. The basic functionality and purpose for creating dashboards has not changed since PerformancePoint was released as a server product in 2007. The article "PerformancePoint Server Case Studies" at *http://technet.microsoft.com/en-us/library/cc811597(office.12).aspx* consolidates some of these older case studies.

Scenario: Tenaska

Tenaska, located in Omaha, Nebraska, is one of the largest independent power producers in the U.S. It builds power plants and provides energy risk-management services. Tenaska previously used manual processes for gathering data, which was stored in Microsoft Excel 2010 spreadsheet software, paper files, and various databases. These disparate sources meant that the company spent 50 percent of its time gathering data rather than analyzing it. There was also no central location for store contracts, performance reports, and other business documents.

After using SQL Server 2008 R2 Integration Services to collect raw data, validate it, clean it, and load it into analytic cubes, Tenaska integrated PerformancePoint Services so that users could view KPIs, scorecards, and charts on their desktops.

PerformancePoint Services Architecture

The following diagram is a physical depiction of PerformancePoint Services. It is similar to the diagram in Chapter 1 but focuses on elements specific to Dashboard Designer, the possible data sources for a dashboard, and databases. It also shows that you can export data from a dashboard to an Excel spreadsheet.

The front-end web server runs on Internet Information Services (IIS) and hosts the PerformancePoint Services Web Parts, web services, and the proxy required for communication between the client and the PerformancePoint Services service application.

Presentation Tier

Export → to Excel 2007 and 2010 from Details Report

Report viewing	Report authoring
Browser	PerformancePoint Dashboard Designer

Application Tier

SharePoint 2010 Business Intelligence

Front-end Web servers

SharePoint Data sources
· Excel & PowerPivot for Excel
· SharePoint lists
· Excel Services

PerformancePoint Services

Application server: Secure Store Service

Data Tier

Other Data sources

Line of Business data
with Business Connectivity Services

SQL Server

SharePoint database servers

PerformancePoint Services Database

Data Warehouse (relational)

SQL Server Analysis Services (multidimensional)

SQL Server Reporting Services

PerformancePoint Services Configuration

This chapter doesn't cover setup information (which is found on TechNet), and instead contains steps to apply security, as well as high-level steps that point you to relevant conceptual documentation. Additionally, these instructions are simplified because in our configuration, we first ran the Configuration Wizard to establish default service applications for our server. When you do this, the Configuration Wizard creates and starts the PerformancePoint

Services service application, which is ready-to-use after you configure Secure Store Services for security. Note When you install the pre-configured VM as described in Appendix A, the PerformancePoint Services service application is already running.

PerformancePoint Service Application Configured

It is a good idea to ensure that the service application for PerformancePoint Services has been started. You may also want to view the default settings or configure PerformancePoint Services.

To manage PerformancePoint service applications in Central Administration

1. In Central Administration, under Application Management, select Manage Service Applications as shown in the following illustration.

 Note You can also use Windows PowerShell to view running service applications.

Site Actions ▾ Browse **Service Applications**	CONTOSO\administrator ▾

New Connect Delete Manage Administrators Properties Publish Permissions

Create | Operations | Sharing

System Settings	Access Services	Access Services Web Service Application Proxy	Started
Monitoring	Application Discovery and Load Balancer Service Application	Application Discovery and Load Balancer Service Application	Started
Backup and Restore			
Security	Application Discovery and Load Balancer Service Application Proxy_3bacb7f8 -a44a-46c2-940d-e402ae8e61d9	Application Discovery and Load Balancer Service Application Proxy	Started
Upgrade and Migration	Application Registry Service	Application Registry Service	Started
General Application Settings	Application Registry Service	Application Registry Proxy	Started
Configuration Wizards	Business Data Connectivity Service	Business Data Connectivity Service Application	Started
	Business Data Connectivity Service	Business Data Connectivity Service Application Proxy	Started
	Excel Services Application	Excel Services Application Web Service Application	Started
	Excel Services Application	Excel Services Application Web Service Application Proxy	Started
	Managed Metadata Service	Managed Metadata Service	Started
	Managed Metadata Service	Managed Metadata Service Connection	Started
	PerformancePoint Service Application	PerformancePoint Service Application	Started
	PerformancePoint Service Application	PerformancePoint Service Application Proxy	Started
	Search Administration Web Service for Search Service Application	Search Administration Web Service Application	Started
	Search Service Application	Search Service Application	Started
	Search Service Application	Search Service Application Proxy	Started
	Secure Store Service	Secure Store Service Application	Started

2. On the Service Applications tab, click Manage to view and manage the items shown in the following illustration.

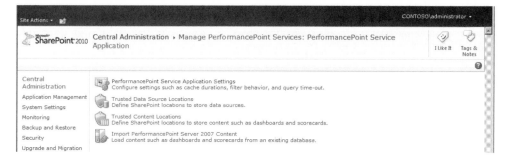

To list running service applications with Windows PowerShell

1. On the Start menu, click All Programs.

2. Click Microsoft SharePoint 2010 Products.

3. Click SharePoint 2010 Management Shell.

4. From the Windows PowerShell command prompt (that is, PS C:\>), type the following command and then press Enter:

   ```
   PS C:/>Get-SPPerformancePointServiceApplication
   ```

Manage and Maintain PerformancePoint Services

The features that you can manage in a service application for PerformancePoint include the following:

- PerformancePoint Applications Settings enable you to manage settings that affect performance, security, and data connection refreshes.

 Note This is where you configure the Unattended Service Account credentials, which is essential for connecting to external data sources.

- Trusted Data Source Locations enable you to restrict access to data sources from PerformancePoint dashboards. You'll see how to configure these in the next section.

Tip Configure trusted data sources to specific sites, particularly when the Unattended Service Account you configure for the data source has access to sensitive information such as financial or personnel data.

- Trusted Content Locations enables you to restrict access to PerformancePoint objects such as KPIs, scorecards, indicators, and reports. You'll see how to configure these in the next section as well.

Import PerformancePoint 2007 Content

The PerformancePoint Services product team blog says it best:

> *"Most of the customers who have been using PerformancePoint Server 2007 have accumulated several months, if not years, worth of dashboards and data. Their KPIs, grids, charts, scorecards, and custom objects have gone to good use, providing a great deal of corporate discussion about how to handle business decisions and to help plan for the future.*
>
> *Understandably, most companies want to build on top of their old dashboards in 2010. And the idea of starting from scratch is unthinkable. Fortunately, Microsoft has a nice migration path so that you can migrate all of your existing objects to the new version. The migration process is straightforward, but to help ensure that things go smoothly, we've created a set of steps to follow."*

The steps to upgrade from PerformancePoint 2007 are located on the Blog post "Upgrading PerformancePoint Server 2007 to PPS 2010," at *http://blogs.msdn.com/b/performancepoint/ archive/2010/02/25/upgrading-performancepoint-server-2007-to-pps-2010.aspx*.

Configure Security for PerformancePoint

In addition to restricting trusted data source and content lists, you must also configure the Secure Store Service.

If you have opened up the Application Settings and see a warning that you do not have the Secure Store Service (SSS) application and Proxy running, you must "generate" a key and then configure an Unattended Service account. The Unattended Service account is an Active Directory domain account that is used for accessing PerformancePoint Services data sources.

> **Note** We specify "for PerformancePoint" in the following procedure because it's important to remember that SSS configuration is performed differently for PerformancePoint than for the other services. The other services are discussed in more detail in Appendix C, "SharePoint As a Service—'Office 365'."

Fortunately, many of the steps are automated for PerformancePoint SSS configuration. You must be a Service Application Administrator for the SSS instance.

To configure SSS for PerformancePoint

1. In Central Administration, click Manage Service Applications.

2. Click Secure Store Service in the list of service applications.

3. On the Service Applications tab, click Manage.

4. On the Edit tab, click Generate New Key.

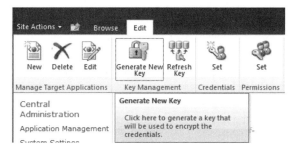

5. In the dialog box that appears, type in a pass phrase that has at least eight characters and at least three element types (numbers, letters, and symbols) to make it more secure (example: Strong;54321).

 Tip The pass phrase is not stored, so you're responsible for keeping it securely.

6. Click Refresh The Key, and when prompted, enter the pass phrase you set in Step 5.

To configure the Unattended Service Account

1. In Central Administration, click Manage Service Applications.

2. Select the PerformancePoint Service Application (or whatever you named it if you manually configured it) in the list of service applications. You should see the window shown in the following illustration.

3. Click PerformancePoint Service Applications Settings. Type the account that has access to the data sources you want available when you create your dashboard, and then click OK.

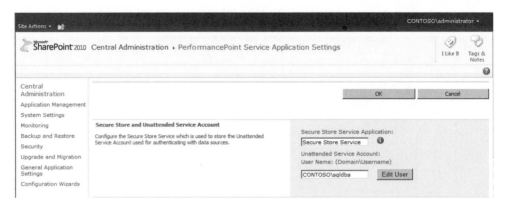

> **Tip** View the first minute of the video "Create a Target Application for SQL Server Authentication," at *http://go.microsoft.com/fwlink/?LinkId=207410*, for configuring the SSS target application to see how SQL Server Authentication is configured. The remainder of the Video is for configuring SSS for Visio.
>
> Be sure to limit the access for the Unattended Service Account to only needed data sources in SQL Server. Also, set this account to read-only access on any data sources so that it has minimum permissions and minimizes vulnerability.

Check the SSS configuration to verify that a target application for PerformancePoint has been created for you.

Configure Data and Content Locations

The following procedures show you how to configure trusted data source and content source locations.

> **Note** By default, these locations are configured to trust all sites on the farm so that PerformancePoint works out-of-box. It is not necessary to configure trusted data source locations if you don't want to limit access.

To configure a trusted data source location

1. Navigate to the Central Administration page for managing the service application for PerformancePoint.

2. Click Trusted Data Source Locations. Notice that All SharePoint Locations is selected by default.

3. Select Only Specific Locations (Current Setting), and then click Apply.

4. Click the Add Trusted Data Source Location link, and in the Edit dialog box, enter the full web address where you want to store data source connections.

5. If necessary, select the type of location, and then click OK.

To configure a trusted content source location

1. Navigate to the Central Administration page for managing the service application for PerformancePoint.

2. Click Trusted Content Locations. Notice that All SharePoint Locations is selected by default.

3. Select Only Specific Locations (Current Setting), and then click Apply.

Site Actions ▾

SharePoint 2010 Central Administration ▸ Trusted Content Locations
Define SharePoint locations to store content such as dashboards and scorecards.

Central
Administration

Application Management

System Settings

Monitoring

Backup and Restore

Security

Upgrade and Migration

Trust content in:

⦿ All SharePoint locations

◯ Only specific locations (current setting)

[Apply]

▭ Add Trusted Content Location

There are no items to show in this view.

4. Click the Add Trusted Data Source Location link, and in the Edit dialog box, enter the full web address where you want to store data source connections.

5. If necessary, select the type of location, and then click OK.

Start PerformancePoint Dashboard Designer

Dashboard Designer is a ClickOnce application hosted by the client without installing an .exe file. You can start it directly from the Business Intelligence Center site, available after you provision the relevant site collection template.

You can also start Dashboard Designer from a SharePoint list configured to support PerformancePoint Services content types. To edit an item, on the drop-down menu simply click Edit In Dashboard Designer. Alternatively, you can create a new item by clicking Add New Item at the bottom of the webpage. Before you install Dashboard Designer, you should make it available on a site the easy way, by creating a site collection using the BI template.

To deploy the Business Intelligence Center using the template

1. In Central Administration, select Create Site Collections, as shown in the following illustration.

 Application Management
Manage web applications
[Create site collections]
Manage service applications
Manage content databases

 System Settings
Manage servers in this farm
Manage services on server
Manage farm features
Configure alternate access mappings

 Monitoring
Review problems and solutions
Check job status
View Web Analytics reports

Backup and Restore
Perform a backup
Restore from a backup
Perform a site collection backup

 Security
Manage the farm administrators group
Configure service accounts

Upgrade and Migration
Convert farm license type
Check product and patch installation status
Check upgrade status

 General Application Settings
Configure send to connections
Configure content deployment paths and jobs
Manage form templates

 Configuration Wizards

2. Enter BizCenter in the Title field, and choose the URL name and path—or create a site at a specific path.

3. On the same page, click the Enterprise tab and click Business Intelligence Center. Enter user names in the Primary Site Collection Administrator and Secondary Site Collection Administrator fields, respectively, and then click OK.

A site collection is created, as shown in the following illustration.

To launch Dashboard Designer

1. Navigate to the Business Intelligence Center site (example: *http://localhost/SP2010-BI*), and under the Create Scorecards With PerformancePoint Services section, click Start Using PerformancePoint Services.

2. Click Run Dashboard Designer to open the Dashboard Designer.

Troubleshoot SQL Server Data Source Configuration

The following are some actions you can perform to troubleshoot SQL Server data source configuration:

- You might need to register the service account to the existing application pool dedicated to PerformancePoint Services. To do this, use Windows PowerShell (as Administrator) and run the following cmdlets:

```
PS C:\> $w = Get-SPWebApplication(" <your web application> ")
PS C:\> $w.GrantAccessToProcessIdentity(" <insert service account> ")
```

> **Note** This action grants db_owner access to the SharePoint content databases.

- Refresh the SSS key.

- Review the Release Notes for "SharePoint Business Intelligence SETUP/ CONFIGURATION," at *http://office.microsoft.com/en-us/sharepoint-server-help/ microsoft-office-servers-2010-faq-readme-HA101793217.aspx?queryid=4dd91eae39694e e586d45d31b5716b32&respos=0&CTT=1&av=OSU140#_Toc276716462.*

- Review existing configuration articles, such as "Deploying PerformancePoint 2010 Soup to Nuts" at *http://blogs.msdn.com/b/performancepoint/archive/2009/11/24/deploying- performancepoint-2010-soup-to-nuts.aspx* and "Set up and configure PerformancePoint Services (step-by-step)" at *http://technet.microsoft.com/en-us/library/ee748643.aspx.*

Providing a Performance Solution

The exercise in this section centers on the sales activities of the Contoso Company. This company manufactures and sells products to various global markets via reseller and Internet channels.

The exercise shows you how to produce a dashboard to publish to users on SharePoint Server 2010. The dashboard enables users to monitor and analyze sales activities and profitability for the company reseller operations.

In the exercise, one KPI is created to support comparisons of sales, sales quotas, and profit margin to a fixed goal of 2 percent, across several fiscal periods, product categories, subcategories, and sales territory regions.

To support the monitoring requirements, two scorecards are created to produce different perspectives of a single KPI. Three reports are created to support analysis requirements.

These scorecards and reports are then embedded in a dashboard that has filters for slicing data by fiscal periods, product categories, and sales territories. The dashboard is deployed to SharePoint so that it can be viewed and explored by Contoso sales management.

Design the KPIs, Scorecards, Reports, and Dashboard

Some or all the documents that this exercise draws from come into play when the Analysis Services Cube is designed and created. As discussed in Chapter 3, this should be an iterative process, and it's the most important step to get right.

Once you know what you want to measure, you must decide what you want to accomplish with the functionality that's available in PerformancePoint. You have many ways to create and configure KPIs and scorecards in Dashboard Designer. Consider putting your rating, actual, target, and how these may aggregate in a spreadsheet, so that you can review them in prototype fashion, adding the potential users and other stakeholders. Additionally, you can find a number of websites where you can review best practices for dashboard design, such as "Dashboard Design 101," on the UXmatters website at *http://www.uxmatters.com/mt/archives/2010/11/dashboard-design-101.php*.

The reports and data sources you choose determine how much you can investigate data and incorporate meaningful visualizations. Consider how you want to filter on available data to give users the right information from which to make decisions. It is also worth reviewing other literature on dashboard design, such as the book *Dashboard Design: The Effective Visual Communication of Data* by Stephen Few.

Create a Simple Dashboard

Before continuing, you should be familiar with the following:

- The definition of "business intelligence" (see Chapter 1)
- The underlying data (see Chapter 2)
- The section "Overview of PerformancePoint Services Components" earlier in this chapter

Dashboard Designer provides a wizard that guides you through importing Analysis Services KPIs into a scorecard. This exercise starts with the KPI because it is the driving element for monitoring and the cornerstone of any performance management initiative. Even though this exercise shows quite a bit of the best dashboard functionality, PerformancePoint provides much more functionality than we can show you in one chapter.

The following list defines the basic sequence of actions for creating a very simplified dashboard that works with the Analysis Services cube data source you created in Chapter 3, an Excel file, and a Visio file, all of which were created in this book:

1. Design your KPIs and Scorecards (already done).

2. Create a data source.

3. Create a set of KPIs.

4. Create dashboard items (report, scorecard).

5. Create filters to control what data is included.

6. Create reports to enable the user to perform analysis on the underlying data.

7. Assemble the dashboard pages.

8. Preview, test, and deploy the dashboard.

Create a Data Source

You can use the procedure in this section to create some data sources for use in your dashboard.

> **Note** Security information for Excel Services is saved in the Trusted Data Connection library.

> **Important** External data sources must reside in the same domain as the SharePoint Server 2010 farm, or authentication will fail. For more information about planning for external data sources, see "Planning considerations for services that access external data sources" at *http://technet.microsoft.com/en-us/library/cc560988.aspx#ConsiderationsForAccessingExternalData*.

> **Tip** Select your authentication method before you type in the server and specify the database.

To create an Analysis Services data source

You must have a data source before you can create FCO (PerformancePoint content).

Although the procedure begins on the Create tab, you can also create a PerformancePoint data source from the Data Connections library on the Documents tab. Either way, Dashboard Designer and the Select A Data Source Template open so that you can create the data source.

1. On the Create tab, right-click Data Connections and select New Data Connection.

2. Analysis Services is selected by default. Click OK.

3. In the Workspace Browser, you are given the option to name the data source. Type the name **Contoso_Retail**.

Note The center pane dynamically depends on the data source you select. In this case, you chose Analysis Services, so the center pane requests specific information for your data source, such as the name of the cube.

4. In the Server field, enter SP2010-BI, In the Database field, enter ContosoRetail OLAP, and in the Cube field, select Sales. Keep the default Authentication Unattended Service Account. Your information should appear as shown in the following illustration.

 Note The Unattended Service Account And Add Authenticated User Name In Connection option, shown in the preceding illustration, applies to Analysis Services only. The Per-User Identity option requires the Kerberos protocol. For an excellent Kerberos resource, see the white paper "Configure Kerberos Authentication for SharePoint 2010 Products," at *http://go.microsoft.com/fwlink/?LinkId=196600*.

Your data source is saved to the data connections library without you having to click Save or OK in the Data Connections library in your BI Center site.

5. On the Time tab, under Reference Member, select a member from the dimension that represents the first day of the year, such as January 1, 2011.

The Time tab is where you configure Time Intelligence before creating a filter that can use in reports and scorecards. It is worth reviewing to see whether you want to configure your data to use Time Intelligence. For more information, see "Configure data sources to work with Time Intelligence by using Dashboard Designer," at *http://technet.microsoft.com/en-us/library/ff701697.aspx*.

The Time Dimension drop-down lists the hierarchies available in the cube, such as Date. Calendar.YWD for (Year, Week, Day).

6. Under Reference Date, enter the same date in your regional format. This allows PerformancePoint to understand how years are structured in the date dimension.

7. Navigate to the Business Intelligence Center, and click Data Connections. You should see the data connections file saved to the Trusted Data Source library.

To save to the workspace and refresh your data sources

1. Click the diskette icon to save your dashboard.

> **Note** As you work on objects as PerformancePoint content, you should regularly click the multi-diskette icon to save all your files. Also, you have the option of clicking the Refresh icon to refresh your data sources.

2. In the File Name field, type **ContosoSalesDashboard**, and then click Save.

The small pencil on the data source indicates that you have not published the dashboard with that data source, although you have saved it. We added the New Data Source, shown in the following illustration, so that you can see the difference.

Create Key Performance Indicators

Now that you have data source connection information stored, you can create a KPI.

To create a KPI

1. Right-click PerformancePoint Content, and then select New | KPI.

2. Click OK.

> **Note** Objective KPIs use only the calculated score of a child KPI, in case you want to compare scores of KPIs instead of values.

As shown in the following illustration, a blank KPI template opens— with no content or data mappings—that includes the actual and target metrics for the KPI. Next, you'll customize two metrics.

3. In the Name column, select Actual and change it to Actual Sales.

4. Click the cell under Data Mappings for Actual Sales, and then click Change Source.

5. On the Workspace tab, select the data source that drives the value of the Actual metric.

6. Double-click SP2010-BI_Contoso-Sales.

7. In the Dimensional Data Source Mapping dialog box, select Sales Quota Amount.

8. In the Dimensional Data Source Mapping dialog box, select New Dimension Filter, and then select Scenario.Scenario Description.

9. In the Select Members dialog box, select Default Member (All Scenario) to select the filter on members of the description dimension.

10. Expand All Scenario, select Actual, and then click OK.

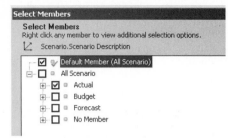

11. In the Dimensional Data Source Mapping dialog box, select New Dimension Filter again, and then select Sales Territory.TerritoryHierarchy.

12. In the Select Members dialog box, select Default Member (All) to select a filter on members of the Sales Territory.Territory.Hierarchy dimension.

13. Expand All, and select Europe as the dimension member.

14. When the Dimensional Data Source Mapping dialog box appears, as shown in the following illustration, click OK.

15. In the center pane, with the KPI selected, select Name, Target, and change it to "Forecast Sales."

16. Repeat Steps 4 through 15 for Forecast Sales, except in Step 10, select Forecast instead of Actual.

17. Click Indicators to see the default. Your KPI should now look as shown in the following illustration.

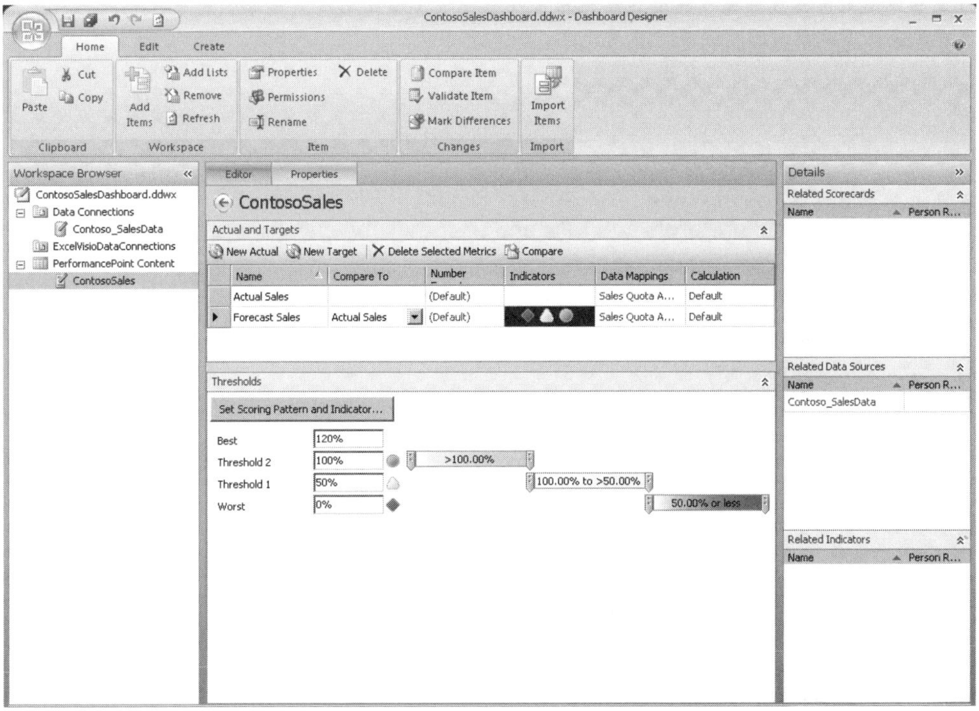

Organize the Workspace Browser

As mentioned earlier, the Workspace Browser offers a new feature from PerformancePoint Server 2007 that allows you to create folders to better organize your PerformancePoint elements.

To create a folder for KPIs

1. Click ContosoSales in the Workspace Browser, and then click the Properties tab in the center pane.

2. In the Display Folder field, type **KPIs**. You should now see ContosoSales under a folder called KPIs.

Create a Scorecard

KPIs are built on measures and presented in scorecards and dashboards. The scorecard is the vehicle for indicators and KPIs and becomes the end-user result of the complete life cycle of a BI solution. That life cycle is described in Chapter 3, where developers prepare data that can be trusted; put that data into a cube so that the cube becomes the ideal data source for the scorecard; and where KPIs display the measures in meaningful ways to assist with data-driven decision making.

Scoring uses some terms that may be unfamiliar, but they're important as we proceed with configuring our scorecard. The following list provides only brief descriptions of an otherwise complex set of concepts:

- **Score**   A calculated value between 0 and 1 that indicates a relative position. 0 is the worst and 1 is the best.

- **Scoring pattern**   The language that describes what is good or bad in a score such as "increasing is better" = "a higher value is better." Or "decreasing is better" = "a lower value is better."

- **Threshold**   The minimum value connected to an indicator that produces a change or specified effect to the indicator.

- **Banding**   The input type for the threshold boundaries. Some are entered as percentages from the target, and others are numeric values with absolute values.

- **Normalize**   In KPI hierarchies where there is a parent-child relationship, normalizing describes how scores are combined to represent the parent or rollup score.

Important Your selections for scoring determine how your indicators and visualizations look.

It is worth your time to review other books that can help you understand how a score is calculated by using the band-by value, how to determine the band value, and how to normalize the score. Other material also discusses rollup scoring. The following are some good books on dashboards and scorecards:

- *Strategy Maps: Converting Intangible Assets into Tangible Outcomes*, by Kaplan and Norton

- *The Strategy-Focused Organization: How Balanced Scorecard Companies Thrive in the New Business Environment*, also by Kaplan and Norton

- *Balanced Scorecard Step-by-Step: Maximizing Performance and Maintaining Results*, by Paul R. Niven

To set the scoring pattern and indicator for the KPI

1. Click the default indicators in the center pane. The Thresholds window appears below the Actual Sales and Forecast Sales in Actuals and Targets.

2. Click Set Scoring Pattern And Indicator to start the wizard shown in the following illustration.

3. Click Next. The Select An Indicator page appears. Indicators dynamically appear to match the scoring pattern selected in the previous screen.

4. For fun, select the smiley faces and click Next. You now specify the worst value. If the score is below the threshold, the score will be zero. Keep the default in this example.

> **Note** We don't suggest you ever use smiley faces in a real world implementation. We use smiley face indicators here only to illustrate that you have a wide range of indicators from which to choose.

5. Click Next. Notice how the visualizations have changed.

You can now edit the thresholds by selecting the target metric row that should be edited. This window may be collapsed, but you can re-expand it by clicking the chevron at the bottom of the center pane.

To create the scorecard

1. Right-Click PerformancePoint Content in the Workspace Browser, and select New | Scorecard.

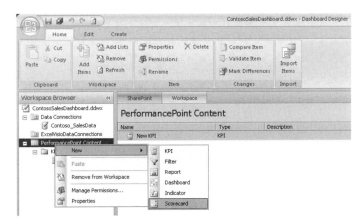

Notice the following options in the Select A Scorecard Template:

- **Microsoft** Analysis Services data source

- **Standard** Blank Scorecard without predefined content or data mappings and Fixed Values Scorecard (user-defined values)

- **Tabular** Includes all the options for tabular data sources such as Excel, Excel Services, SharePoint List, and SQL Server table

2. Select Microsoft and click OK. A Create An Analysis Services scorecard is selected.

3. Select the Contoso_SalesData data source, and then click Next.

4. Make sure Create KPIs From SQL Server Analysis Services Measures is selected, and click Next.

5. A screen appears, with two buttons on the top: Add KPI and Select KPI. Add KPI lets you choose an existing KPI from the data source, if it exists. If it does, you can make more choices such as setting Actual, Band Method, and Targets.

   For this example, select the KPI you created in the exercise titled "To create a KPI," earlier in this chapter. Click Select KPI, and then click OK.

6. Ensure that your KPI is selected, and then click Next.

7. The Add Measure Filters dialog page appears. You already filtered data from the Analysis Services cube when you created the KPIs without using this wizard, so just click Next.

8. The same logic applies to the Add Measure Columns dialog. Just click Next. Your scorecard now updates to reflect the KPI you created previously. The following illustration shows the items expanded in the Details pane so that you can see the available options. If you had not included the KPI, you could drag it into the center pane.

The illustration also shows that we used the Workspace feature to create a folder for Scorecards by clicking the Properties tab. Finally, notice that the Contoso_SalesData data source is selected in the bottom-right corner.

9. Save the scorecard and its associated KPI to the server.

To add dimensions to the scorecard

By adding a dimension, you give users the ability to slice KPIs based on different views available through the data source. Specific details may be required to drill down on operational scorecards.

1. Drag the Geography/Hierarchy dimension to just above the ContosoSales column of the scorecard. The member selector appears.

2. Select the member Europe.

If you right-click the member you selected, other options appear, as shown in the following illustration.

3. Choose Select All Descendants.

Note If you accidently add an unwanted dimension and its members, you can click the Undo icon in the upper-left corner of Dashboard Designer.

Important If you're not familiar with multidimensional tools, we highly recommend that that you experiment with the user interface by dragging and dropping dimensions and selecting members for each value to see the multidimensional views of the Analysis Services data source. Use the Undo tool to return to your original state.

4. Perform the same steps listed in Steps 1 and 2, but this time drag the Forecast Sales column. Your KPI in design view (and now with a "dimension") should look as shown in the following illustration.

5. On the Edit tab, click Update to update the scorecard view. Larger scorecards take time to update.

> **Note** The Update and Refresh buttons do different things. Update is unique to scorecards and refreshes only the scorecard. In contrast, Refresh updates the PerformancePoint content and data sources in the Dashboard Designer on your machine.

Notes About the Scorecard

At this point you have created one KPI and one scorecard and associated one dimension with the KPI. You can build more KPIs and add more dimensions to give business users more options for slicing data they need to view, and much more. Here are a few more scorecard elements that you should explore:

- The Details pane lets you navigate the elements that you can add to the Scorecard, which can dynamically change how your data is visualized.

- You can add metrics on the opposite axes from all KPIs.

- Aggregations on the scorecard enable you to make summations of all the metrics. You simply add the aggregation type above the metric column. Aggregations are limited to columns (no row aggregating).

- Named sets (from the cube) can be placed on a scorecard.

- Set Formulas allows you to add MDX or Time Intelligence expressions to the scorecard to further filter the data that is viewed by the user.

Create a Filter

You want to include one filter on the dashboard to give users the option to select from other territories.

To create a filter

1. Right-click the PerformancePoint Content list in the Workspace Browser.

2. Select New | Filter, and in the resulting dialog box, click Member Selection.

3. Select the Contoso_SalesData data source, and in the Select Members dialog box, click Select Dimension. The Select Dimension dialog box opens.

4. Select Geography.Region Country Name, and then click OK.

5. Click Select Members, and select All Countries under Europe.

6. Select List For The Display Method, and then click Finish.

> **Note** You have the option of editing the filter.

Add a Report

As mentioned earlier in the "Overview of PerformancePoint Services Components" section, there are 10 report types and features that you can use to analyze and investigate data that you monitor using scorecards and KPIs. The reports help you to create a reporting structure that gets the right data to the decision-makers in the right visualization. For example, an analytic bar chart is useful for comparing groups of members, or you might want to show how sales amounts are distributed across different countries or regions.

We recommend that you review the report types and determine which can best fit your needs for enhancing the scorecard experience. In the following example, it makes sense to include several reports, but we focus on the Analytic chart. The Analytic chart and grid are highly interactive, and you can place them on a webpage; however, the data source must be either PowerPivot or Analysis Services.

To add a bar chart

1. Right-click PerformancePoint Content, and select New | Report.

2. Select Analytic Chart, and then click OK. A wizard opens so that you can select the data source.

3. Select the Contoso_SalesData Analysis Services data source, and click Finish. A report authoring environment renders in Dashboard Designer where you can drag measures, dimensions, and named sets from the Details pane.

4. Drag the Date Calendar YQMD dimension hierarchy into the Background section, and click the drop-down arrow to select the members Year 2009, 2010, and 2011.

5. Drag the Sales Territory dimension hierarchy into the Background section, and then select the Europe dimension hierarchy. (This serves as a background filter for the report.)

6. Drag the Sales Amount measure into the Bottom Axis section.

7. Drag the Geography dimension hierarchy into the Series section, and then select dimension members at the country level. Deselect All and Europe.

 Note You can simplify selecting all members under a single parent node by right-clicking and selecting All Children.

The following illustration shows the result of dragging and dropping dimensions and of narrowing by selecting members.

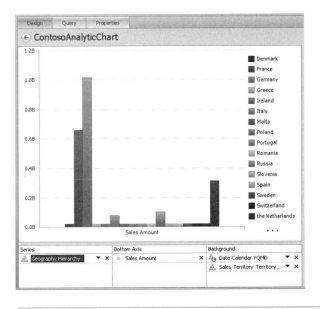

Tip Notice that you have three tabs. The Query tab lets you view the MDX query as a result of dragging and dropping dimensions and selecting members. The Properties tab lets you type in the folder name, Reports, to keep things organized in Workspace Browser.

You can enter Data Elements by right-clicking anywhere on the chart. The following illustration shows the result of choosing options for adding a filter, a pivot, changing the report type, and changing the report format.

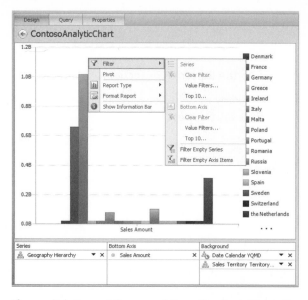

If you click Report Type, and then Stacked Chart, the chart updates to the following visualization. Again, it's well worth your time to explore the options to determine the most meaningful visualization for your decision-makers.

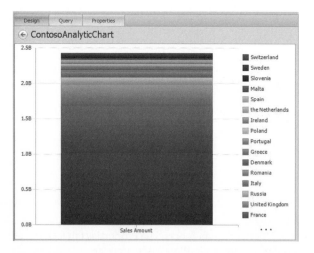

If you select Filter and then Top 10, you'll see the following Top 10 countries. Notice the filter icon, which tells you the report has a filter, and so forth.

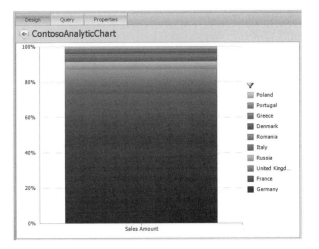

Create a Dashboard

You are now ready to create a dashboard, the vehicle you use to show PerformancePoint objects to business users. Dashboards are nothing but PerformancePoint Services Web Parts put together on a Web Part page with connections configured between the parts to create interactivity. Dashboards are ASPX pages. You must have Designer-level permissions on the SharePoint site to deploy the dashboard.

> **Note** SharePoint Designer also has Web Part pages but does not support creating connections between PerformancePoint Web Parts. Also remember that differences between these authoring tools can be confusing; they are different tools, and their terminology and concepts are different.

You can use the next exercise to put Web Parts together and then configure the connections. Web Part connections include:

- Get Value From
- Send Values To
- Source Value
- Connect To

To create a dashboard

1. Right-Click PerformancePoint Content, and then select New | Dashboard.

2. Select the last layout, Header, 2 Columns. (You can modify this later, after you create the dashboard.) The zones mentioned at the bottom of this screen define how you can position scorecards, reports, and filters on the dashboard.

3. Type a name for your dashboard as it is highlighted in the Workspace Browser. The Details pane on the right lets you drag and drop scorecards, reports, and filters.

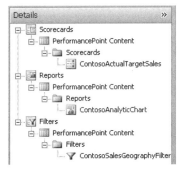

The elements shown in the following illustration are available to create a dashboard.

4. Put a Header on the dashboard by choosing to add to the zone by clicking Add in the bottom-right corner of Dashboard Designer. Select the Header item. Dashboard Designer automatically adds the ContosoSalesGeographyFilter.

5. From the Details pane, open the Scorecards node and search until you find the ContosoActualTargetSales scorecard. Drag it onto the Left Column zone.

6. From the Details pane, open the Reports node and look for the ContosoAnalyticChart report. Drag that report onto the Right Column zone.

Notice that you cannot see the scorecard or chart you created yet. You must deploy the dashboard first.

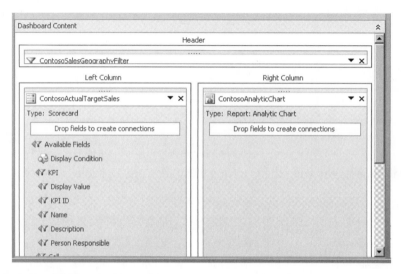

7. Right-click the dashboard in the Workspace Browser, and then select Deploy To SharePoint.

8. Choose the document library where you want to store this dashboard.

9. Choose the master page you want to use.

> **Note** You can modify all subsequent deployments for this dashboard by using the dashboard Deployment Properties tab, which is an additional tab next to the Editor tab, to change the target location or master page.

10. Click OK.

The dashboard is deployed using the PerformancePointDefault master page, and it fills the entire browser window.

	Actual Sales	Forecast Sales		
ContosoSales			☺	
Europe	$19,164,654,491.76	$19,431,033,138.72	☺	-1%
Denmark	$171,660,921.38	$174,299,705.09	☺	-2%
France	$5,232,844,247.10	$5,309,767,414.99	☺	-1%
Germany	$8,060,226,425.89	$8,168,283,898.30	☺	-1%
Greece	$171,052,751.52	$173,667,300.23	☺	-2%
Ireland	$171,057,767.37	$173,725,189.48	☺	-2%
Italy	$624,616,631.43	$634,062,367.51	☺	-1%
Malta	$169,703,354.49	$172,434,878.02	☺	-2%
Poland	$171,271,121.13	$174,150,067.85	☺	-2%
Portugal	$171,136,505.32	$173,922,985.05	☺	-2%
Romania	$172,913,828.98	$175,608,006.82	☺	-2%
Russia	$789,377,297.60	$789,501,122.34	☺	0%
Slovenia	$168,423,240.95	$171,058,655.48	☺	-2%
Spain	$170,598,221.83	$173,314,191.68	☺	-2%
Sweden	$167,651,916.44	$170,311,222.73	☺	-2%
Switzerland	$165,880,191.89	$168,486,555.02	☺	-2%
the Netherlands	$170,783,166.46	$173,595,053.41	☺	-2%
United Kingdom	$2,415,456,902.00	$2,454,844,524.72	☺	-2%

Modify Your Zones

You can add, remove, and split zones as necessary.

To modify a zone

1. Right-click a zone.

2. Click Zone Settings on the context menu to open the Zone Settings dialog box, and then click the Size tab.

To learn more about zone size and orientation, see the product team blog post "PerformancePoint Dashboard Sizing Explained," at *http://blogs.msdn.com/b/performance-point/archive/2008/01/07/performancepoint-dashboard-sizing-explained.aspx.*

Other Options in Dashboard Designer

In addition to the procedures you've seen in this chapter, you can also:

- Add another page or existing dashboard using the Editor tab when the focus is on your dashboard in Workspace Browser. This enables you to separate and organize content by region, product, and so forth. Additionally, it is easy to help users navigate between pages on the Properties tab.

- You can modify the filters you created so that users can filter on information they see.

Summary

This chapter provides a taste of the rich functionality available in Dashboard Designer. In this chapter, you explore PerformancePoint Services to understand the following:

- The components and architecture of PerformancePoint, including what's new.

- How to configure security for a data source.

- How to author and publish a dashboard to SharePoint 2010 by using Dashboard Designer.

Along the way, the various sources for more information should give you steppingstones to more information about the concepts presented here. Finally, it's worth noting (again) that PerformancePoint is far too complex to cover fully in a single chapter, so you should plan to spend some time exploring the various features and options to gain a full sense of what's possible.

Quick Reference

To	Do this
Manage PerformancePoint Services service applications in SharePoint Central Management	To view the default settings for PerformancePoint Services or configure the settings, use SharePoint Central Administration and click Manage Service Applications, click the PerformancePoint service application, and then click Manage. TO learn more, see the section "After Running the SharePoint Configuration Wizard."
Configure SSS for PerformancePoint Services	Before you connect to SQL Server data sources, you must configure SSS from Central Administration. See the section "Configure Security for PerformancePoint" to learn more.
To deploy the Business Intelligence Center from the enterprise templates and start Dashboard Designer	Consider setting up a single repository for all of your BI assets, including your Visio and Excel files, PerformancePoint dashboards, and more. This is where you also start the PerformancePoint Dashboard Designer. Simply go to Central Administration and click Create Site Collections. When you select a template, make sure you select the Enterprise tab and then Business Intelligence Center. To learn more, see the section "Launch PerformancePoint Dashboard Designer."
To create a basic dashboard	See the section "Providing a Performance Solution."

Chapter 8
Bringing It All Together

After completing this chapter you will be able to:

- Understand the basic concepts of BI dashboards in SharePoint.

- Understand how SharePoint supports the concurrent use of multiple BI products.

- Create a SharePoint dashboard that uses several different Microsoft BI products and features.

Introduction

Users in organizations often need to gain insights from data across many different sources. They may need to look at sales data alongside orders data or forecast data. While the requirement itself seems straightforward, the data often resides in many different places— or the people who analyze the data perform that analysis in different ways, using different products. You don't always have a clear "one size fits all" answer to the question of which product to use to best visualize a particular data source. You might also need to determine which product to use based on the maturity of an organization, its capabilities, or simply the user's comfort level with the technology.

For example, one user might use Reporting Services to show insights about customer trends, and another might use Excel Services to show how a particular customer segment lines up with cost projections. Management in the organization might actually want to see both analyses side by side, to help answer a business-critical question. The simplest way to do this would be to allow these products to work in a side-by-side fashion, providing integrated views of the data, rather than forcing yet another user to copy each BI report and regenerate it using a single tool.

One of the strengths of SharePoint is that it gives users the ability to bring data and insights from different products together in a holistic way. Whether the data comes from a SQL Server data source, from an Analysis Services cube, from within a SharePoint list, from an Excel file, or from any one of a number of other places, the Microsoft BI stack with SharePoint gives you the tools to easily view insights from the various data sources in a single integrated view. BI developers can choose to use any of the products described in this book, because through SharePoint, all the products can deliver side-by-side analyses to help business users gain deeper insights while still allowing individual users to use the products that make the most sense to them, based on the specific data being used or on their comfort level with a particular product or technology.

Dashboards

The concept of a dashboard is probably very familiar to most readers. At the simplest level, a dashboard brings visualizations of data and status together into a single place, so users can easily—usually at a glance—view how a particular business effort is doing. Dashboards are suitable for many different purposes, including measuring status against goals, monitoring progress, and managing business process. The best dashboards provide a way to take action on the information they show, such as quickly sending an alert or email to the right individual if something needs to be done.

Dashboards can be constructed from many different types of content: charts, icons showing status (usually referred to as key performance indicators, or KPIs), key numbers and statistics, fully interactive reports, tables, or just about any other visualization that shows how well an organization is tracking toward its goals.

You can use all the products discussed in this book to create meaningful views. The previous chapters have provided a good overview of when to use the individual products and how to get started with them. This chapter focuses on what the end user sees, by first walking through some straightforward examples that show how to gather insights created using each product, and then combining those insights onto a single dashboard page so that end users can consume the information easily.

Tools in SharePoint for Authoring Dashboards

While you can use each product discussed in this book to create a single full-page report that functions much like a dashboard, you can also combine views from each product into a single dashboard page.

Here are the three primary tools you can use to do this:

- **PerformancePoint Dashboard Designer**   PerformancePoint is a different dashboard experience altogether. You should distinguish the dashboard experience described in Chapter 7, "PerformancePoint Services," from the Web Part experience explained in this chapter. You can use a PerformancePoint dashboard to display PerformancePoint objects in a browser. The authoring tool, PerformancePoint Dashboard Designer, is a OneClick application available when PerformancePoint Services is configured. Dashboard Designer allows you to build integrated BI solutions that bring the published results of the other authoring tools together into interactive dashboards. To learn more about Dashboard Designer, see Chapter 7.

- **SharePoint page/dashboard user interface**   You can use the SharePoint interface for all the other dashboard-building products. For example, using the native SharePoint user interface, you can customize Web Parts, SharePoint KPIs, and SharePoint pages to combine insights from such products as Excel Services, Visio Services, and more. This chapter discusses the basic elements, such as Web Parts, Web Part pages, filters, and SharePoint KPIs.

- **SharePoint Designer**   Using SharePoint Designer, you can fully customize pages in SharePoint, making it easy to add a custom look-and-feel while taking advantage of advanced functionality such as configuring custom behaviors for alerts or workflows. SharePoint Designer is the premier tool for creating great no-code customized solutions. It's mentioned here for completeness, but this chapter doesn't cover it in any detail. See the Microsoft product page at *http://sharepoint.microsoft.com/en-us/product/Related-Technologies/Pages/SharePoint-Designer.aspx* for more information about SharePoint Designer.

Report Builder is another available tool for BI developers; it is the report authoring environment for creating reports with SQL Reporting Services. Discussion of Report Builder features is out of scope for this book, but if you'd like more information about Report Builder, see "Getting Started with Report Builder 3.0," at *http://technet.microsoft.com/en-us/library/dd220460.aspx*.

Which Dashboard Tool Should I Use?

It is not Microsoft's intention to confuse customers with several different dashboards. Often, the BI tools that you should use depend on the specific problems that you are trying to solve, the BI maturity level of your organization (see Chapter 2, "Choosing the Right BI Tool"), the expertise of people who build or use the dashboard, and other considerations, such as the KPI functionality offered by a SharePoint Web Part dashboard versus a KPI authored in PerformancePoint Dashboard Designer.

Basically, you don't want to use a jackhammer when all you need is a small ping hammer to help users make decisions. The functionality of many of these tools overlaps. You might decide which tool to use based on your familiarity or proficiency with the tool. In any case, the following guidelines can be helpful when choosing which dashboard-creation technology to use.

> **Note** The following are high-level suggestions that stem from a generalized dashboard-usage perspective only. See the individual chapters for more in-depth explanations of the strengths of each product and when to use it.

Use Performance Point to create comprehensive KPIs, scorecards, reports, filters, and dashboards when:

- You want to include any of the following multidimensional data sources:

    ❑ SQL Server Analysis Services

> **Note** An Analysis Services cube is a multidimensional data source that is ideal for a rich KPI. Analysis Services KPIs, discussed in Chapter 3, "Getting to Trusted Data", can be imported into a scorecard by using the PerformancePoint Scorecard Wizard.

    ❑ PowerPivot model

> **Note** A PowerPivot model must first be created by using the PowerPivot add-in for Excel and then published to a SharePoint site that has PowerPivot services enabled.

- You want to include tabular data sources such as the following:

    ❑ SharePoint list

    ❑ Excel Services

    ❑ SQL Server table

    ❑ Excel workbook

    ❑ Custom data source

- You need visualizations that allow you to drill down, such as decomposition trees to see the underlying data for a particular value.

- Need more advanced KPIs that support the following:

    ❑ Multiple data sources with which KPIs can perform calculations

    ❑ More complex visualizations (such as gauges)

    ❑ A large number of states—important when you want to display and communicate the current state of your business as well as its desired future state (or multiple forecasts)

- You want dynamic hierarchies that refresh when the data source is updated.

- You want Time Intelligence features that allow you both to filter and to create variations on the filter that allow the user to select a single "current date."

- You want to create or include any of the following reports or report features in your dashboard:

> **Note** Some reports or report features are created Dashboard Designer, while others are already created in another BI tool, such as SQL Server Reporting Services. The distinction is discussed in Chapter 7, "PerformancePoint Services."

- ❑ Analytic chart
- ❑ Analytic grid
- ❑ KPI details
- ❑ Show details
- ❑ Decomposition tree
- ❑ Reporting Services report
- ❑ ProClarity Analytics Server Page report

Use "native" dashboard tools, such as Excel Services, SharePoint dashboard pages, KPIs, and filters, when:

- You want to include any of the following data sources:
  - ❑ Analysis Services
  - ❑ PowerPivot
  - ❑ SQL Server
  - ❑ Excel workbook
  - ❑ Visio diagram
- The BI reports or logic are already based in Excel (often the case, given Excel's widespread usage).
- The needs around your KPIs are fairly simple and don't have more than a few states (up to 5 states).
- You need KPIs on a page or series of pages, have very simple KPI needs, and don't want to spend the time creating and managing more complex solutions such as a Performance Point scorecard or workbook file.
- You need to prototype a solution quickly. (For example, experienced Excel users can build a full report faster in Excel, using conditional formatting, and so on.)
- You need a solution that can be manipulated on-the-fly. (It's easy to edit Excel reports or use the SharePoint user interface to tweak dashboard pages with little or no training.)

Dashboard (Web Part) Pages in SharePoint

The lightest-weight dashboard authoring tool is a simple web browser that takes advantage of the user interface that SharePoint has provided to build dashboard pages that use Web Parts.

Web Parts are logical containers in SharePoint pages that can display content. The Web Part framework in SharePoint provides easy drag-and-drop interactivity, includes a Settings page, and includes other user-interface features to make configuring pages fairly simple. Web Part pages are generally essential for creating a dashboard-like experience in SharePoint. You would typically use Web Parts when you need to display content from different files or products (such as Excel Services, Visio Services, Reporting Services, and so on) in a page, when you want to display that content side by side with other SharePoint content, or when that content needs to interact with other SharePoint entities in the same page (such as lists or other Web Parts).

PerformancePoint dashboard pages are ordinary Web Part pages that contain various components as connected Web Parts. The Filter, Scorecard, Report, and Stack Web Part are discussed in more detail in the section "Create a Dashboard" in Chapter 7.

To create a dashboard page in SharePoint

1. Go to the SharePoint site where you want to add your dashboard page, expand the Site Actions drop-down list, and choose More Options, as shown in the following illustration.

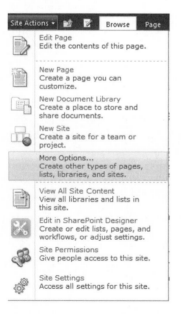

2. When the Create page opens, on the right-hand side of the page, under Pages And Sites, choose Web Part Page.

Pages and Sites

Page
Web Part Page
Blog
Team Sites
Sites and Workspaces

Alternatively, depending on whether Silverlight is enabled, you might see a slightly different user interface. On the Create page, in the Browse From list, choose Filter By Page and then choose the Web Part Page option as shown in the following illustration. Then click Create (on the right-hand side of the page).

Create

Browse From:

Installed Items >   Title ▲ Type
Office.com

Filter By:

All Types
Library
List
Page >
Site

Page   Web Part Page

Now you must make some choices. As shown in the following illustration, you need to select your preferred page layout, enter a name for the page, and specify where to store the page.

Name

Type a file name for your Web Part Page. The file name appears in headings and links throughout the site.

Name:

WebPartPage   .aspx

☐ Overwrite if file already exists?

Layout

Select a layout template to arrange Web Parts in zones on the page. Multiple Web Parts can be added to each zone. Specific zones allow Web Parts to be stacked in a horizontal or vertical direction, which is illustrated by differently colored Web Parts. If you do not add a Web Part to a zone, the zone collapses (unless it has a fixed width) and the other zones expand to fill unused space when you browse the Web Part Page.

Choose a Layout Template:

Header, Footer, 3 Columns
Full Page, Vertical
Header, Left Column, Body
Header, Right Column, Body
Header, Footer, 2 Columns, 4 Rows
Header, Footer, 4 Columns, Top Row
Left Column, Header, Footer, Top Row, 3 Columns
Right Column, Header, Footer, Top Row, 3 Columns

Save Location

Select the document library where you want the Web Part Page to be saved.

Document Library

Site Assets

Create   Cancel

3. Accept the defaults, and name the page WebPartPage. Feel free to experiment with the different layout options available—whatever you find pleasing. The Save Location is the document library where SharePoint stores your new page.

4. Click Create to display a new blank Web Part page, as shown in the following illustration.

Use Excel Services in the Dashboard

To make the dashboard more interesting, you can use the next exercise to get some data from an Excel workbook and show it on the page by using the Excel Web Access Web Part. Before doing that though, you need an Excel workbook.

You can use almost any workbook to do this. The following example walks you through the steps to create a simple workbook that works with some of the filters you can add to the page in later sections of this chapter.

Create the Excel Workbook

The workbook creation process has two parts. First you need to add a pivot table connected to OLAP data in Analysis Services, and then you can generate a chart from that data.

To add a pivot table to a workbook

1. Start the data connection wizard in Excel, click the Data tab, click From Other Sources, and select From Analysis Services, as shown in the following illustration.

2. Complete the Data Connection Wizard to connect to the Contoso Retail DW database, select the Sales cube, and click Finish.

3. In the Import Data dialog box, choose PivotTable Report to create a new pivot table report in your sheet.

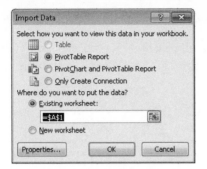

4. In the PivotTable Field List dialog box, choose Sales from the topmost filter to see only those fields relevant for the Sales data.

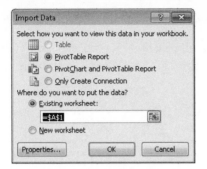

5. Scroll through the field list, selecting the check box next to the following fields: Sales Amount, Product, and Calendar YWD. This adds the primary data to the spreadsheet that we are working with.

6. Drag the Calendar YWD field from the Column Labels area to the Report Filter area, as shown in the following before-and-after illustrations.

Before   After

You should end up with a pivot table in your workbook, as shown in the following illustration.

	A	B	
1	Calendar YWD	All	▾
2			
3	**Row Labels** ▾	**Sales Amount**	
4	⊞ AUDIO	$150,703,104.28	
5	⊞ TV & VIDEO	$1,348,482,541.08	
6	⊞ COMPUTERS	$2,937,030,931.13	
7	⊞ CAMERAS & CAMCODERS	$2,536,738,529.70	
8	⊞ CELLPHONES	$884,480,287.07	
9	⊞ MUSIC, MOVIES & AUDIO BOOKS	$164,279,314.28	
10	⊞ GAMES & TOYS	$149,919,633.87	
11	⊞ HOME APPLIANCES	$3,915,829,318.64	
12	**Grand Total**	**$12,087,463,660.05**	
13			

To add a simple chart to the workbook

1. Continuing with the same file you created in the preceding procedure, make sure your cell selection is located in the pivot table, and on the Insert tab, click Pie to choose a Pie chart.

2. To format the chart so that it looks a little better in the report, move the chart and then grab its corner to resize it so that it fits next to your pivot table.

3. Optionally, choose a chart style that you like from the chart ribbon.

4. On the Chart Analyze tab, in the Field group, click Hide All.

    You should now have a finished report that resembles the following illustration.

	A	B	C	D	E	F
1	Calendar YWD	All ▼				
2						
3	**Row Labels** ▼	**Sales Amount**				
4	⊞ AUDIO	$150,703,104.28				
5	⊞ TV & VIDEO	$1,348,482,541.08				
6	⊞ COMPUTERS	$2,937,030,931.13				
7	⊞ CAMERAS & CAMCODERS	$2,536,738,529.70				
8	⊞ CELLPHONES	$884,480,287.07				
9	⊞ MUSIC, MOVIES & AUDIO BOOKS	$164,279,314.28				
10	⊞ GAMES & TOYS	$149,919,633.87				
11	⊞ HOME APPLIANCES	$3,915,829,318.64				
12	**Grand Total**	**$12,087,463,660.05**				
13						
14						
15						

5. Save the workbook to SharePoint, and view it in a browser by using Excel Services.

When you view the workbook on the server, make sure the pivot table refreshes and that all your data connectivity is working. If it isn't, see the section "External Data Configuration" in Chapter 4, "Excel Services," for some steps that should help.

Prepare the Workbook for the Dashboard: Add Parameters

Because the ultimate goal is to end up with multiple Web Parts on a dashboard page, you need a way to filter the data on the page at the same time. You can use a SharePoint filter to do this. A SharePoint filter is yet another Web Part on the page that takes a given value and sends it to other Web Parts on the page. Then, based on the value provided by the SharePoint filter Web Part, the other Web Parts can change or filter the data they display. This simple mechanism enables users to choose a given value and then see all the different Web Parts on the page get filtered by their choice. SharePoint filters are created either in a SharePoint Web Part page user interface or in SharePoint Designer.

Before configuring the Excel Services Web Parts so that they can be filtered, you need to make some simple modifications to the workbook file so that it can be filtered in the dashboard. You must modify the workbook so that it can accept a filter value and recalculate based on that value. You do this by specifying workbook parameters.

A workbook parameter is a single cell in Excel that accepts input values when the file is loaded on the server. This provides a way to modify a cell's contents even in read-only or view-only permission situations, without allowing the rest of the workbook to be edited. Workbook parameters are single-cell named ranges that don't contain any formulas.

To specify a workbook parameter

In the following exercise, the goal is to allow users to change the date filter for the pivot table. First you need to give it a name.

> **Note** This exercise uses the same workbook you created earlier in the chapter.

1. In column B of row 1, select the date filter cell (showing "All" in the following illustration) on the pivot table, type **DateFilterCell** in the box to the left of the formula bar, and press Enter. Now you can refer to that cell by name, which makes it easy to specify it as a parameter later.

2. Click File, click Save & Send, and then click Save To SharePoint.

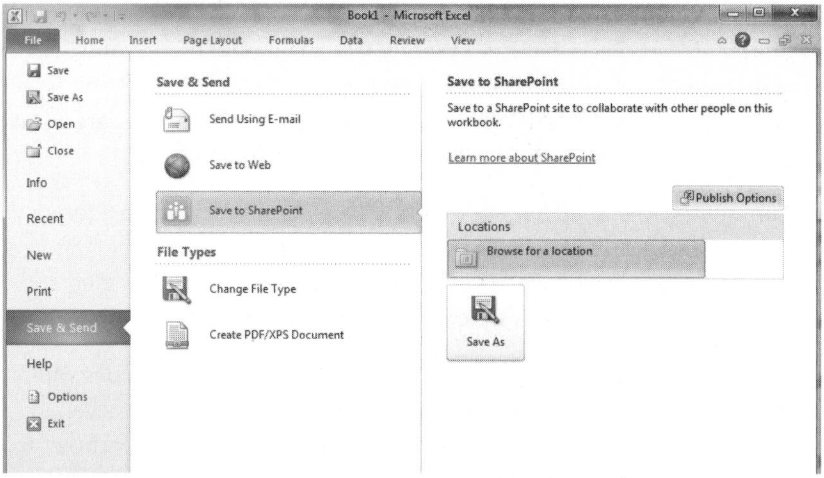

3. Click Publish Options (as shown in the right pane of the preceding illustration) to open the Publish Options dialog box, and then, to define the workbook parameters, click the Parameters tab, shown in the following illustration.

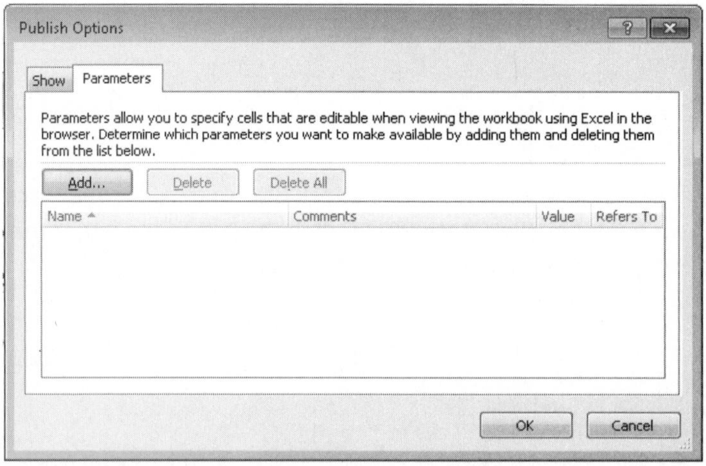

4. In the Publish Options dialog box, click Add to display the Add Parameters dialog box, shown in the following illustration, where you can choose which single-cell named ranges to add as parameters.

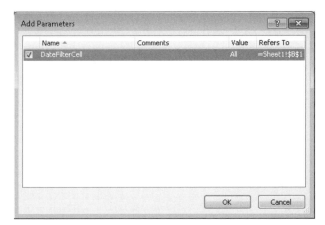

5. In the Add Parameters dialog box, select the DateFilterCell cell that you defined earlier and click OK.

6. Click OK to close the Publish Options dialog box.

7. Save the file in SharePoint. (If you opened the file directly from SharePoint, you can simply click Save, or you can click Save As to overwrite the earlier version of the file.)

The workbook you just saved in SharePoint now allows users to set values in the DateFilterCell cell even if the workbook is in read-only or view-only mode. Changing the cell value triggers a refresh of both the pivot table and pivot chart. You'll use this parameter later when we associate it with a SharePoint filter.

Show the Workbook in Web Parts

Now it's time to show the pivot table and chart in separate Web Parts on the dashboard page. The first step is to add the Excel Web Access Web Parts to the page and configure them.

To add an Excel Web Access Web Part

1. From the Page tab of your browser, navigate to the Web Part page you created before. (Remember that it might be in the Site Assets library of your site, depending on where you saved it.)

2. Pick a zone, and then click Add A Web Part to expand the top of the page so that you can choose which Web Part to add.

3. As shown in the preceding illustration, select Business Data in the Categories area, choose Excel Web Access in the Web Parts area, and then click Add to add the Web Part to the page in the zone you selected previously.

4. You should now have an empty Excel Web Access Web Part on the page. You can use this Web Part to load and display Excel workbooks using Excel Services.

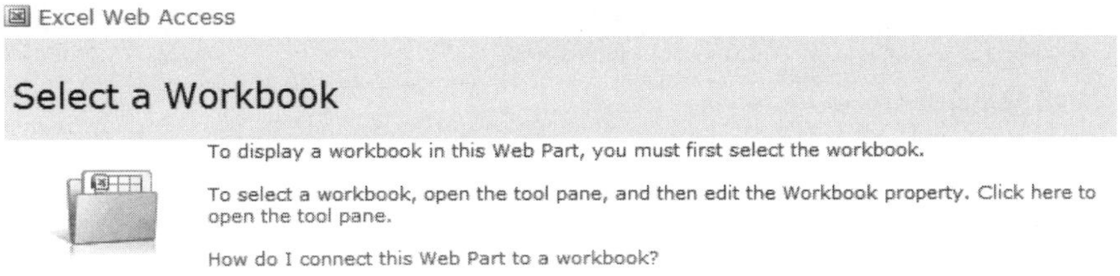

Excel Web Access

Select a Workbook

To display a workbook in this Web Part, you must first select the workbook.

To select a workbook, open the tool pane, and then edit the Workbook property. Click here to open the tool pane.

How do I connect this Web Part to a workbook?

To configure the Web Part

Now you can configure the Web Part to display the workbook you created earlier.

1. In the Select A Workbook page, shown in the preceding illustration, click the Click Here To Open The Tool Pane link to expand the tool pane for the Web Part, displaying all the configuration options.

2. Under the Workbook Display area, click the blue button to browse for a workbook to display. A webpage dialog box opens, enabling you to navigate within SharePoint to pick a workbook. Use that dialog box to select the workbook you saved in SharePoint from the previous steps, or just type the URL to the workbook directly.

   You should end up with a URL for the workbook you want to display, as shown in the following illustration.

   Excel Web Access   ×

   Workbook Display   ≈

   Workbook:

   http://sp2010-bi/bi site/Shared

   Named Item:

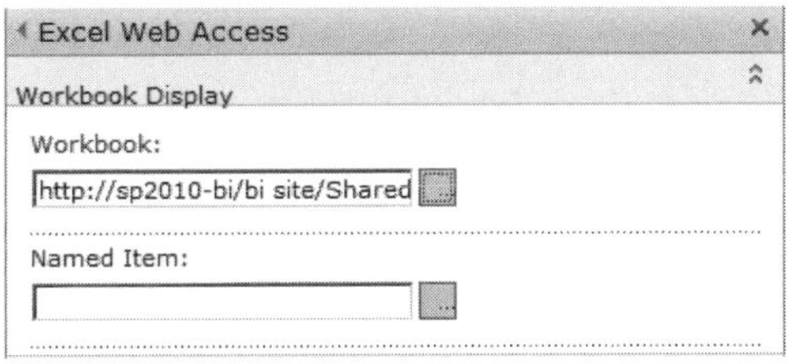

3. Scroll down to the bottom of the Web Part properties tool pane, and click OK. You should now see your workbook displayed in the Web Part, as shown in the following illustration.

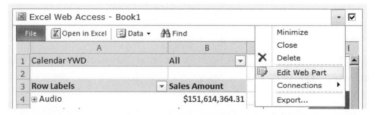

Notice that the workbook looks just like an Excel file at this point. You can click the sheet tabs, see the chart, interact with the pivot table, and so forth.

You can control what the Web Part actually shows—for example, you can have it show only the chart.

4. Click the drop-down arrow and select Edit Web Part, as shown in the following illustration, to open the Web Part Properties tool pane.

5. In the tool pane, under Named Item, type in **Chart 1**. (This works only if you have created a workbook with at least one chart in it and have not changed the default name of the chart. If you did rename your chart, type the name you gave to the chart.)

6. Click either OK or Apply at the bottom of the Web Part Properties tool pane, and the Web Part displays the chart named Chart 1, as shown in the following illustration.

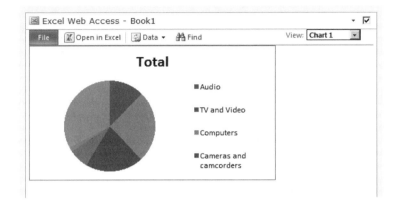

Notice that the Web Part no longer displays this page as a spreadsheet. Instead, it displays each item, one at a time, in the Web Part. This viewing mode is referred to as the Named Item View. When users expand the View drop-down list, they can choose to display any of the other items in the workbook.

The Named Item View is the view used in most Web Parts, because most people just want to see the parts of a workbook that are interesting and related in a dashboard. This is also the mode that is used when the workbook author publishes only a selection of items from Excel (as described in the "To publish and Excel file" procedure in Chapter 4). That is, because the workbook author chose to display only certain items rather than full sheets, each item appears in Named Item View.

Therefore, in the case where the author chose to show only a set of items from the workbook, the Web Part shows whichever is the first item in the workbook (sorted alphabetically)—even if you don't specify the name of an item in the Named Item Web Part Text box. However, you can also specify which item should appear first in the workbook by using the Named Item text box in the Web Part properties task pane.

Set Other Web Part Properties

Open the Web Part properties tool pane again. Notice that many properties that can affect how the workbook is displayed are listed. You won't explore all the properties here, but generally, you can find properties for controlling whether the toolbar is visible, what commands are on the toolbar (if it is visible), whether or not the Named Item drop-down list is displayed, and what types of interactivity you want to allow for the Web Part (such as sorting, filtering, recalculation, and so on).

For now, turn the toolbar off. Under Type Of Toolbar, choose None from the drop-down list, as shown in the following illustration.

Then scroll down and expand the appearance section. Notice the width and height controls. These controls are used frequently for adjusting dashboards that have many objects on the page, to get the right look and feel. You need to adjust these to make the Web Part fit the displayed Excel content in a way that doesn't show unnecessary scrollbars. Finally, click OK to close the Web Part Properties tool pane.

Add More Web Parts and Finish

Repeat the steps in the preceding section, but this time set the Named Item to PivotTable1 to display the pivot table you created earlier. Notice that in the Excel client you can see the name of each item in the ribbon for that item. Feel free to add any other Web Parts to the page as well.

On the ribbon at the top of the SharePoint page, click Stop Editing. Until now, the Web Part page has displayed in Edit mode. This mode shows all the various zones, drop-downs for displaying edit menus, editing ribbons, and so forth. When you click Stop Editing, the Web Part page displays in the way that visitors to the site will see it. This page has many other settings that you can use to make the page cleaner (such as turning off Web Part titles). You can freely experiment with these options to learn how they modify the look and feel of the page.

As shown in the preceding illustration, our example has two Web Parts on the page—one showing a chart and the other showing a pivot table. Both come from the same workbook. However, at this point, when you drill down on the pivot table, the chart does not update. This is because each Web Part loads its own copy of the workbook—that is, it gets its own session on the server. Each session is completely separate, so changes from one session don't affect other sessions. This is the reason why you can have a single Web Part page viewable by many users at the same time, yet one user's operations (filter, sort, drill, and so on) affect only that user.

> **Note** The example in this section is for illustrational purposes only. It's intended to show how you can have multiple Web Parts interacting on the same page. In a real-world scenario, the power of multiple Web Parts becomes apparent when you have items from different workbook files that can be viewed side by side, rather than items from the same file.

The next section shows you how to put a single filter on the page that enables both the chart and the pivot table to update.

Add a SharePoint Filter to the Page

SharePoint provides many different kinds of filters right out of the box. You can also add new custom filters to SharePoint—but that is beyond the scope of this book. The filters that ship as part of SharePoint can take data from many different sources, including a SharePoint list, a predefined set of values, Analysis Services, user-entered values, and many more.

This section focuses on using an Analysis Services filter. The goal is to allow users to select a date from Analysis Services and then see other Web Parts on the page update to reflect the chosen date.

Create a Reusable Data Connection

Because you want to use the Analysis Services filter in SharePoint, you first need to provide it with the Analysis Services connection information. The ideal way to do that is to reuse the same connection that the workbook uses. SharePoint and other Office products (like Excel) provide features for connection reuse, sharing, and management. While most of those topics are out of scope for this book, the following "bare minimum" procedure shows you how to easily reuse the connection you created earlier for the workbook.

The goal here is to save the connection information from the Excel workbook as a separate connection file (an .odc file) to SharePoint so that other workbooks, Visio files, or SharePoint filters can easily reuse the same connection.

To save the connection information to SharePoint

1. Open the Excel workbook that contains the pivot table and chart you have been working with in this chapter.

2. On the Data tab, click Connections, as shown in the following illustration.

The Workbook Connections dialog box opens.

3. For each connection (only one is shown in the preceding illustration, but there could be more if you have more connections in your workbook), select the connection and then click Properties.

4. In the Connection Properties dialog box, click the Definition tab, as shown in the following illustration.

5. Click Export Connection File to open the File Save dialog box.

6. In the File Save dialog box, type the path to the SharePoint site where you are creating your dashboard, and press Enter to save your file.

> **Note** Don't worry about typing the name of the connection file at this point. Just type the name of the SharePoint site; the dialog box lets you navigate to the specific library where you want to save it.

7. When the dialog box displays the SharePoint user interface, as shown in the following illustration, you can choose where to save your file. In this case, you should save it in a Data Connection Library (if you have one); if not, in the Document Libraries list, simply double-click Shared Documents to save it there.

8. Type the name of the file that you want to use—Contoso Retail DW Sales in this case—and click Save.

Now the data connection information is neatly packaged up as a file that you can reuse for other workbooks, diagrams, or, in this case, for filters on the page. Now you can add the Analysis Services filter.

Add the Filter to the Dashboard

Many types of filters are available in SharePoint, but for this example, the goal is to let users filter by date (the year), in the same Analysis Services cube that the workbook is using.

To add an Analysis Services filter to a dashboard page

1. Navigate to the dashboard page in your browser, and make sure it is in Edit mode. (You might need to click the Page tab on the webpage and then click Edit Page to get to Edit mode.)

2. Click the Add a Web Part link in the left-column zone of the page.

3. Under Categories, choose Filters. Under Web Parts, choose SQL Services Analysis Services Filter, and then click Add.

You should now have an empty filter on the page, ready to be configured.

SQL Server Analysis Services Filter

Open the tool pane to configure this filter.

Configure the Filter

Now you need to configure the filter to get the right data from Analysis Services. At this point, it is connected to the cube but isn't getting the date values. The goal is to grab values from the same date field that the pivot table and chart use so that you can pass those values to the other Web Parts on the page.

To configure the Analysis Services filter

1. In the filter Web Part, as shown in the preceding illustration, click the Open The Tool Pane link to open the properties task pane for that filter.

2. Under the Pick a Data Connection From section, select A SharePoint Data Connection Library, and then click the Browse icon next to the Office Data Connection File text box.

3. Use the SharePoint dialog box to navigate to where you saved the .odc file earlier, select it, and click OK to close the dialog box.

4. In the properties task pane, in the Dimension drop-down list, choose Date. (You might have to wait a few seconds for the Dimension combo box to enable, because the page needs to refresh and populate the drop-down list from Analysis Services.)

5. Choose Calendar YWD from the Hierarchy drop-down list, as shown in the following illustration.

6. Click Ok to close the task pane.

The filter is now connected to Analysis Services. If you expand the filter, you can see the same calendar year date choices as you saw in our pivottable in Excel.

Connect the Filter to Other Web Parts

At this point, you have a filter that allows users to choose date values from Analysis Services on the page, but changing the selected date has no effect on the rest of the dashboard. To make the filter meaningful, you need to connect it to the other Web Parts on the page so that it can pass the selected date value and so that the other Web Parts can filter their data accordingly.

To connect a filter to other Web Parts

1. In the Web Part containing your chart, click the drop-down arrow that appears at the upper-right corner of the Web Part page. This displays a drop-down list containing options for the Web Part.

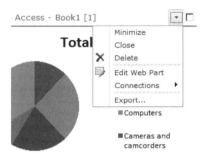

2. From the drop-down list, choose Connections | Get Filter Values From | SQL Server Analysis Services Filter, as shown in the following illustration. The Configure Connection -- Webpage Dialog dialog box opens. (You might need to allow pop-up windows in your browser to view this dialog box.) This dialog box shows all the available workbook parameters to which you can send the filter value. In this example, there is only one: the DateFilterCell parameter you created earlier.

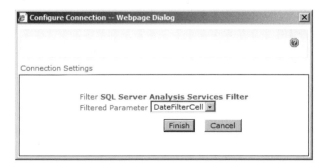

3. In the Configure Connection -- Webpage Dialog dialog box, shown in the following illustration, make sure that the DateFilterCell parameter is selected and then click Finish to accept the parameter.

The filter is now be connected to the Web Part and should refresh automatically after the dialog box closes. Depending on your server's settings, you might be prompted to continue with a data refresh in the Excel Web Access Web Part. The Excel Services administrator can control this setting. (It is a Trusted File Location setting—see the "Server Security" section in Chapter 4 for more information.)

4. Repeat Steps 1–3 to connect the filter to the Web Part that shows the pivot table.

5. Click Stop Editing, as shown in the following illustration, to take the page out of edit mode.

The filter is now connected and should work. To test it, expand the filter drop-down list, choose values (you can choose multiple values), and notice how both of the Excel Services-based Web Parts update.

Note The Contoso data set might not be fully populated—that is, not all years contain data. If you get an empty pivot table and chart, change the filter to another year. The years 2008 and 2009 should have data.

SQL Server Analysis Services Filter		Excel Web Access - Book1 [2]	
Year 2008; Year 2009		Calendar YWD	(Multiple Items)

Excel Web Access - Book1 [1]

Total

- Audio
- TV and Video
- Computers
- Cameras and camcorders

Row Labels	Sales Amount
Audio	$121,879,692.40
TV and Video	$933,449,760.50
Computers	$2,062,957,144.84
Cameras and camcorders	$1,459,329,856.58
Cell phones	$528,385,673.22
Music, Movies and Audio Books	$90,828,945.15
Games and Toys	$107,266,790.79
Home Appliances	$2,547,618,790.38
Grand Total	**$7,851,716,653.87**

Add SharePoint KPIs

SharePoint natively provides some simple KPIs and some detailed views of them, along with some Web Parts to integrate them into dashboards. Other products, like Excel or PowerPivot, have KPIs or formatting that you can use to create KPIs. But if you don't need a full spreadsheet, don't have more advanced calculations for KPIs, don't want to spend the time developing Performance Point KPIs, and just want something quick and simple, SharePoint KPIs might be the way to go.

SharePoint KPIs are stored as items in a list (like most things in SharePoint). This list is a special type of list—a status list.

To create a new status list

1. Navigate to the site where your Web Part page is located.

2. From the Site Actions menu, choose More Options.

3. From the Create dialog box, under the Filter By section in the left-hand side of the dialog box, select List, and then select Status List in the main dialog box section. On the far right-hand side of the dialog box, give your new list a name, and click Create. A new, empty status list appears in the browser.

Four basic types of KPIs can be added to your list. The KPIs can be based on values from a SharePoint list, values from a cell in an Excel spreadsheet (recalculated using Excel Services when the user views the KPI), KPIs stored and managed in Analysis Services, and a KPI that has a goal, threshold, and current value that are manually entered and updated. In this exercise, we want to create a KPI based on Analysis Services data.

4. Expand the New drop-down list on the toolbar in your status list, and choose SQL Server Analysis Services Based Indicator to open the New Item dialog box.

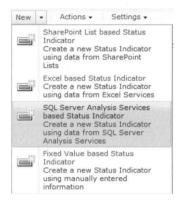

5. In the New Item dialog box, click the browse icon next to the Data Connection text box.

Data Connection

Select the data connection that contains the connection information for the SQL Server 2005 Analysis Services server, database and cube that contains the KPI.

Data Connection:

Examples:
http://portal/dataconnections/datacube.odc
or /dataconnections/datacube.odc

Note You might see some red text under the text box shown in the preceding illustration, warning you about your connection not being encrypted. You can ignore this text because you're most likely learning about these technologies in a test environment. In general, when setting up solutions in a production environment, make sure that your configuration is in compliance with whatever local security policies your company might have in place.

6. In the Select an Asset – Webpage dialog box that enables you to browse and choose a data connection file, choose the Contoso Retail DW Sales.odc file you used in Step 3 of the procedure "To configure the Analysis Services filter," earlier in this chapter.

7. Select Revenue under the Status List section from the right-hand side of the dialog box, and leave the Include Child Indicators check box selected.

KPI:

Only display KPIs from display folder *

All KPIs

Status List *

Channel Revenue
Product Gross Profit Margin
Revenue

☑ Include child indicators

8. Type **Revenue** for the name of your KPI in the Name text box, and then click OK to close the dialog box and create the KPI. You should end up with a single KPI in your list, as shown in the following illustration.

Indicator	Goal	Value	Status
Revenue	12413657608.8876	$12,413,657,608.89	⚠️➡️

The next step is to add a detailed view of this KPI to the existing dashboard.

To add the KPI to the dashboard

1. Navigate to your dashboard page, and on the Page tab, click Edit Page to put the page into edit mode.

2. In the middle column of the page, click the Add A Web Part link. Under Categories, choose Business Data, select Indicator Details under Web Parts, and click Add to add the Web Part to the dashboard.

Categories	Web Parts		About the Web Part
📁 Lists and Libraries	📊 Business Data Actions	📊 Indicator Details	Indicator Details
📁 Business Data	📊 Business Data Connectivity Filter	📊 Status List	Displays the details of a single Status Indicator. Status In-
📁 Content Rollup	📊 Business Data Item	📊 Visio Web Access	important measure for an organization and may be obtain
📁 Filters	📊 Business Data Item Builder		sources including SharePoint lists, Excel workbooks, and
📁 Forms	📊 Business Data List		Analysis Services KPIs.
📁 Media and Content	📊 Business Data Related List		
📁 Outlook Web App	📊 Chart Web Part		
📁 PerformancePoint	📊 Excel Web Access		
📁 Search			
Upload a Web Part ▼	← →		Add Web Part to: Middle Column ▼
			Add

3. SharePoint adds an unconfigured KPI Details Web Part to the page. Click the Open The Tool Pane link to display the Indicator Details tool pane.

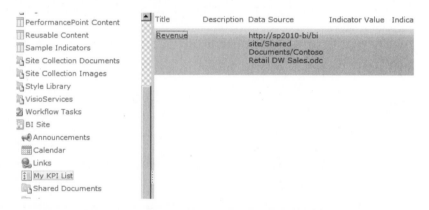

Indicator Details   ▾ ☐

   ℹ️ Status Indicators display important measures for your organization and show how your organization is performing with respect to your goals. <u>Open the tool pane</u> to configure this Web Part.

4. In the Indicator Details pane, click the icon next to the Status List text box to open the Select An Asset Web Page dialog box.

5. In the Select An Asset Web Page dialog box, browse to and select the Revenue KPI that you created in the preceding exercise, and click OK.

6. Click OK to close the properties tool pane for the Web Part.

You have now added a SharePoint KPI, based on data provided by Analysis Services.

Indicator Details		▾ ☑
	Title	Revenue
	Description	
	Comments	
	Value	$12,413,657,608.89
	Goal	12413657608.8876
	Cube	Operation
	Data Connection	http://sp2010-bi/bi%20site/Shared%20Documents/Contoso%20Retail%20DW%20Sales.odc
	Status Indicator	Revenue
	Trend	➡

Connect the Filter to the KPI

To really bring the dashboard together, you want to connect the KPI to the Analysis Services filter on the page. Then, when users filter by a certain time frame, the KPI updates to reflect the filtered time period.

To connect a filter to a KPI

1. In the Indicator Details Web Part, click the drop-down arrow at the upper-right corner of the Web Part to display the options menu.

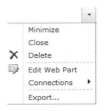

2. From the drop-down list, choose Connections | Get Filter Parameter From | SQL Server Analysis Services Filter.

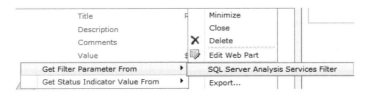

3. In the Configure Connection—Webpage Dialog dialog box, expand the drop-down list and choose the [Date].[Calendar YWD] value, which is the expression value that the Analysis Services filter is currently using.

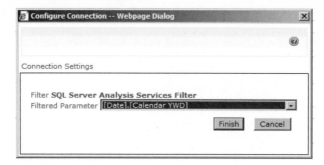

4. On the Page tab, as shown in the following illustration, click Stop Editing to take the page out of edit mode.

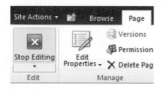

You have now connected your KPI to your Analysis Services filter, and users can now filter the entire dashboard page by a selected calendar year. Notice that the values of the chart, pivot table, and KPI change whenever you change the filter value on the page. Your dashboard should now resemble the following illustration.

Year 2009			

Indicator Details

Title	Revenue ▼
Description	
Comments	
Value	$3,740,483,119.18
Goal	3740483119.18223
Cube	Operation
Data Connection	http://sp2010-bi/bi%20site/Shared%20Documents/Conto 20Retail%20DW%20
Status Indicator	Revenue
Trend	➡

Excel Web Access - Book1 [1]

Total

- Audio
- TV and Video
- Computers
- Cameras and camcorders

Excel Web Access - Book1 [2]

Calendar YWD	Year 2009	

Row Labels	Sales Amount
⊞ Audio	$68,947,296.35
⊞ TV and Video	$460,183,910.90
⊞ Computers	$1,072,783,640.15

Your result might not match the preceding illustration exactly. For example, toolbars may appear for some Web Parts, so you might want to clean up the overall look-and-feel of your dashboard. You have many ways to do this—for example, you can change the size of the chart in Excel workbook or change the size of the web part using the properties tool pane. You can also use the properties tool panes to disable features you aren't interested in showing, and by dragging Web Parts to different zones on the page, you can clean up the look-and-feel of the page. If you create a rough design for the dashboard ahead of time, you can also choose different templates to get different zone layouts when you create the initial dashboard page.

Add a Visio Web Drawing

Visio Services allows you to embed Visio Web Drawings in other SharePoint pages. Using the Visio Web Access Web Part, you can embed either static or data-driven Visio Web Drawings in SharePoint pages.

The Visio Web Drawing is a new Visio file type (*.vdw) that allows diagrams to be rendered in full fidelity in the browser using Visio Services on SharePoint 2010.

You can easily connect your diagrams to one or more data sources, including Microsoft Excel, SQL Server, and SharePoint Server lists, by using the Data Selector and Automatic Link wizards.

> **Note** Visio 2010 connects to SQL Server Analysis Services only when using the PivotDiagram feature.

You can keep the data in your diagrams up to date by using the Automatic Refresh feature.

In this example, store managers at Contoso are also responsible for the accounting. As part of the workflow, the managers must send their paperwork to the auditor.

To create a Visio diagram

1. Open Visio 2010 Premium, click File, and then click New. The templates categories appear.

2. Under Template Categories, select Flowchart, and then Work Flow Diagram.

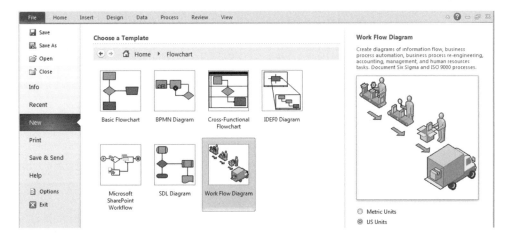

3. Click Create. A blank Visio diagram appears, with the Shapes section on the left.

4. Click Department (US Units) and drag the Accounting shape and then the Auditing shape into the display pane. Now click Arrow Shapes (US Units), and drag an arrow into the center of the display pane, as shown in the following illustration.

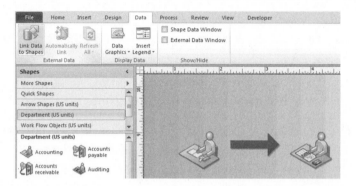

5. On the Data tab, click Link Data To Shapes. Then on the Data Selector page, select Microsoft SQL Server database and click Next.

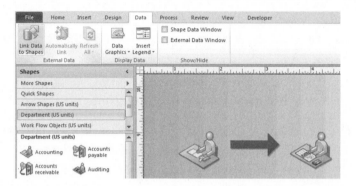

6. On the Connect To Database Server page, in the Server Name field, type **SP2010-BI**. Keep the default credentials (Use Windows Authentication), as shown in the following illustration, and click Next.

7. On the Select Database And Table page, select the ContosoRetailDW database and then select the DimEmployee table, as shown in the following illustration.

8. Click Next, and then click Finish to create an ODC file automatically named SP2010-BI ContosoRetailDW DimEmployee.odc.

Note If you already have an ODC file, a warning message appears, asking whether you want to replace the existing file.

If you want the diagram to auto-refresh in a SharePoint pages, you should select the Always Attempt To Use The File To Refresh Data option shown in the following illustration.

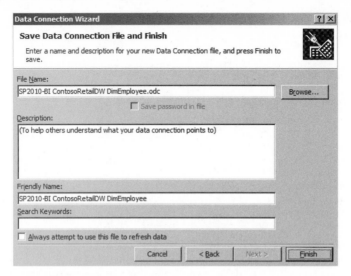

9. Click Next to see the Select Data Connection page, as shown in the following illustration, and then click Next again.

On the Connect To Data page, shown in the following illustration, you can select the data that you want to be available for your data-driven drawings. You can choose from the available columns and rows of Employee dimension data. Your Data Selector should resemble the following illustration after you complete Steps 10 and 11 of this procedure. To learn more about dimension table data, see Chapter 3, "Getting to Trusted Data."

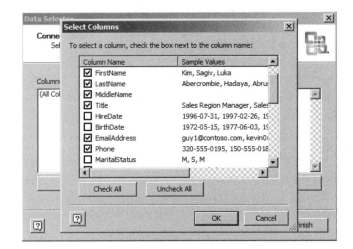

10. Click Select Columns to open the Select Columns dialog box, as shown in the following illustration, click Uncheck All in the dialog box, and then select the following columns:

- ❑ EmployeeKey

- ❑ FirstName

- ❑ LastName

- ❑ Title

- ❑ EmailAddress

- ❑ Phone

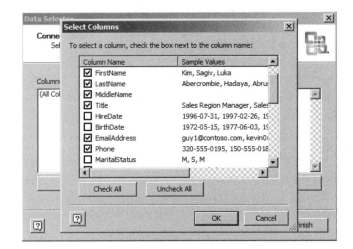

11. On the Connect To Data page, shown in Step 9 of this procedure, click Select Rows and then expand the Title drop-down list. To filter the results of your query, in the Title drop-down list, select Sales Store Manager.

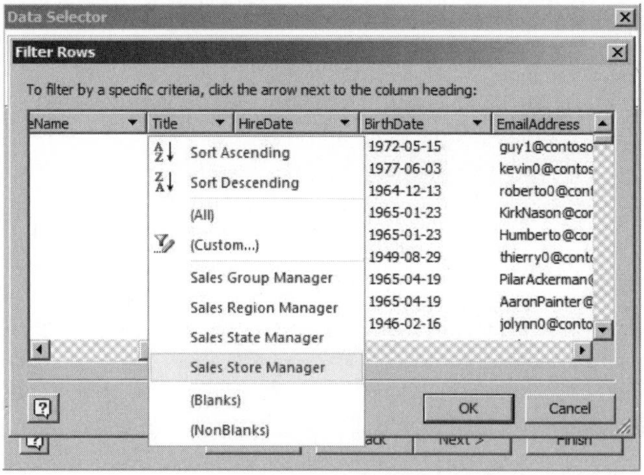

12. Click Next, and then click Finish to close the wizard. An External Data section appears under your Visio drawing, as shown in the following illustration.

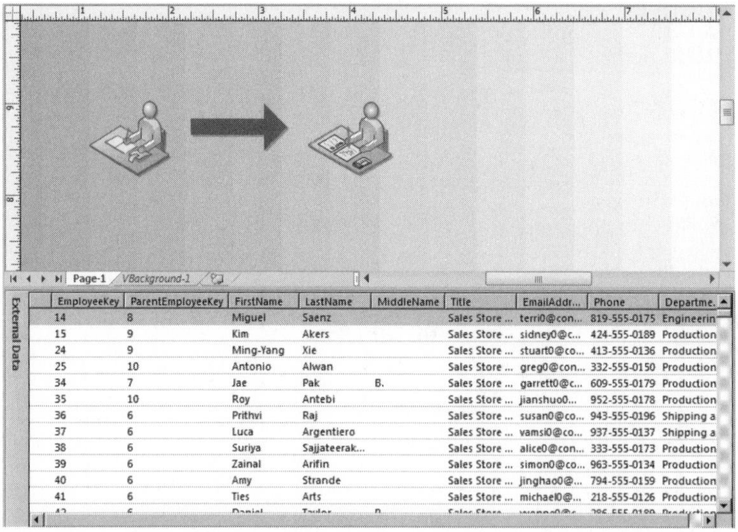

To link data to your diagram

1. Drag the first record (14, Miguel), shown in the preceding illustration, onto the Accounting shape on the left of the diagram. The diagram is now linked or "bound" to data that will refresh and remain current. You have the option to show more data by right-clicking the diagram and selecting Edit Data Graphic.

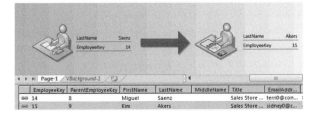

To publish to SharePoint

1. On your Business Intelligence Center site, click Libraries, and then click Create.

> **Note** The Business Intelligence Center is a site collection template that you can cre-
> ate after farm configuration. The Business Intelligence Center provides a good place to
> store all of your business intelligence assets, such as Visio diagrams, Visio Web Drawings,
> PerformancePoint Dashboard elements, and more.

The Create page, shown in the following illustration, opens when you click Create.

2. Double-click the Visio Process Repository. You can now upload the diagram you created previously. Be sure to upload the Visio file you saved as a Visio Web Drawing (.vdw file).

3. Type **AccountingWorkflow** for your title and URL.

4. When the file appears in your Visio Process Repository, expand the AccountingWorkflowGraphic drop-down menu, and select View In Web Browser.

The diagram is now viewable and appears in your browser, as shown in the following illustration.

To embed the Web Drawing as a Web Part

1. On the WebPartPage, click Add A Web Part.

2. As shown in the following illustration, under Categories, select Business Data, select the Visio Web Access Web Part, and then click Add.

An embedded Visio Web Drawing container appears in the Web Part location. You can use this to select your published Visio Web Drawing.

Left Column

Add a Web Part

▣ Visio Web Access ▾ ☐

Select a Web Drawing

To display a Web Drawing in this web part, you must first select the Web Drawing.
To select a Web Drawing, open the tool pane, and then edit the Web Drawing URL web part setting.
Click here to open the tool pane.

How do I connect this web part to a Web Drawing?

3. Click the Click Here To Open The Tool Pane link.

4. In the Web Drawing URL text box, as shown in the following illustration, type the URL for the Web Drawing, or click the Browse icon to navigate to the SharePoint folder where the drawing is located. After the URL is in the input field, click Apply at the bottom of the configuration panel.

◀ **Visio Web Access** ✕

☐ Web Drawing Display

Web Drawing URL

`http://sp2010-bi/sites/VisioRep` ▢

☑ Override the Web Drawing's default initial view using the web part's current page, pan and zoom

☐ Force raster rendering

Automatic Refresh Interval (in minutes)

0

Expose the following shape data items to web part connections

☐ Toolbar and User Interface

☑ Show Refresh

☑ Show Open in Visio

☑ Show Page Navigation

You can now customize the Visio Web Access Web Part with the features below the Web Drawing URL, or you can simply click OK or click Apply to see your Web Drawing embedded in the page.

Add a PerformancePoint Web Part

Because PerformancePoint in 2010 is part of the SharePoint infrastructure, you can share dashboard Web Parts across sites. That means you can create a dashboard from within SharePoint by using PerformancePoint objects that have already been published to SharePoint lists.

> **Important** PerformancePoint Dashboard Designer terminology is a little different from that of SharePoint Designer. In the section "Which Dashboard Tool Should I Use?" earlier in this chapter, we point out where those differences are and try to differentiate clearly between a SharePoint dashboard and a PerformancePoint dashboard.

> **Note** Before you can add a Web Part from an existing PerformancePoint object, such as a scorecard or KPI, you must have already created the objects in PerformancePoint Dashboard Designer.

After you create your dashboard in Dashboard Designer, you can publish your completed PerformancePoint dashboard to your SharePoint Dashboards library. After you publish, all of your dashboard objects are essentially placed within the SharePoint Web Part gallery and are then usable in any way that you want.

> **Note** Although you can create Web Part pages in SharePoint Designer by using SharePoint 2010 filters, you can create connections between PerformancePoint Web Parts only in a browser.

Here's a high level view of the steps you need to follow, based on two possible methods. We assume that you have looked at Chapter 7 and have an understanding of the elements of Dashboard Designer and of PerformancePoint dashboards. The procedure in this section uses a very simple example to show that you can add available PerformancePoint Web Parts to a SharePoint dashboard.

- **Method 1**:
    - ❑ Configure SharePoint.
    - ❑ Configure a PerformancePoint-enabled site.
- **Method 2** Simply create a site collection using the Business Intelligence Center template (on the Enterprise tab).

Let's build a dashboard with PerformancePoint!

To start PerformancePoint Dashboard Designer

1. After running the Farm Configuration wizard to get your service applications running, create a site collection from the Enterprise template tab, and then open the Business Intelligence Center.

2. Navigate to your site collection. You can locate it by going to Central Administration and clicking Application Management and then clicking Site Collection List. Highlight the URL, and paste it into a browser.

3. Click the Start Using PerformancePoint Services link.

4. As shown in the following illustration, on the TeamBI tab of the TeamBI page, click Run Dashboard Designer. Dashboard Designer is a ClickOnce application.

The screen shown in the following illustration appears.

Next, let's create the dashboard.

To create a dashboard

> **Note** The steps in this procedure are intentionally very high level. You can review all these steps in more detail in Chapter 7, "PerformancePoint Services."

1. In Dashboard Designer, create a data source.

2. Create the dashboard items (KPI, scorecard, reports, and filters).

> **Important** Different from a SharePoint filter, in PerformancePoint a filter is a Web Part object, created using Dashboard Designer, that modifies the data presented in a published PerformancePoint dashboard. The available filters include Custom Table (or a tabular data source), MDX Query, Member Selection, Named Set, Time Intelligence, and Time Intelligence Connection Formula. Display filters, such as List, Tree, and Multi-Select Tree, give users intuitive controls to navigate hierarchies and values. To learn more about creating filters in Dashboard Designer, see Chapter 7, "PerformancePoint Services." You can create a PerformancePoint filter "natively" in SharePoint if it was previously created in Dashboard Designer.

3. Assemble the dashboard by adding what you have created in the way of KPIs, scorecards, reports, and filters.

4. Preview, test, and deploy the dashboard.

Next, let's add some Web Parts.

To add Web Parts to the Web Parts page

1. Just as you would in Excel Services and Visio Services, click Add A Web Part on the Web Parts page.

2. Select the PerformancePoint Scorecard Web Part. This is an empty scorecard Web Part from which you can point to the published scorecard. PerformancePoint objects are stored in lists, in a trusted location.

3. Type in the location and click OK. The PerformancePoint Scorecard dialog box should appear in the Web Part, as shown in the preceding illustration.

To complete the dashboard, add some KPIs. You can use the standard connection framework in SharePoint to associate PerformancePoint filters with standard SharePoint Web Parts.

The Web Part Page

As a result of creating the Web Parts without positioning, your page will look like the following image.

You can see how the Web Parts are interactive when published by clicking on Stop Editing in the Page tab. Note in this image that we have selected Denmark to cascade and drill in on the PerformancePoint Scorecard Web Part.

Summary

This chapter looks at some of the basic features that SharePoint includes for creating dashboards and includes step-by-step walkthroughs to help get you started.

Microsoft has many products that can help you achieve great BI. Sometimes you might want to choose one product instead of another—for technical reasons, because of BI maturity, or to meet the comfort level of a particular user. One of the strengths of SharePoint is its ability to store documents related to many BI reports or solutions, and it can also surface BI functionality from many different features and products. So even if your company discovers insights by using different tools or features, you can use SharePoint to bring them together and enjoy the advantage of using them in a single place. In particular, SharePoint dashboards are extremely useful for bringing all the data and insights together into one place.

Quick Reference

To	Do this
Determine if you want to create a dashboard "native" to SharePoint or a PerformancePoint dashboard	See the section "Which Dashboard Tool Should I Use?"
Create a page where you can surface reports, KPIs, and other BI insights side by side—when the initial reporting was created with different features or products	Create a dashboard page in SharePoint. See the section "Dashboard (Web Part) Pages in SharePoint."
Surface Excel-based reporting in a dashboard in SharePoint	Create Excel reports that show the desired BI insights. See the section "Create the Excel Workbook."
	Add and configure Excel Web Access Web Parts on your dashboard page. See the section "Show the Workbook in Web Parts."
View diagrams as part of a larger dashboard BI solution	Add Visio Web Drawings to your dashboard page. See the section "Add a Visio Web Drawing."
Filter an entire dashboard page (including multiple Web Parts on the page) by the same value or set of values	Add a SharePoint Filter to the page, and connect it to the appropriate Web Parts. See the sections "Add the Filter to the Dashboard" and "Configure the Filter."
Add a Visio Web Part to the dashboard	Click Add a Web Part in the WebPartPage and navigate to a VDW file. Click OK. See the "Add a Visio Web Drawing" section in this chapter.
Add a "native" KPI to a SharePoint dashboard page	In general, you can use Excel Services or Performance Point to surface KPIs. The simplest type of KPI is natively part of SharePoint. See the section "Add SharePoint KPIs" in this chapter.
Create a Web Part derived from a PerformancePoint Report or Scorecard	Review the high-level steps for creating a PerformancePoint Web Part in section "Add a PerformancePoint Web Part".

Appendix A
Virtual Machine Setup and SharePoint Configuration

In this appendix, we provide you with the following two options for server setup so that you can use the tools discussed in this book.

Option 1:

- You can download and install the 2010 Information Worker Demonstration and Evaluation Virtual Machine (RTM). The virtual machines (VMs) are already pre-configured for you.

Option 2:

- Follow the guides and relevant links in this appendix to create the VMs from scratch and set up a test configuration. The VMs enable you to work along with the exercises with minimal effort and with minimal impact on your other machines.

- Perform the required SharePoint 2010 installation and configuration procedures. These procedures are essential for you to succeed in following the exercises. This section references resources such as articles and videos to help you get up to speed.

- Perform the necessary security configuration steps. This is essential for connecting to external data. It is also extremely important for securing business intelligence (BI) assets.

Options for Software Installation and Configuration

The authors went back and forth between two viable options for setting up an environment in which you can test the tools. On one hand, you have the option to download a VM onto an existing machine that has Windows 2008 R2 with Hyper-V enabled. On the other hand, you might want to start from scratch by installing Windows 2008 R2, enabling Hyper-V, and creating your own VMs by installing and configuring the available 180-day evaluation software. The benefits and tradeoffs of each method are described in the following table.

	Benefits	Tradeoffs
Preconfigured VM	You get a large variety of software features already installed and configured on one VM.	The size of the VM and number of pre-configured platforms require a robust machine with a minimum of 4 GB of RAM, with 8 GB recommended. The files might take more than an afternoon to download.
	Much simpler and quicker than manually installing and creating your VMs.	Some troubleshooting is required.
Manual setup	You get the IT professional experience and understanding from setting up your own VM, which can prove helpful if you need to set up a development or production environment in the future.	This option requires more research about installing and configuring the software that is needed for each VM, and thus requires more time. You will need to seek out various online resources to find out how others overcame some of the potential blocking issues.
	You have the option of choosing the minimum configuration to test the tools.	You must download and install more software if you want to try out all that the pre-configured VMs have to offer.

In the preconfigured VM, Active Directory has been configured for more than 200 "demo" users with metadata in an organizational structure. All these user profiles have been imported and indexed for search within SharePoint Server 2010 but are not necessary for the exercises in the book.

SharePoint Server 2010 has been configured in a "complete" farm, using Kerberos authentication and the default SQL Server 2008 instance for data, and has a site collection created by using the Team Site template at *http://intranet/* and a FAST Search Center at *http://intranet/ search/*.

You can also create other site collections after you have set up VM "a". To learn more, see Chapter 7, "PerformancePoint Services," which shows you how to create a site collection using the Business Intelligence Center template.

Overview of Hyper-V, for Both Options

For both manual setup and pre-configured setup, you must install Windows Server 2008 R2 and enable the Hyper-V role. It gives you the tools and services to create and manage a VM-based computing environment. You can manage and run multiple VMs on one physical computer using Hyper-V. You can use the available trial version for 180 days.

The computer you choose as the host also matters, because it must have a Hyper-V-capable processor.

Option 1: Set Up a Pre-configured VM

The following is a modified version of the Virtual Machine Setup Guide.docx, which you get when you download the install files.

Download

The download is very large and usually requires some time. We recommend that you use the Akamai Download Manager to download faster; it also can pause and resume if the download is interrupted. Make sure to locate the faster download links at the bottom of the main download page at *http://www.microsoft.com/downloads/en/details. aspx?FamilyID=751fa0d1-356c-4002-9c60-d539896c66ce&displaylang=en.*

Of the files you find on that page, you need the following:

- Virtual Machine 2010-7a parts 1-12

- Virtual Machine 2010-7a parts 13-20, SFV & Setup Guide

- Virtual Machine 2010-7b (needed only if you want to run Exchange Server)

What Comes with the Download and Other Considerations

Everything you need to work through the exercises in this book is included on one VM, except for the exercises in Chapter 3, "Getting to Trusted Data." The download includes an Active Directory domain and CONTSOS.COM with DNS and WINS configured.

Virtual Machine "a"

The 2010-7a VM contains the following pre-configured software:

- Windows Server 2008 R2 Standard Evaluation Edition x64, running as an Active Directory Domain Controller for the "CONTOSO.COM" domain with DNS and WINS

- Microsoft SQL Server 2008 R2 Enterprise Edition with Analysis, Notification, and Reporting Services

- Microsoft Office Communication Server 2007 R2

- Microsoft Visual Studio 2010

- Microsoft SharePoint Server 2010 Enterprise Edition

- Microsoft Office Web Applications

- FAST Search for SharePoint 2010

- Microsoft Project Server 2010

- Microsoft Office Professional Plus 2010

- Microsoft Visio 2010

- Microsoft Project 2010

- Microsoft Office Communicator 2007 R2

(Optional) Virtual Machine "b"

The 2010-7b VM contains the following pre-configured software:

> **Note** VM 2010-7b is optional; it is not required to work through the exercises in the book.

- Windows Server 2008 R2 Standard Evaluation Edition x64, joined to the "CONTOSO. COM" domain

- Microsoft Exchange Server 2010

System Requirements

To install VM "a", you will need the following:

- Supported Operating Systems: Windows Server 2008 R2

- Windows Server 2008 R2 with the Hyper-V role enabled

- Drive Formatting: NTFS

- Processor: Intel VT or AMD-V capable

- RAM: 8 GB or more (more is always nice)

- Hard disk space required for install: 50 GB

Pre-configured VM Setup

The following are steps and considerations as you setup VM "a" for going through the exercise in the book.

Performance Considerations

Unpack and run the VM image on a fast hard drive (7200 RPM or better). This drive will work better if it is different from the drive containing the operating system of the host machine. If you are installing the VM on a laptop, a second internal drive or external eSATA drive works best, although a USB 2.0 (make sure it's 2.0, because 1.1 is too slow) or FireWire connection is acceptable. For the absolute best performance, use a second internal SSD drive.

Host Configuration

You can use the following procedure to configure the VM host.

To prepare the host machine

1. Install the Hyper-V role on your Windows Server 2008 R2 host.

> **Note** Use Windows Server 2008 R2. Older versions of Hyper-V cannot import the VM package, can trigger activation of the software included in the image, and are likely to give you reduced performance.

2. Extract the VM image.

    a. Copy the archive files for the VM to local disk.

    b. Extract the VM image by running the self-extracting executable.

    c. Set the extraction location on a separate drive as suggested in the previous section, "Performance Considerations."

> **Note** Extracting can take some time, depending on your machine's resources.

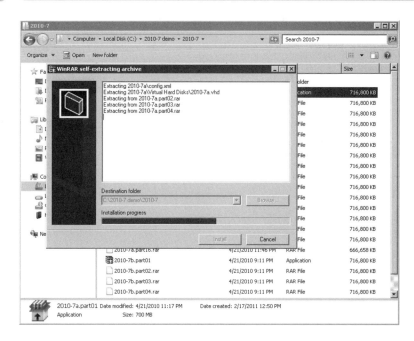

Configure Hyper-V for the VM

You must configure Hyper-V so that it runs in a protected virtual network. This is because the VM does not contain any antivirus software, and items such as MAC addresses, IP addresses, host names, and so on might conflict with other running instances of the VM or with potentially unrelated physical machines. The internal virtual network configuration that you create in the following procedure allows the host machine to access the VM by using Remote Desktop. We recommend that you do not use an external network for this VM.

If you choose to run the VM with external access, set up a second network card (NIC) on the physical machine and configure the Hyper-V to use that NIC. The primary NIC for the host is configured to use a static IP address—and changing this setting will produce server errors. Your external network configuration in Virtual Network Manager might resemble the following illustration.

To configure Hyper-V for the VM

1. Configure the Hyper-V Manager.

2. Start Hyper-V Manager from Control Panel -> Administrative Tools.

3. Confirm that the local host machine appears in the Hyper-V Manager list, and select it if it's not already selected.

4. Under Actions, click Virtual Network Manager.

> **Note** After you perform this step, the VM is configured with a different NIC card.

5. Confirm that you have created an internal virtual network named "Internal." Internal networks limit connectivity to only VMs and the host. If no such network exists, create one now by performing the following steps:

   a. Click Virtual Network Manager in the Actions pane.

   b. Choose New Virtual Network in the Virtual Networks pane.

   c. Choose Internal from the type list, and click Add.

   d. Type **Internal**, and then click OK.

To learn more about the different types of virtual networks, see the blog post, "Hyper-V: What are the uses for different types of virtual networks?" at *http://blogs. technet.com/b/jhoward/archive/2008/06/17/hyper-v-what-are-the-uses-for-different-types-of-virtual-networks.aspx*.

To import and configure the VM

Due to the activation and expiration models in Windows Server 2008 and R2, you should retain a copy of the VMs you downloaded and create a snapshot before you first run the VMs. For more information, see the "Activation and Expiration" section later in this appendix.

1. Under Actions, click Import Virtual Machine.

2. Click Browse to select the folder where you extracted the VM package. Keep the default settings.

3. Click Import, and wait for the import operation to complete—you can see the import status in the Operations column.

4. Select the newly imported VM, and then click Settings in the right pane of the Hyper-V Manager.

5. Confirm (and correct if necessary) that the Network Adapter "VM Bus Network Adapter" is connected to the "Internal" network from Step 5d of the preceding procedure ("To configure Hyper-V for the VM"). Please do not add a new Network Adapter (unless you must add the Internal Network).

6. Close the VM Settings dialog box. The new VM should appear in your Virtual Machines list.

> **Note** The machine we use has 12 GB of memory and an I7 Intel processor, which allows us to run four VMs at a time (the preconfigured VM, 2010-7a, and the two-machine setup we describe later in this appendix. The other machines, 2010-7b and MOSS-BI, are turned off to save on machine resources. Serious performance issues could occur if you have them all running at the same time.

7. Start the virtual image.

8. After the machine starts, log in as Administrator (press Ctrl+Alt+End). The password is **pass@word1**.

If you were unable to import the VM, we suggest that you use the following procedure to create a new VM and restore the 2010-7a.vhd that you extracted.

To restore VM 2010-7a.vhd

1. In Hyper-V Manager, under the Actions pane, click New and then click Virtual Machine to start the New Virtual Machine Wizard.

2. Click Next. On the Specify Name And Location page, shown in the following illustration, determine where you want to store the new virtual machine, and then click Next.

3. In the Assign Memory dialog box, assign 4000 MB, and then click Next.

4. In the Configure Networking dialog box, select Internal if you have already configured it in Network Manager in the Hyper-V Manager. If not, you can change it later in the VM's Settings dialog box in Hyper-V Manager.

5. On the Connect Virtual Hard Disk page, shown in the following illustration, select Use An Existing Virtual Hard Disk. Click Browse to locate the extracted 2010-7a VM, and then click Next.

6. In the Installations Options dialog box, click Next. The 2010-7a VM appears in your Hyper-V Manager under Virtual Machines, as shown in the following illustration. However, notice that it is now shut off.

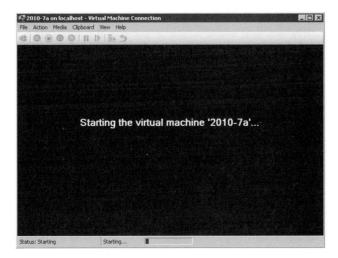

7. Double-click the new VM, and then click the green button to turn on the VM. When it turns on, you should see it starting, as shown in the following illustration.

After you log in as Administrator (password: pass@word1), the installation requires about 10 to 15 minutes to finish the configuration, because it must detect the host hardware and install the appropriate drivers. Then you must reboot the machine. After the machine reboots, use the following procedure to configure the network adapter in the VM (not in the host).

To configure the network adapter

1. Open the Network and Sharing Center in Control Panel.

2. Click Change Adapter Settings.

3. Right-click the adapter and click Properties.

4. Select Internet Protocol Version 4 (TCP/IPv4), and click Properties.

5. Select Use The Following IP Address, and then type the following values:

   ❑ IP Address: **192.168.150.1**

   ❑ Subnet Mask: **255.255.255.0**

   ❑ Default Gateway: (leave blank)

   ❑ Preferred DNS Server: **192.168.150.1**

Your Network and Sharing Center should resemble the following illustration.

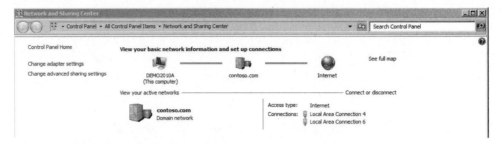

Your Internet Protocol (TCP/IPv4) Properties should resemble the following illustration.

Now the VM is ready to use. Enjoy!

Snapshots and Saved State

Hyper-V introduces the concept of "snapshots," which you can use to revert a VM to a previous configuration state.

To create a snapshot

1. Open or return to the Hyper-V Manager.

2. Select the VM, and under Actions, click Snapshot.

3. Wait for the snapshot captures to complete.

4. (Optional) Select each VM, and rename the snapshots you have just created.

To apply a snapshot

1. Open or return to the Hyper-V Manager.

2. Select the VM, right-click the snapshot you want to use, and choose Apply. You will be prompted to save the current state as a snapshot. Doing so retains your current state, skipping discards it.

Start the VM

Before each VM session, use the following procedure to set up the environment.

To start the 2010-7a VM

1. Return to or start the Hyper-V Manager.

2. Select the VM.

3. Click Start.

4. Click Connect. When the Virtual Machine Connection window appears, wait for the VM to boot up and reach the login screen.

> **Important** The VM Connection uses Ctrl-Alt-Home instead of the normal Ctrl-Alt-Del sequence for login.

Log in to the image using the Virtual Machine Console as the following user:

- ❑ User: **administrator**
- ❑ Password: **pass@word1**
- ❑ Domain: **CONTOSO**

To stop the VM image

1. Click Shut Down from the Virtual Machine Connection or from the Hyper-V.

Activation and Expiration

The VMs contained in this package are inactivated 180-day evaluations. These evaluation copies require activation, or rearming, after a 10-day period; otherwise, they shut down after 2 hours of continuous operation. It is optional to activate the operating system in the VM.

> **Important** Avoid performing the following procedure, unless your initial 10-day evaluation period has expired.

To reset the activation or "rearm" the VM

You can perform the "rearm" procedure only a limited number of times—generally four, but even fewer in some cases. The authors highly recommend that you use one of the options described earlier in this chapter, in the section "Configure Hyper-V for the VM," to avoid being left without a functioning VM.

1. Start up and login to the VM.

2. Open an elevated (Run as Administrator) command prompt.

3. Run "slmgr –rearm" (no quotes) in the command prompt.

4. Wait for the pop-up confirmation that the configuration changes are complete.

5. Reboot the VM.

6. Repeat for each Windows Server 2008 R2 VM in the set.

To activate the VM, you need an Internet connection. For that, you must add a second NIC to the VM by using the Hyper-V Management Console, and then connect it to an external network connection that has Internet access. You can then activate Windows from within the VM. Windows still expires after 180 days but does not prompt for activation or shut down after 2 hours.

Post-Setup Performance Tweaks

This section provides procedures you can perform for the host machine that can help you get best performance.

To restore the Microsoft Contoso BI Demo Dataset for Retail Industry

1. Go to the download Link to see instructions at the bottom of the page: *http://www.microsoft.com/downloads/en/details.aspx?displaylang=en&FamilyID=868662 dc-187a-4a85-b611-b7df7dc909fc.*

2. The Contoso_Retail.abf and Contoso_RetailDW.bak are located on the VM demo2010a C: drive.

To defragment all host drives

1. Open Windows Explorer, right-click the C: drive icon, and click Properties.

2. On the Tools tab, click Defragment Now.

3. Confirm that the C: drive is the selected volume, and then click Defragment.

4. Wait for the defragmentation to complete. This can take anywhere from a few seconds to a few hours, depending on the size of the drive and how fragmented it is. You might need to run this multiple times for full effect.

5. Repeat for all other host hard drives.

To set the host video resolution

1. Right-click the desktop, select Properties, and then select Settings.

2. Confirm that the resolution is at least 1024 × 768 (the minimum recommended resolution is 1280 × 1024) and that the color depth is at least 16-bit.

3. Open the Control Panel and select Date And Time.

4. Confirm that the date and time are accurate; if they're not, correct them.

To disable virus scanning

Follow the procedures for your antivirus software to disable any "real-time" scanning of the Hyper-V processes and the folder where you unpacked the VM files. For more details, see the support information at *http://support.microsoft.com/kb/961804*.

To convert the VM's dynamic Virtual Hard Drive (VHD) to a static VHD

If you have sufficient drive space, consider performing this conversion procedure. The fixed VHD is considerably larger—135 GB—but provides better performance.

1. Open the Hyper-V Manager on the host. Select the VM in the Virtual Machines pane.

2. Click Settings in the Actions pane.

3. Choose the Hard Drive under IDE Controller 0 in the Hardware pane.

4. Directly below the path of the VHD file, click Edit.

5. Choose the Convert option, and then click Next.

6. Supply a file path and name for the new fixed disk.

7. Click Finish, and wait for the edit operation to complete.

8. Click Browse to navigate to the VHD file, and choose the fixed VHD you just created.

9. Click OK to apply the change, and then close the settings window.

10. Defragment the host drive containing the new fixed VHD.

Option 2: Set Up Your Own VMs on Windows 2008 R2

Rather than install Windows 2008 R2, provision it for Hyper-V, and create a machine to import the 2010-7a VM, you have another option. This section describes that second option, which is to create an environment from scratch so that you can perform the exercises in this book. Because it would be all too easy to write another entire book about installing and configuring all of the software you need, this section provides only an overview of how to set up a particular architecture and configuration so that you can apply the BI tools introduced in the chapters in this book.

Architecture for Server Configuration

The following illustration shows what software is installed on what machines for the configuration the authors used while writing this book. To ensure that our configuration could be duplicated by readers, we used 180-day trial versions for all software.

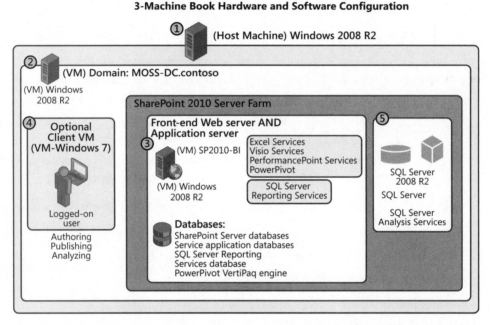

3-Machine Book Hardware and Software Configuration

The numbered items in the following list correspond to the circled areas in the image:

1. *Host machine*: Your host machine is the machine on which you need to install Windows Server 2008 R2, either by using a physical DVD or installing and learning to use ISO image software.

2. *VM (or guest machine)*, MOSS-DC.contoso: Contains your Active Directory domain structure, in which you need to create user accounts for your SharePoint, SQL Server roles, and client roles, such as the Unattended Service account and SharePoint Admin account. This machine becomes your domain, and it will probably need a physical IP address. You will join the other VMs to the domain.

3. *Second VM (or guest machine)*, SP2010-BI: Includes Windows Server 2008 R2 + SQL Server 2008 R2 + SharePoint 2010, in that order. Note that the databases for your SharePoint Server are different from those used as data sources in the exercises. Some people separate the two by creating a separate instance for their data sources. Another option is to use a different VM or a separate machine, as described in item 5 of this list. See the section "Install Software on Your VMs," later in this appendix, for installation files.

4. *(Optional) Third VM*: To truly test the user accounts and security of your configuration, it is a good idea to create a VM that can play the role of the client in test environment. On this VM, install Windows 7 and Office 2010.

> **Note** If you want to get serious about testing security configurations such as Kerberos or NTLM, you should consider taking installation and configuration to the next level by creating another VM to host the data sources, SQL Server and 2008 R2 Analysis Services. Because memory resources are typically scarce after running three VMs on a physical host machine, you might consider adding another physical computer to your configuration that you can allocate to Analysis Services data sources. The configuration options available depend on the resources you have, such as memory and processor speed.

Select a Host Computer with Windows 2008 R2

The computer you choose as the host matters, because it must have a Hyper-V capable processor. In addition, you need enough processing power and memory to run the VMs. You might also need to enable Hyper-V for your processor in the system BIOS to make virtualization possible.

The first step is to locate the right processor. If you already have a computer, check to see whether the processor is listed in the Hardware section of the Windows Server catalog at *http://go.microsoft.com/fwlink/?LinkId=111228*. To see the list of servers that have been tested to run Hyper-V, in the Hardware section of the Windows Server catalog, under Product category, click Servers, and then under Additional Qualifications, click Hyper-V.

You can also review the more comprehensive documentation for Hyper-V by reading the TechNet topic "Hyper-V Getting Started Guide," at *http://technet.microsoft.com/en-us/library/cc732470(WS.10).aspx*.

Install and Configure Windows 2008 R2 for Hyper-V

This section simply points you to useful links containing instructions for installing Windows 2008 R2 and configuring your server for Hyper-V.

Install Windows 2008 R2 on Your Physical Host Machine

For detailed information about this process, see the TechNet topic "Installing Windows Server 2008 R2," at *http://technet.microsoft.com/en-us/library/dd379511(WS.10).aspx*.

Configure Hyper-V

Following are the basic steps to perform as you navigate through the Hyper-V documentation on TechNet (at *http://technet.microsoft.com/en-us/library/cc730764.aspx*) or as you view instructions from a blog or video:

- Create VMs. We created two for our configuration.
- Create VHDs. We used fixed VHDs.
- Configure Hyper-V:
    - Configure memory and processors.
    - Configure networking.
    - Configure disks and storage.
- Install a guest operating system.
- Connect to a VM.

It's also helpful to view the document titled "Checklist: Configure Virtual Machines for Development and Test," at *http://technet.microsoft.com/en-us/library/cc754062.aspx*.

Re-configure Your Virtual Networks

After installing updates, we switched our external network to a private network to protect it from security attacks and to simplify security between machines.

The TechNet article "Manage Virtual Networks" at *http://technet.microsoft.com/en-us/library/cc732197.aspx*, is particularly helpful.

Additionally, the blog post "Hyper-V: What are the uses for different types of virtual networks?", at *http://blogs.technet.com/b/jhoward/archive/2008/06/17/hyper-v-what-are-the-uses-for-different-types-of-virtual-networks.aspx*, provides a visual explanation of the purpose of the optional virtual network configuration.

Install Software on Your VMs

You should plan to install the following software on your VMs.

Server software	Download link
Windows 2008 R2 You can also download the VHD Windows Server 2008 R2 Enterprise and Server Core evaluation images, configured for Hyper-V (64-bit only).	*http://www.microsoft.com/windowsserver2008/en/us/ trial-software.aspx*
SQL Server 2008 R2 You can download 64-bit versions for AMD or Intel.	*http://www.microsoft.com/sqlserver/2008/en/us/R2Downloads. aspx* Server Software: Microsoft Contoso BI Demo Dataset for Retail Industry Download Link: *http://www.microsoft.com/downloads/en/ details.aspx?displaylang=en&FamilyID=868662dc-187a-4a85- b611-b7df7dc909fc*
SharePoint Server 2010 Enterprise	*http://technet.microsoft.com/en-us/evalcenter/ee388573.aspx*
Microsoft Office Professional 2010	*http://office.microsoft.com/en-us/try*
Microsoft Visio 2010 (Premium)	*http://technet.microsoft.com/en-us/evalcenter/ee390821.aspx*

Install Windows 2008 R2 on Your VMs

The authors recommend that you purchase and install mounting software so that you can mount ISO images from which to install when you connect and start your newly created VMs. You cannot access installation files easily from the host machine unless you install the mounting software.

Install SQL Server 2008 R2

For detailed information about this process, see the MSDN topic "How to Install SQL Server 2008 R2," at *http://msdn.microsoft.com/en-us/library/ms143219.aspx*.

Install SharePoint Server 2010

For detailed information about this process, see the topic "How to Install SharePoint Server 2010 on a Small Farm," on the ES2010 site at *http://www.endusersharepoint.com/ EUSP2010/2010/06/09/how-to-install-sharepoint-2010-on-small-farm-part-1-full-installation- on-small-farm-up-to-managing-service-applications/*.

SharePoint 2010 Installation and Configuration

Install SharePoint Server 2010

You must install SharePoint Server 2010. For helpful information about how to do this, visit the video library at *http://go.microsoft.com/fwlink/?LinkId=187074*. The author of this video guide, Asif Rehmani, is a SharePoint MVP, MCT, and is president of SharePoint-Videos.com. Also view the TechNet SharePoint Server deployment topic "Deployment for SharePoint Server 2010," at *http://technet.microsoft.com/en-us/library/cc262957.aspx*.

Configure SharePoint Server 2010

After installing Microsoft SharePoint Server 2010, you must perform an initial configuration. We encourage you to run the Configuration Wizard to complete the exercises in this book. You must perform some additional security configurations to connect to external data sources. These additional requirements are discussed in the next section, "Security for the Services Dedicated to BI."

The following is a list of the necessary service applications that are started for you when you run the SharePoint Configuration Wizard and accept all the defaults:

> **Note** Additional considerations apply for configuration with PowerPivot.

- PerformancePoint Services
- Visio Services service application and proxy
- Secure Store Service application and proxy (previously known as Single Store Sign on)
- Excel Services (if you want to connect Visio diagrams to Excel workbooks)

It doesn't hurt to check to ensure that these required service applications are started. Central Administration provides a web-based user interface that enables you to configure all the service settings for Visio Services.

> **Note** You can use Windows PowerShell to accomplish all the following tasks if you prefer a scripting environment.

To view service applications in Central Administration

1. In Central Administration, under Application Management, select Manage Service Applications.

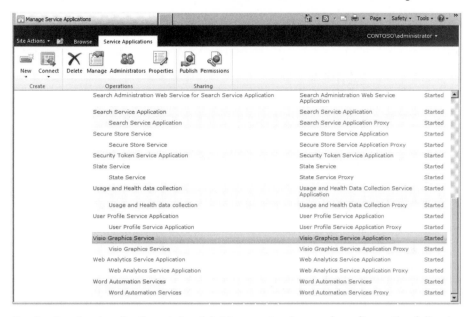

2. On the Service Applications tab, click Manage to view and configure the following:

   ❑ **Global Settings**   Use to manage settings for performance, security, and refreshing data connections.

> **Note** At the bottom of the Global Settings window, you set the target application ID, which is used to reference the Unattended Service Account credentials. This is required for connecting to external data sources external to your SharePoint farm.

   ❑ **Trusted Data Providers**   Use this feature to add or remove data providers for refreshing data connections. The list is extensive and includes providers for Oracle, IBM DB2, SQL Server, and more.

To list running service applications with Windows PowerShell

1. On the Start menu, click All Programs.

2. Click Microsoft SharePoint 2010 Products.

3. Click SharePoint 2010 Management Shell.

4. From the Windows PowerShell command prompt (that is, PS C:\>), type the following command and then press Enter:

```
PS C:/>Get-SPVisioServiceApplication
```

Security for the Services Dedicated to BI

You must be able to connect to external data sources. The following sections include helpful links and some instructions to make sure you can successfully walk through the exercises provided in this book.

Different Names

You configure security for Excel, Visio, and PerformancePoint Services differently for each product. The language used for authentication methods may be specific to each service application. Refer to the TechNet article "Configure a SharePoint Server 2010 farm for business intelligence by using NTLM," at *http://technet.microsoft.com/en-us/library/gg266385.aspx*.

Excel and Visio Services

The following videos can help you configure your SQL Server account, which will be used as the Unattended Service Account while you use the Secure Store Service (SSS) application. They will also help you configure Excel Services and Visio Services security using the SSS. To download a copy of the video file, right-click the link and then click Save Target As.

- To configure a Secure Store target application: Watch the video at *http://go.microsoft.com/fwlink/?LinkId=207410*.

> **Note** The preceding video also has a valuable piece in the beginning that shows you how you must first create an identity in SQL Server 2008 R2.

- To configure a target application for the Unattended Service Account: Watch the video at *http://go.microsoft.com/fwlink/?LinkId=207411*.

- To configure Excel Services: Watch the video at *http://go.microsoft.com/fwlink/?LinkId=207412*.

- To configure Visio Services: Watch the video at *http://go.microsoft.com/fwlink/?LinkId=207413*.

For more information, see the following TechNet topics:

- "Configure Excel and Excel Services with SQL Server Analysis Services (SharePoint Server 2010)" (*http://technet.microsoft.com/en-us/library/ff729457.aspx*)

- "Use Secure Store with SQL Server Authentication (SharePoint Server 2010)" (*http://technet.microsoft.com/en-us/library/gg298949.aspx*)

Configure the .odc file

When you have a local .odc file on your computer and you want to publish a Visio 2010 or Excel 2010 file to SharePoint 2010, you must upload the .odc file to the SharePoint Server. You can do this by modifying the file.

For this example, the following procedure was performed using Excel 2010.

> **Note** Although you can create a reusable .odc file in Visio 2010 by using the data connection wizard, it is a common practice to create and modify the file in Excel 2010, to make it available to both Excel and Visio in SharePoint.

To publish an existing Office Data Connection file (.odc) to SharePoint

1. Open the Excel file connected to the data source that you want to publish to SharePoint. Click Data, and then select Refresh All.

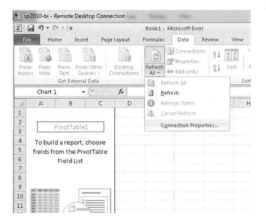

2. Select Connection Properties to open the Connection Properties dialog box.

3. In the Connection Properties dialog box, on the Definition tab, click Export Connection File. If you have enabled the Desktop Experience Feature, you can copy and paste the URL where your Data Connections Web Part resides, or you can enter the location of your trusted data connection library. After you paste the URL, you should see the URL in the connection name at the top of your Connections Properties dialog box.

4. Click Export again.

5. Your .odc file is now located on the SharePoint Server, so users can click to connect to external data from any browser where permissions are granted.

To learn more about .odc files and external data connections, see the TechNet topic "Plan External Data Connections for Excel Services," at *http://technet.microsoft.com/en-us/library/cc262899(office.12).aspx*.

Note You can also embed a SQL Server login information for authentication. Consider the scenarios where you might incorporate this method instead of using an .odc file that is published to SharePoint for shared, but limited access.

PerformancePoint Services

Create and configure a Secure Store Service application and proxy. This is required for storing the Unattended Service Account password for a PerformancePoint Services service application.

To initialize the Secure Store Service application, refer to the following sections of the TechNet topic "Configure the Secure Store Service (SharePoint Server 2010)," at *http://tech-net.microsoft.com/en-us/library/ee806866.aspx*:

- "Initialize an instance of a Secure Store Service application"
- "Refresh the encryption key"

Finally, see the TechNet topic "Configure the Unattended Service Account for PerformancePoint Services," at *http://technet.microsoft.com/en-us/library/ee836145.aspx*.

Resources for Configuring Security

Resources that you might find useful when configuring security include:

- "Configure a SharePoint Server 2010 farm for business intelligence by using NTLM" (*http://technet.microsoft.com/en-us/library/gg266385.aspx*)
- "Configuring Kerberos Authentication for Microsoft SharePoint 2010 Products" (*http://www.microsoft.com/downloads/en/confirmation. aspx?FamilyID=1a794fb5-77d0-475c-8738-ea04d3de1147&displaylang=en*)

The Kerberos authentication topic is a comprehensive guide that walks you through the process of setting up Kerberos for the BI tools discussed in this book—and more—providing scenarios, configuration, and server setup guidance.

Conclusion

The information in this appendix should help you get started with the demos in each chapter. The options are personal preference. Some of the authors have always started from the ground up to install all of the software in a new VM. Other authors have benefited from the pre-configured VM and saved valuable time. In this appendix, we cover both for your benefit so that you can choose the method you prefer. We encourage you to try both and see which is most useful.

Appendix B
DAX Function Reference

This appendix lists the functions currently available in DAX.

Date and Time Functions

The basic date and time functions available in PowerPivot mainly operate as converters between text and datetime types. Also, other "time intelligence" functions are specific to PowerPivot and are covered in the subsection "Time Intelligence Functions" later in this appendix.

Function	Description
DATE(<year>, <month>, <day>)	Returns the specified date in datetime format.
DATEVALUE(date_text)	Converts a date in the form of text to a date in datetime format.
DAY(<date>)	Returns the day of the month, a number from 1 to 31.
EDATE(<start_date>, <months>)	Returns the date that is the indicated number of months before or after the start date. Use EDATE to calculate maturity dates or due dates that fall on the same day of the month as the date of issue.
EOMONTH(<start_date>, <months>)	Returns the date in datetime format of the last day of the month, before or after a specified number of months. Use EOMONTH to calculate maturity dates or due dates that fall on the last day of the month.
HOUR(<datetime>)	Returns the hour as a number from 0 (12:00 A.M.) to 23 (11:00 P.M.).
MINUTE(<datetime>)	Returns the minute as a number from 0 to 59, given a date and time value.
MONTH(<datetime>)	Returns the month as a number from 1 (January) to 12 (December).
NOW()	Returns the current date and time in datetime format.
SECOND(<time>)	Returns the seconds of a time value, as a number from 0 to 59.
TIME(hour, minute, second)	Converts hours, minutes, and seconds given as numbers to a time in datetime format.
TIMEVALUE(time_text)	Converts a time in text format to a time in datetime format.
TODAY()	Returns the current date.

Function	Description
WEEKDAY(<date>, <return_type>)	Returns a number from 1 to 7 identifying the day of the week of a date. By default, the day ranges from 1 (Sunday) to 7 (Saturday).
WEEKNUM(<date>, <return_type>)	Returns the week number for the given date and year according to the specified convention. The week number indicates where the week falls numerically within a year.
YEAR(<date>)	Returns the year of a date as a four digit integer in the range 1900-9999.
YEARFRAC(<start_date>, <end_date>, <basis>)	Calculates the fraction of the year represented by the number of whole days between two dates. Use the YEARFRAC worksheet function to identify the proportion of a whole year's benefits or obligations to assign to a specific term.

Information Functions

Information functions are used to analyze the type of an expression. They all return a TRUE or FALSE value and can be used in any logical expressions.

Function	Description
ISBLANK(<value>)	Checks whether a value is blank, and returns TRUE or FALSE.
ISERROR(<value>)	Checks whether a value is an error, and returns TRUE or FALSE.
ISLOGICAL(<value>)	Checks whether a value is a logical value, and returns TRUE or FALSE.
ISNONTEXT(<value>)	Checks whether a value is not text (blank cells are not text), and returns TRUE or FALSE.
ISNUMBER(<value>)	Checks whether a value is a number, and returns TRUE or FALSE.
ISTEXT(<value>)	Checks whether a value is text, and returns TRUE or FALSE.

Filter and Value Functions

Filter and Value functions are used to evaluate and manipulate the context.

Function	Description
ALL(<table_or_column>)	Returns all the rows in a table or all the values in a column, ignoring any filters that might have been applied.
ALLEXCEPT(<table>,column1>,<column2>,...)	Overrides all context filters in the table except filters that have been applied to the specified columns.
BLANK()	Returns a blank.

Function	Description
CALCULATE(<expression>,<filter1>,<filter2>...)	Evaluates an expression in a context modified by the specified filters.
CALCULATETABLE(<expression>, <filter1>, <filter2>,...)	Evaluates a table expression in a context modified by filters.
DISTINCT(<column>)	Returns a one-column table that contains the distinct values from the specified column.
EARLIER(<column>, <number>)	Returns the current value of the specified column in an outer evaluation pass of the mentioned column.
EARLIEST(<table_or_column>)	Returns the current value of the specified column in an outer evaluation pass of the mentioned column.
FILTER(<table>,<filter>)	Returns a table that represents a subset of another table or expression.
RELATED(<column>)	Returns a related value from another table.
RELATEDTABLE(<table>)	Follows an existing relationship, in either direction and returns a table that contains all matching rows from the specified table.
VALUES(<column>)	Returns a one-column table that contains the distinct values from the specified column. This function is similar to the DISTINCT function, but the VALUES function can also return an Unknown member.
ALLNONBLANKROW(?)	In a table or column, returns all the rows except for blank rows and disregards any context filters that might exist.
FIRSTNONBLANK(<column>,<expression>)	Returns the first non-blank values in a column, filtered by expression.

Logical Functions

Logical functions return a TRUE or FALSE value and are used to implement logical conditions in a DAX expression.

Function	Description
AND(<logical1>,<logical2>,...)	Checks whether all arguments are TRUE, and returns TRUE if all arguments are TRUE.
FALSE()	Returns the logical value FALSE.
IF(logical_test>,<value_if_true>, value_if_false)	Checks whether a condition provided as the first argument is met. Returns one value if the condition is TRUE, and returns another value if the condition is FALSE.

Function	Description
IFERROR(value, value_if_error)	Returns value_if_error if the first expression is an error. Otherwise, the function returns the value of the expression itself.
NOT(<logical>)	Changes FALSE to TRUE, or TRUE to FALSE.
TRUE()	Returns the logical value TRUE.
OR(<logical1>,<logical2>,...)	Checks whether one of the arguments is TRUE to return TRUE. The function returns FALSE if all arguments are FALSE.

Math and Trig Functions

The following mathematical and trigonometric functions are available in DAX.

Function	Description
ABS(<number>)	Returns the absolute value of a number.
CEILING(<number>, <significance>)	Rounds a number up to the nearest integer or to the nearest multiple of significance.
EXP(<number>)	Returns e raised to the power of a given number. The constant e equals 2.71828182845904, the base of the natural logarithm.
FACT(<number>)	Returns the factorial of a number, equal to the series 1*2*3*...*, ending in the given number.
FLOOR(<number>, <significance>)	Rounds a number down, toward zero, to the nearest multiple of significance.
INT(<number>)	Rounds a number down to the nearest integer.
LN(<number>)	Returns the natural logarithm of a number. Natural logarithms are based on the constant e (2.71828182845904).
LOG(<number>,<base>)	Returns the logarithm of a number to the base you specify.
LOG10(<number>)	Returns the base-10 logarithm of a number.
MOD(<number>, <divisor>)	Returns the remainder after a number is divided by a divisor. The result always has the same sign as the divisor.
MROUND(<number>, <multiple>)	Returns a number rounded to the desired multiple.
PI()	Returns the value of pi, 3.14159265358979, accurate to 15 digits.
POWER(<number>, <power>)	Returns the result of a number raised to a power.
QUOTIENT(<numerator>, <denominator>)	Performs division and returns only the integer portion of the division result. Use this function when you want to discard the fractional remainder of a division operation.

Function	Description
ROUND(<number>, <num_digits>)	Rounds a number to the specified number of digits.
ROUNDDOWN(<number>, <num_digits>)	Rounds a number down, toward zero.
ROUNDUP(<number>, <num_digits>)	Rounds a number up, away from zero.
SIGN(<number>)	Determines the sign of a number, the result of a calculation, or a value in a column. The function returns 1 if the number is positive, 0 (zero) if the number is zero, or -1 if the number is negative.
SQRT(<number>)	Returns the square root of a number.
TRUNC(<number>,<num_digits>)	Truncates a number to an integer by removing the decimal, or fractional, part of the number.
[vb] RAND()	Returns a random number greater than or equal to 0 and less than 1, evenly distributed. The number that is returned changes each time the cell containing this function is recalculated.
[vb] RANDBETWEEN(<bottom>,<top>)	Returns a random number between the numbers you specify.

Statistical Functions

Statistical functions aggregate data that returns a scalar value. Usually these functions operate on all rows of the table that contains the specified column. This column has to be a numeric or date type.

Function	Description
AVERAGE(<column>)	Returns the average (arithmetic mean) of all the numbers in a column.
AVERAGEA(<column>)	Returns the average (arithmetic mean) of the values in a column. Handles text and non-numeric values.
AVERAGEX(<table>, <expression>)	Calculates the average (arithmetic mean) of a set of expressions evaluated over a table.
COUNT(<column>)	Counts the number of cells in a column that contain numbers.
COUNTA(<column>)	Counts the number of cells in a column that are not empty.
COUNTAX(<table>, <expression>)	Counts nonblank results when evaluating the result of an expression over a table.
COUNTBLANK(<column>)	Counts the number of blank cells in a column.
COUNTROWS(<table>)	Counts the number of rows in the specified table or in a table defined by an expression.

Function	Description
COUNTX(<table>, <expression>)	Counts the number of rows that contain a number or an expression that evaluates to a number, when evaluating an expression over a table.
MAX(<column>)	Returns the largest numeric value in a column.
MAXA(<column>)	Returns the largest value in a column. Logical values and blanks are counted.
MAXX(<table>, <expression>)	Evaluates an expression for each row of a table and returns the largest numeric value.
MIN(<column>)	Returns the smallest numeric value in a column. Ignores logical values and text.
MINA(<column>)	Returns the smallest value in a column, including any logical values and numbers represented as text.
MINX(<table>, < expression>)	Returns the smallest numeric value that results from evaluating an expression for each row of a table.
SUM(<column>)	Adds all the numbers in a column.
SUMX(<table>, <expression>)	Returns the sum of an expression evaluated for each row in a table.

Text Functions

The following functions for evaluating and handling text strings are available in DAX.

Function	Description
CODE(<text>)	Returns a numeric code for the first character in a text string, in the character set used by your computer.
CONCATENATE(<text1>, <text2>,...)	Joins multiple text strings into one text string. The joined items can be text, numbers, or Boolean values represented as text, or a combination of those items. You can also use a column reference if the column contains appropriate values.
EXACT(<text1>,<text2>)	Compares two text strings and returns TRUE if they are exactly the same, and returns FALSE otherwise. EXACT is case-sensitive but ignores formatting differences. You can use EXACT to test text that is entered into a document.

Function	Description
FIND(<find_text, within_text, start_num)	Returns the starting position of one text string within another text string. FIND is case-sensitive.
FIXED(<number>, <decimals>, <no_commas>)	Rounds a number to the specified number of decimals and returns the result as text. You can specify that the result be returned with or without commas.
LEFT(<text>, <num_chars>)	Returns the specified number of characters from the start of a text string.
LEN(<text>)	Returns the number of characters in a text string.
LOWER(<text>)	Converts all letters in a text string to lowercase.
MID(<text>, <start_num>, <num_chars>)	Returns a string of characters from the middle of a text string, given a starting position and length.
REPLACE(<old_text>, <start_num>, <num_chars>, <new_text>)	Replaces part of a text string, based on the number of characters you specify, with a different text string.
REPT(<text>, <num_times>)	Repeats text a given number of times. Use REPT to fill a cell with a number of instances of a text string.
RIGHT(<text>, <num_chars>)	Returns the last character or characters in a text string, based on the number of characters you specify.
SEARCH(<search_text>, <within_text>, [start_num])	Returns the number of the character at which a specific character or text string is first found, reading left to right. SEARCH is case-sensitive.
SUBSTITUTE(<text>, <old_text>, <new_text>, <instance_num>)	Replaces existing text with new text in a text string.
TRIM(<text>)	Removes all spaces from text except for single spaces between words.
UPPER (<text>)	Converts a text string to all uppercase letters.
VALUE(<text>)	Converts a text string that represents a number to a number.
FORMAT(<value>, <format_string>)	Converts a value to text according to the specified format.

Time Intelligence Functions

The Time Intelligence functions perform complex operations on dates, such as comparing aggregated values year over year or calculating the year-to-date value of a measure.

Function	Description
CLOSINGBALANCEMONTH (<expression>, <dates>, <filter>)	Evaluates the specified expression at the calendar-date end of the given month. The given month is calculated as the month of the latest date in the dates argument, after applying all filters.
CLOSINGBALANCEQUARTER (<expression>, <dates>, <filter>)	Evaluates the specified expression at the calendar-date end of the given quarter. The given quarter is calculated as the quarter of the latest date in the dates argument, after applying all filters.
CLOSINGBALANCEYEAR (<expression>,<dates>,<filter>)	Evaluates the specified expression at the calendar-date end of the given year. The given year is calculated as the year of the latest date in the dates argument, after applying all filters.
DATESINPERIOD (<date_column>, <start_date>, <number_of_intervals>, <intervals>)	Returns a table of dates that can be found in the specified date column, beginning with the start date and continuing for the specified number of intervals.
DATESBETWEEN (<column>, <start_date>, <end_date>	Returns a table of dates that can be found in the specified date column, beginning with the start date and ending with the end date.
DATEADD (<date_column>, <number_of_intervals>, <interval>)	Returns a table that contains a column of dates, shifted either forward in time or back in time from the dates in the specified date column.
FIRSTDATE (<datecolumn>)	Returns the first date in the current context for the specified date column.
LASTDATE (<datecolumn>)	Returns the last date in the current context for the specified date column.
LASTNONBLANK (<datecolumn>, <expression>)	Returns the last value in the column, filtered by the current context, where the expression is not blank.
STARTOFMONTH (<date_column>)	Returns the first day of the month in the specified date column.
STARTOFQUARTER (<date_column>)	Returns the first day of the quarter in the specified date column.
STARTOFYEAR (<date_column>[,<YE_date>])	Returns the first day of the year in the specified date column.
ENDOFMONTH(<date_column>)	Returns the last day of the month in the specified date column.

Function	Description
ENDOFQUARTER(<date_column>)	Returns the last day of the quarter in the specified date column.
ENDOFYEAR(<date_column>)	Returns the last day of the year in the specified date column.
PARALLELPERIOD(<date_column>, <number_of_intervals>,<intervals>)	Moves the specified number of intervals and then returns all contiguous full months that contain any values after that shift. Gaps between the first and last dates are filled in, and months are also filled in.
PREVIOUSDAY(<date_column>)	Returns the previous day date from the date column.
PREVIOUSMONTH(<date_column>)	Returns the set of dates in the previous month from the date column.
PREVIOUSQUARTER(<date_column>)	Returns the set of dates in the previous quarter from the date column.
PREVIOUSYEAR(<date_column>)	Returns the set of dates in the previous year from the date column.
NEXTDAY(<date_column>)	Returns the next day date from the date column.
NEXTMONTH(<date_column>)	Returns the set of dates in the next month from the date column.
NEXTQUARTER (<date_column>)	Returns the set of dates for the next quarter from the date column.
NEXTYEAR (<date_column> [,<YE_date>])	Returns the set of dates for the next year from the date column.
DATESMTD(<date_column>)	Returns the subset of dates from the date column for the interval that starts at the first day of the month and ends at the latest date in the specified dates column, for the month that is the corresponding month of the latest date.
DATESQTD (<date_column>)	Returns the subset of dates from the date column for the interval that starts at the first day of the quarter and ends at the latest date in the specified dates column, for the quarter that is the corresponding quarter of the latest date.
DATESYTD (<date_column> [,<YE_date>])	Returns the subset of dates from the date column for the interval that starts the first day of the year and ends at the latest date in the specified dates column for the year to date.
SAMEPERIODLASTYEAR (<dates>)	Returns a table that contains a column of dates shifted one year back in time from the dates in the specified dates column, in the current context.

Function	Description
OPENINGBALANCEMONTH (<expression>, <dates>,<filter>)	Evaluates the specified expression at the calendar-date end of the month prior the given month. The given month is calculated as the month of the latest date in the dates argument, after applying all filters.
OPENINGBALANCEQUARTER (<expression>,<dates>,<filter>)	Evaluates the specified expression at the calendar-date end of the quarter prior to the given quarter. The given quarter is calculated as the quarter of the latest date in the dates argument, after applying all filters.
OPENINGBALANCEYEAR (<expression>,<dates>,<filter>)	Evaluates the specified expression at the calendar-date end of the year prior to the given year. The given year is calculated as the year of the latest date in the dates argument, after applying all filters.
TotalMTD (<expression>,<dates>,<filter>)	Evaluates the specified expression for the interval that starts at the first day of the month and ends at the latest date in the specified dates column, after applying all filters.
TotalQTD (<expression>,<dates>,<filter>)	Evaluates the specified expression for the interval that starts at the first day of the quarter and ends at the latest date in the specified dates column, after applying all filters.
TotalYTD (<expression>,<dates>,<filter>)	Evaluates the specified expression for the interval that starts at the first day of the year and ends at the latest date in the specified dates column, after applying all filters.

Appendix C
SharePoint As a Service—"Office 365"

If you have ever wanted to use SharePoint in your organization but have been afraid that you don't have the IT knowledge, budget, or expertise to install, manage, and maintain the machines or software, this appendix is for you. This appendix explains how Microsoft allows disparate businesses—from the smallest one-person home office to the largest enterprises—to get the benefits of SharePoint without needing to know how to install, manage, deploy, patch, back up, scale out, or generally maintain the machines or software.

This appendix is relatively short because you can do most of the same things with Office 365 and SharePoint Online that you can do with SharePoint on-premises. But this appendix does highlight a few important exceptions and concepts.

A Basic Overview of Software, Services, and the Cloud

Words and phrases such as "software as a service," "software plus services," "cloud services," or simply just "the Cloud," have been buzzing around in the industry for a while. Various pundits have heralded these as the "next big change" in computing, on par with how the Internet or the graphical user interface changed computing.

The upshot of all this buzz is that if you don't know much about services or service-based computing, you're probably starting to feel left out in the cold. Don't worry, you're not too far behind; many people and companies are only just now starting to understand what services are, how to leverage them, and how to ascertain their proper role in business productivity.

But what are services? What is the Cloud? Why is it important? And, more importantly, how can it benefit you and what does it have to do with SharePoint BI?

A "Service" at the Most Basic Level

The notion of a service is not a new concept. People have been consuming services for a long time. Services are simply about having someone else perform a task or job—that is, a "service" that is useful to you. Simple day-to-day examples of services are exactly what you might think they would be: having someone do your dry cleaning, wash your car, do your taxes, or pick up your trash. In all these cases, someone else does work for you, and you don't have to understand how they do those jobs, what tools they use, and so on. In other words, there's nothing new or novel about services. The definition of service hasn't magically changed somehow just because large computer companies have started using it.

A "Service" in the Computing World

So how does the simple notion of services apply to software and computing? The confusion starts with the many different meanings assigned to this combination. But fundamentally, the concept is still exactly the same—it's still about someone performing a service that is useful to you. The only difference is that in this context, the services pertain to computing.

Here are some simple examples of computing-based services that you'll probably be familiar with:

- **Buying and selling items on your favorite auction website**   You don't have to worry about where the site stores pictures, how it manages bids, how buyers and sellers connect, nor do you need to worry about applying security updates, site scalability, or anything of that nature.

- **Doing taxes online**   You don't have to install the tax software, run the machines, update it for security issues, and so on. You just log in and use it.

- **Using an Internet search engine**   You don't have to know how a search engine works or how to run the computers to perform a successful search. It is even possible to install a search engine on your local network and have search capability "powered by Bing."

- **Hosting a website**   Many people have their own homegrown websites these days. In most cases, the provider performs all the hosting tasks (the actual running of the computers that contain your website), domain registration, and so on. In the early days of the Internet, this wasn't the case. Today you have the option of doing all the steps separately, but more often than not, cheap providers are ready to do all these things for you. Once it is up and running, you generally need to worry only about the content on your website. How often the machines are updated, patched, and so forth is usually not a concern.

The preceding simple cases should illustrate the point. Even in the context of computing, the idea of a service is fairly straightforward. The services described above purposely use simple examples to illustrate the concept. You'll see more complex examples of services later in this appendix.

The Cloud

Another often-misunderstood term is "the Cloud" and how it pertains to services. Generally the distinction between the cloud and services is minor and can usually be ignored altogether.

People often use these terms interchangeably. But sometimes the cloud can imply a few distinctions that are worth discussing.

When people refer to the cloud, they usually mean a system that resides in some location (in fact, usually spread across many locations) that users can access from anywhere. In most cases, this really just means that there are a bunch of server computers in dark air-conditioned rooms somewhere, often called "datacenters." In fact, there are probably many such rooms spread out over many different cities, states, and even countries—all networked together in some way, with data stored redundantly in multiple locations. This scheme means that regardless of local interruptions, such as a power outage or even a catastrophe such as a fire or flood, the data stored on those machines, and likely even the service itself, won't be lost.

So the cloud implies both redundancy and infrastructure, ensuring that the computer programs providing the services and any data they store are maintained and always available. Services "live" in the cloud.

All the computing-specific services described so far must run on a computer. You may think that they are running on *your* computer, but your computer usually just shows you an interface and the results in a browser. The Bing search engine doesn't use your computer to scour the Internet. The auction website doesn't use your computer to store or calculate sales costs for all the items in the various auctions. Your computer shows only what you need to see (the search results, the current bid, and so forth); in other words, when using services, your computer simply displays some content in a webpage. The real work that must occur for the service to be useful is done on the large network of machines known as the cloud.

Not All Clouds Are Equal

As you may have guessed, not all clouds are the same. You would probably prefer a white fluffy cloud to low-lying fog. It takes money, people, good hardware, great software, and general know-how to run a large enough network of server machines to make up a great cloud. If you need to choose between two different services that live in the cloud, one consideration is the relative strength of each operation.

To evaluate a service, take a look at the EULA and support level agreement (SLA) for each service. Among the things you should try to discover are:

- What kind of security and privacy guarantees the service operators make

- What kind of downtime they expect to have (we all know computers can fail; computers making up the cloud are no different)

- How much redundancy is in place to avoid catastrophes

- What kind of customer support they have when support issues arise

- How large and how quickly they can scale if the number of customers, the sales volume, or processing load increases for your business

- How or whether they plan to reimburse you if something goes wrong

Different services offer different levels of support. Most services don't talk about clouds versus the service (again, those terms are often used interchangeably), but each service should offer the information to answer these and other questions you might have around how reliable the service is and how well it can meet your needs.

The Microsoft Cloud

Microsoft has invested heavily in running services in the cloud and already has a number of major cloud services available. Microsoft has years of experience running services such as Windows Update, MSN, Xbox Live, Hotmail, and many others. In fact, SharePoint Online has been available at scale since October of 2008.

"Software"—What It Means in a Services World

You may have been thinking of all of this as software, including programs that run on the Internet and those that run on your home computer. That's true. It *is* all software—that is, code running on a computing device. However, the term "software" has taken on a slightly different meaning in many of the cloud/service discussions.

Software has come to mean programs that you install and maintain on a machine that you own. For example, installed games, photo editing programs, or applications such as Microsoft Office on your computer are traditional types of desktop software. You need to maintain all those applications, meaning you have to install them, update them when a security patch gets released, troubleshoot issues that come up if something isn't working right, and so on. On the other hand, services are not programs that you own; someone else owns, installs, and maintains them. You typically only use them or subscribe to them.

Tradeoffs: Service vs. Software

This section goes into more detail on the tradeoffs between software and services to help you understand when and why you might choose each.

Key Advantages of Software

Traditional software has some advantages over services that you should not overlook. Software running on machines you own typically runs much faster. The machine is under your desk or in your company datacenter, not miles or hundreds of miles away over a far-reaching network. The software applications running on your desktop leverage your computer in a native way; desktop applications tend to be much more powerful than their counterparts that run only in a browser over the Internet. They're also often much richer visually, and typically have more functionality. You also "own" the software you have purchased. You can update it or uninstall it as you see fit. If the manufacturer provides an update you don't want, you don't have to install it. You also have a greater degree of control over who is using the software; for example, you can limit which users can use which physical machines. Imposing such control is usually straightforward. And, because you own the machines, you can control what other software programs are installed on those machines.

Key Advantages of Services

Services have a huge advantage in terms of ease of setup and maintainability. This becomes particularly obvious for more complex server products that might need to scale out over many machines. Installing SharePoint on tens or hundreds of machines is a far different task than installing it on a single computer sitting under your desk. Even a single local installation can be complex—that installation still has to be patched, and you have to troubleshoot it if problems occur. In a world where people are inundated with information and have business-critical tasks to perform, there's a price for each employee's time—and increasingly, your employees' time is better spent on business needs rather than on locating and downloading a patch or a Service Pack, deploying it, and configuring and testing everything to ensure that it continues to run smoothly.

Another advantage of services is that you don't have to buy and maintain the hardware. Like software, hardware acquisition must be planned, and new hardware must be set up, updated, and generally maintained over time. Again, these tasks consume costs and time that service consumers can avoid completely.

Services can provide advantages in situations that require central compliance, reporting, and governance as well. For example, if users can access files only through a service application (which may limit functionality, according to policy), you gain a single point of control and a single place to restrict what users can do with those files.

Which Is Right for You?

As you've seen, software and services each have their advantages and disadvantages. Software installed on-premises may be a better fit for you or your organization depending on your level of trust or comfort with the technology or with the company providing the service, and also depending on your security needs and how tightly you need to manage your users' computing environments.

For many businesses, the need to tightly manage their users' desktops actually arises from the difficulty of maintaining those machines. It can be easier to lock them down than to have to patch, reinstall, upgrade, or troubleshoot them later. With services, businesses gain most of the functionality without all the setup and maintenance overhead. If you want to skip the hardware purchase, the scale-out, and the maintenance costs, and if you don't mind not "owning" the software itself, and if you also want to avoid having to patch, upgrade, and troubleshoot software, services would be a great choice for you. Many companies find that the cost savings alone, just from not having to purchase and maintain hardware and software, make services much more cost-effective as well.

Ultimately, the best approach may be to have both—the power of software running locally while tightly integrated with cloud-based services in a hybrid approach. This is true in cases where you need extremely fast client-side software applications but where your files and environment can be stored or managed as a service. This is exactly the kind of offering that Office 365 provides. You'll see more details about the hybrid approach later in this appendix.

More Traditional Productivity Applications As Services

Earlier in this appendix, you saw some examples of services (auctions, search, and so forth) that illustrate the basic concept of what a service is. You may feel as if you have been using services for many years already—and you would likely be right. If that's the case, your reaction probably runs toward confusion or even disappointment over the buzz around services. After all, isn't the whole concept simply renaming capabilities that have been around since the 1990s? The answer is "no"; services are not just a renaming of what has already been available.

Indeed, a fundamental shift is occurring around services, and the concept is extending far beyond the kinds of "Internet-based things" already in existence that were cited as examples earlier. The notion of services has expanded to encompass computing tasks that were traditionally performed on premises, such as building and maintaining traditional databases, monitoring machine performance, document management, or even using core productivity applications such as Office.

More complex examples include the following:

- Databases, such as SQL Azure, which can host data for use by individuals or companies. These include complex systems for sales data, forecasting data, and so on, which can be made available from anywhere that has a connection. Traditional software programs can access the data, but the data itself is hosted as part of a service.

- Monitoring programs, such as Windows Intune, that can monitor the health of various individual machines at a company. This is an example of a service that can monitor computers under users' desks for malware like viruses, determine which programs have been installed, schedule updates, and so forth. Although the actual program that does the monitoring and aggregation of the data runs as a service, its useful task happens to be applied to a local computer. Microsoft provides such services as part of the Windows Azure wave of services.

- The Office Web Applications hosted on *www.skydrive.com* or by *www.hotmail.com*. After all, what could be more "software" than Microsoft Office? If you attach an Excel document to an email, a recipient receiving the message can view it using "Excel" right inside their browser. Or they can go to SkyDrive and author a new Excel file. In other words, they get most of the advantages of Excel without having to actually install Excel on their computers. This is an example of a traditional productivity application offered as a service.

In general, offloading complex or intense computing tasks to an operating system or machine in the cloud. Many developers are now beginning to leverage the Windows Azure environment to perform complex computations and data storage in the cloud. So the program might run locally, but it can hand off some tasks to a service, such as scrubbing large amounts of data or performing intense computations.

> **Note** See *http://www.microsoft.com/windowsazure/evidence/* for more examples of the way many companies are leveraging the Windows Azure service.

In the future, we expect to see many more computing solutions performed as a service or in some combination of software ("on-premises") and services in the cloud.

SharePoint As a Service in Microsoft Office 365

With the basic concepts of services explained, we'll move on to consuming SharePoint as a service. The chapters in this book have generally assumed that you are either planning to install or have installed SharePoint on one or more machines at your home, small business, or company. But if you don't "own" SharePoint or some of the other BI products—and don't want to install it—there is another way to use SharePoint: as a service called SharePoint Online, which is part of the Office 365 offering.

What Is Office 365?

Office 365 is Microsoft's core offering of productivity services. It includes subscription-based services such as Exchange Online, Lync Online, SharePoint Online, and Office Pro Plus (the full desktop of Office 2010 served up as a download). Office 365 is a service in the cloud that provides thin applications (browser-based versions of popular Office applications) and other functionality that works seamlessly with software applications you have installed on your local computers. This means Office 365 allows you to:

- Access your data, documents, contacts, email, and other solutions from any location and from many different devices.

- Work using your existing software applications (Office, Outlook, Lync, and so on) in conjunction with the Office 365 online services. Many of these desktop applications have service-based companion versions, so if you have the client applications installed on your machine, you can choose which to use.

- Leverage the power of SharePoint for features such as document management, dashboards, wikis, lists, content management sites, search, company portals, and collaborative sites to simplify working with colleagues and external partners.

You can subscribe to any of several different versions of Office 365. There is a version for small businesses, one for enterprises, and one for educational institutions. In addition, there is also a Kiosk Worker SKU, which is unique to the cloud-based service. This SKU is intended for businesses whose employees spend most of their time away from a computer or share a computer with others—often called "kiosk workers." It may be important to the business to keep those employees connected even though they don't spend much time working on a computer. To get a more in-depth overview, see the Microsoft Office 365 product page at *http://office365.microsoft.com/en-US/online-services.aspx.*

This book doesn't cover all the Office 365 capabilities; it provides only a high-level overview with a focus on SharePoint. At the time of this writing, Office 365 was in the early stages of development, so some of the capabilities or user-interface features may have changed by the time you read this book.

To help you get started, the remaining sections of this appendix describe basic SharePoint and Office functionality and configuration.

Using Office

You can now choose from two versions of Office—the Office Web Apps and the Office thick-client programs that you might already be using on your computer today. Both versions are useful in many different scenarios.

The Office Web Apps are particularly useful when individuals in your organization do not have an Office client at all. For those who do, the Office Web Apps are also useful as companion applications in scenarios where you are on the go and just need to read a document or maybe do some light editing, or maybe you need to work with documents on other machines or devices. In Office 365, the Office Web Apps are already configured and available. To use them, simply click the Office file you see in a SharePoint document library.

The thick-client applications are useful when you need the full power and functionality of the Office client. If you are doing more than lightweight editing or simple viewing, you will want to use the thick client because much of the more advanced functionality of Office is available only in the desktop version.

Connecting the Office Client

The key to being able to use your Office clients with Office 365 is to get them connected in a way that allows seamless operation with SharePoint Online. To do this, you must first download and install the Microsoft Online Services Connector. This helps you configure your Office client for proper authentication to enable you to directly save, open, and edit files stored in SharePoint Online.

Using SharePoint Online

Generally speaking, from the point of view of most users, most of SharePoint Online looks and behaves the same as if you were running SharePoint on-premises, providing sites, site collections, team sites, document libraries, lists, user permissions, and so on.

After you subscribe to Office 365, you can set up your *tenancy*—that is you can think of yourself as being a tenant in a larger system. There might be many users, companies, small businesses, and so on also using the service; in this case, you are one of many "tenants." As an administrator (or tenant) for a service, you can configure many settings that control email, communications, management of users, sites, site collections, and so forth, for the end users in your organization. Most of the user interface elements are the same, so you don't need much SharePoint Online-specific knowledge. That's part of the beauty of services done well. Some of the key differences between using SharePoint Online as part of Office 365 and using SharePoint on-premises, which you have installed and configured, are discussed in the following sections.

SharePoint Online vs. SharePoint On-Premises

This section looks at how factors such as hardware, configuration settings, and data connectivity are affected, depending on whether you choose online or on-premises versions of SharePoint.

Hardware

Microsoft owns the hardware and servers that run Office 365 and SharePoint Online. You don't need to worry about drivers, support, configuration, and so on for any hardware. The tradeoff is that because you don't own the hardware, you can't customize it to fit your specific needs. Generally, most users and organizations won't see this as much of a tradeoff—in fact, this is probably a net benefit to anyone who has been through the process of buying and configuring a bunch of servers. Most users won't even care about not owning the hardware, because they generally care only about using the software, which they can see. But for completeness, Office 365 users are using shared hardware resources managed by Microsoft at scale.

Even though the hardware is shared, the entire Office 365 ecosystem is designed with security in mind. The system contains multiple layers to ensure complete data isolation between different tenants—including both the physical security of the datacenters and the logical security built into the software.

Configuration Settings

Generally speaking, service administrators in Office 365 have fine-grained control over their tenancy in the SharePoint Online environment, but they don't have control over settings that can globally affect the health of the service or machines the service is running on. Eliminating administrator access to such settings prevents one tenant from doing something that adversely affects other users of the service.

If you have adjusted the global settings of your SharePoint environment because you need them to be specific to the types of solutions your organization creates, it would be worth your time to contact Microsoft Support, or you can read the available documentation to see how well the various Office 365 services would work for you. The public service descriptions on the Microsoft Download Center, at *http://go.microsoft.com/fwlink/?LinkId=207232*, are a good starting place for exploring the documentation.

You likely don't need to worry about any configuration in SharePoint that you may have altered for hardware performance, security, or deployment reasons. All those settings have been taken care of for you and are appropriate for most users. But you may want to audit your Service Application settings, to determine exactly what you changed from the default values. As an example, one such setting in Excel Services is the Maximum Workbook Size. You may have changed this setting to support very large workbooks in your deployment. Such workbooks might not work on Office 365, because they're dependent on the Maximum Workbook Size setting. In Office 365, the Maximum Workbook Size is considered a global setting for Excel Services because it can globally impact server resource usage. Therefore, you, as a tenant, can't have direct control over it. This is only one example, but the concept applies to all global settings in SharePoint Online and Office 365.

Data Connectivity in Office 365

Because this book is about BI, and a lot of BI revolves around data, it is worth a quick discussion about data connectivity in SharePoint Online within Office 365.

Most organizations have a SharePoint server behind a firewall, as well as a data source (such as Analysis Services) that is also behind a firewall on-premises. It is usually fairly straightforward to get data refresh working for applications such as Performance Point, Excel Services, or Visio Services. You simply set up the data refresh accounts on the server (see the Unattended Account referenced in Chapter 4, "Excel Services"), or you configure Kerberos between your machines. You make sure there is network access between your SharePoint server and your data source (if there are firewalls or other barriers in place). Then you simply have your users create their Excel workbooks as they normally would, and in most cases, when those files are loaded on SharePoint, the data can be refreshed. So a picture of a typical setup might look something like the following diagram.

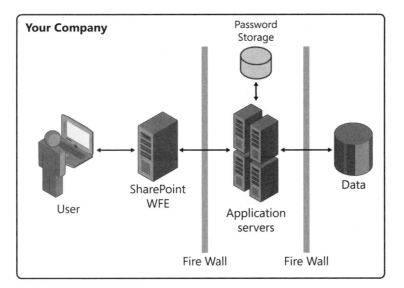

The data refresh in the above scenario is possible because the back-end SharePoint machine can directly open a connection to the data source machine (assuming firewalls, and so on, are configured correctly).

However, this picture changes in the Office 365 world for the following reasons:

- Your data source might still be required to live on-premises, behind your firewall.

- The SharePoint machine is now in the cloud—so you can't change the configuration on the physical SharePoint machines.

- Kerberos configuration is not possible, because you don't own either the domain or the physical machines.

- You don't control the network from end to end because you don't own the SharePoint machines.

- You can't configure server accounts in Secure Store Service anymore because:

  - You don't have access directly to the Secure Store Service.

  - You don't know the domain that the SharePoint service is running on.

  - Depending on policy, tenants might not be allowed to store end user passwords in a service like Secure Store Service in Office 365.

- You can't configure server accounts such as the Unattended Service account (which depends on the Secure Store Service) for service applications like Visio Services and Excel Services.

- So now the picture looks closer to something like the following illustration.

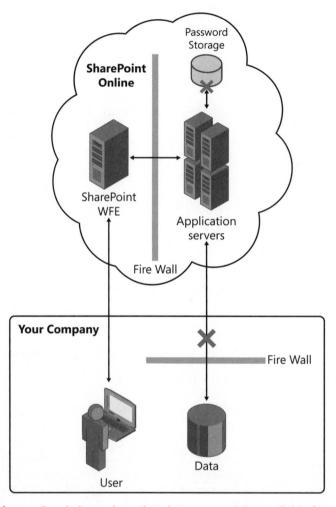

The factors listed above show that data connectivity available for service applications running on SharePoint Online within Office 365 is more limited than the data connectivity available to you in an on-premises version of SharePoint.

So what are the options for data connectivity for service applications like Excel and Visio? You can get connected to SQL data that uses a SQL user name and password. Excel gives you the option to save a SQL user name and password in the connection string (which is then saved in the file). In this case, when you open up your data source for read access over the network, Excel Services from Office 365 should be able to connect to it. Another option is to store even your SQL data in the cloud by using SQL Azure. You would connect to SQL Azure in the same way from a service application as you would using Excel Services in SharePoint. The downside of this is that the password is stored in the workbook file, which raises security concerns. So that scenario makes sense only when the file is tightly secured, the password used is a read-only account, and the data is not mission-critical or highly sensitive.

For data connections that connect to data stored in SharePoint Online, things should generally work without any major changes, but connectivity might be limited for data sources running on-premises.

For many, this is a small tradeoff when considered against the off-loaded expense of hosting SharePoint on-premises. Microsoft Office 365 can handle all of that for you. Also, because it is a live service, you get the newest software as soon as it is available, without having to go through a painful upgrade process. Also, Microsoft is working on data connectivity and other issues that don't work seamlessly in Office 365. You can expect to see new features in the future that help address some of these issues, because Microsoft updates the live service continually.

Availability of Service Applications and BI in Office 365

Office 365 is a new offering from Microsoft, and the first version won't support the full range of services in SharePoint 2010. At the time of this writing, neither PowerPivot nor PerformancePoint Services are supported in Office 365, but Visio Services and Excel Services are both supported (though with the limitations around data connectivity noted earlier in this appendix).

Because many of the BI products described in this book aren't yet available in SharePoint Online in Office 365, and because the data connectivity story is still limited, Office 365 can't yet be considered as a cloud-only BI solution. BI isn't center stage for this service offering, at least not yet. While some simple reporting solutions built on Excel Services can work for some scenarios, many hallmark BI scenarios won't. Because Office 365 is a live service and is just getting started, we have to watch for service updates over time. Office 365 will most likely add support for missing services and offer solutions to help better solve data connectivity issues, enabling a much stronger services-based BI story in the future.

Summary

Services in the cloud are all about someone else providing valuable computing resources and capabilities to you at a fraction of the cost of ownership of hosting comparable software on-premises. In the computing industry, a fundamental shift that revolves around services is well under way. Large companies, small businesses, and even single users are adopting services, reaping the benefits of simplicity—getting up and running without all the overhead from setup, upgrade, patching, troubleshooting, general maintenance, and without worrying about the cost of buying and maintaining hardware. Services are easy to adopt, always up to date, and easy to use from anywhere.

SharePoint, Office, Exchange, and more are being taken broadly into the world of services with the release of Office 365, which is Microsoft's premier bundle of services for large, medium, small, and single-operator businesses, and for educational institutions.

> **Note** To learn more about SharePoint Online, visit *http://office365.microsoft.com/en-US/sharepoint-online.aspx*. To learn more about the Office 365 services, visit *www.office365.com*.

Index

Symbols

A

B

G

Y

Z

Norm Warren

Norm Warren is a writer for PerformancePoint Server 2007 and SharePoint Server 2010 at Microsoft and has written articles on PerformancePoint® Server for the information worker, IT Pro, and SQL Server® BI developer audiences. He has a Master's degree in computer information technology and is currently earning an MBA with an emphasis in financial accounting. At Microsoft, Norm gives guidance to the BI community in the way of a blog, Norm's PerformancePoint Server blog (*http://blogs.msdn.com/normbi/*). He is also a member of The Data Warehouse Institute (TDWI).

Mariano Teixeira Neto

Mariano Teixeira Neto is a software design engineer on the SQL Server Analysis Services team. For the last three years he's been working on PowerPivot for SharePoint.

John Campbell

John Campbell is a program manager with Microsoft's Excel Services team.

Stacia Misner

Stacia Misner is the founder of Data Inspirations (*www.datainspirations.com*), which delivers global business intelligence (BI) consulting and education services. As a consultant, educator, mentor, and author specializing in business intelligence and performance management solutions that use Microsoft technologies, she has more than 25 years of experience in information technology and has focused exclusively on Microsoft BI technologies since 2000. She is the author of multiple books related to Microsoft SQL Server®, and most recently co-authored *Introducing Microsoft SQL Server 2008 R2* and *Building Integrated Business Solutions with SQL Server 2008 R2 and Office 2010*. Stacia is also a Microsoft Certified IT Professional-BI and a Microsoft Certified Technology Specialist-BI. She currently lives in Las Vegas, Nevada, with her husband, Gerry, where you can contact her via email at *smisner@datainspirations.com*.

What do you think of this book?

We want to hear from you!

To participate in a brief online survey, please visit:

microsoft.com/learning/booksurvey

Tell us how well this book meets your needs—what works effectively, and what we can do better. Your feedback will help us continually improve our books and learning resources for you.

Thank you in advance for your input!

Stay in touch!

To subscribe to the *Microsoft Press® Book Connection Newsletter*—for news on upcoming books, events, and special offers—please visit:

microsoft.com/learning/books/newsletter